AF352631

Lenchitudes

Lenchitudes

Sapphic Representation in Contemporary Mexican Narrative

ALEJANDRA MÁRQUEZ

SUNY PRESS

Cover credit: Ana Luisa Zavala, *Lenchitudes*, 2025. Used with permission.

Published by State University of New York Press, Albany

© 2026 State University of New York

EU GPSR Authorised Representative:
Logos Europe, 9 rue Nicolas Poussin, 17000, La Rochelle, France
contact@logoseurope.eu

For information, contact State University of New York Press, Albany, NY
www.sunypress.edu

Library of Congress Cataloging-in-Publication Data

Name: Márquez, Alejandra, 1988– author.
Title: Lenchitudes : sapphic representation in contemporary Mexican narrative /
    Alejandra Márquez.
Description: Albany : State University of New York Press, [2026]. | Series:
    SUNY series, Genders in the Global South | Includes bibliographical
    references and index.
Identifiers: LCCN 2025023489 | ISBN 9798855805147 (hardcover : alk. paper) |
    ISBN 9798855805161 (epub) | ISBN 9798855806946 (PDF)
Subjects: LCSH: Lesbianism in literature. | Mexican literature—20th century—
    History and criticism. | Mexican literature—21st century—History and criticism. |
    Lesbians in literature. | LCGFT: Literary criticism.
Classification: LCC PQ7122.H66 M37 2025
LC record available at https://lccn.loc.gov/2025023489

Para mi mamá, Cecilia Guajardo,
la norteña de mis amores

Contents

Acknowledgments

I completed this book amid a global pandemic and following the devastating loss of my mother, Cecilia Guajardo, in May 2023. Strangely enough, the act of writing *Lenchitudes* gave me strength, anchoring me through a period of intense grief. My mother was always my number one fan; her unwavering love, support, and belief in me continue to inspire my every word.

I am deeply thankful to Rebecca Colesworthy, and the Genders in the Global South series editors, Debra A. Castillo and Debarati Sen, for their support and enthusiasm for this project. To the brilliant readers whose generosity helped make *Lenchitudes* a reality, thank you for your work and for pushing me to think harder. To everyone at SUNY and beyond who helped in the making of this book. To my friend Fran Dennstedt, who accompanied me as I wrote *Lenchitudes* and gave me invaluable feedback. I am indebted to three of the organizers of the Marcha Lencha who generously spoke with me: Sofía J. Poiré, Ana de Alejandro, and Raquel Medina. This project started a decade ago, and though it has transformed over time, I am grateful to Rosa Perelmuter, Sam Amago, Juan Carlos González Espitia, Robert McKee Irwin, and Oswaldo Estrada for their careful reading and critical insights.

Oswaldo's countless hours spent mentoring me, reading my work, and preparing me for academic life have been as meaningful as his friendship, kindness, and emotional support. My heartfelt thanks go to him, Cristina Carrasco, and Elena Alegría, who became family to both my mother and me during my time in Chapel Hill and to this day. To Rosa, thank you for being my academic mom and showing me love through Cuban sandwiches, coffee, and Sor Juana. The years I spent at UNC were among the happiest in my life, and I owe that to many exceptional people. Special thanks to Sarah Booker, whose translation skills have rescued me many times and whose intellectual curiosity continues to inspire me. To my NC friends—Bob Noffsinger, Ariana Vigil, Sandra García Gutiérrez, Kyle McQuillan, Etna Ávalos, Héctor Rendón, Jhonn Guerra Banda, Amaia Valparís, Cristóbal Clemente Rodrigálvarez, Sam Krieg, Paco Chen-López, Nefi López-Chen, Rhi Johnson, and Sarah Blanton—I am grateful for your constant laughter and companionship.

At Michigan State I have found an invaluable community. I am particularly grateful to Rocío Quispe-Agnoli, whose mentorship, thoughtful advice, stimulating conversations, and unwavering support have been indispensable. Many thanks to Danny Méndez for his guidance, encouragement, and friendship. To my first friend in Michigan, Silvina Bongiovanni, who immediately made me feel at home and whose humor and companionship have kept me going whenever I've felt like giving up. Deep thanks to Brian Buccola, Thea Knowles, and my nephew Lorenzo Buccola, who inspire me to look forward to many years ahead. Deep gratitude to the rest of my chosen Michigan family for making winters bearable and summers feel like paradise: Nilü Akalin, Aaron Schultz, Nazita Lajevardi, Megan Dean, Keith Underkoffler, Alan Barbalena, Ignacio González, Sofía Farah, Carmel Nemirovsky, Stephen Przybylinski, Karthik Durvasula, Becky Crisenberry, and Maya Durvasula. I am beyond grateful to Laurie Medina and the Center for Latin American and Caribbean Studies for always making my ideas come to fruition. A very special thanks to Deborah Johnson, Micaela Flores, and all of the friends I have made through the Diversity Research Network. The DRN has been a lifeline for me and for many other scholars and has allowed us to build community and feel seen. Lastly, Beth Bonsall and Alex Tekip have supported and encouraged my work to reach wider audiences, and I feel honored and fortunate to work with them every chance I get.

My deepest gratitude belongs to my people in and beyond Mexico. To my best friend, Carlos Meade, thank you for your unconditional love and friendship. To my San Miguel and Mexico City family: Dalia Herrera, Lydia Franke, Nati Franke, Dahlia and Alison Bastien, Abner Burnett, Chantal Naves, Lali Babot, Pam and Frida Mason, David Dykes, Carlos Velázquez, Frances Boyd, Sonia Ortega Stark, Erika Alvizo, and Ana Julia Salcedo Alvizo. To the Zavala Cerroblanco family, especially my dear friend Ana Luisa Zavala (the talented artist who helped design this book's cover), I owe tremendous gratitude. I am grateful for my colleagues who have become treasured friends—Olivia Cosentino, Carina Guzmán (Islandia),

Juanma Ramírez Velázquez, Ángel Díaz Miranda, Giovanna Urdangarain, Luis Martín Ulloa, Armando García, Elena Madrigal (mi hada madrina lésbica), and Artemisa Téllez. To my Sarah Pettit Lesbian Summer Camp friends for their feedback on the very early stages of this project: Caitlin O'Neil, Krystal Cleary, and Melina Moore.

Heartfelt thanks to those who made Laredo home: Cristina Martínez, Sandra Contreras, Kesia Rodríguez, Alyson Martínez, Alejandra Ávila, Griselda Guerrero (in loving memory), Enrique Reyes, José Cardona-López, Irma Cantú, Agustín Martínez-Samos, and Lola Norris. A special thank you to John Kilburn for convincing me to do a PhD. My path toward literature began thanks to my great-aunt, María Dolores de la Peña, and my grandmother, Luz de la Peña Hinojos. Wherever my mother is now, I know she is in good company with them and my stepfather, Fernando Caraballo. Deepest thanks to Mary Ellen Clery, whose kindness and wise words feel like a warm hug, and to the Clery, Logemann, and Monroe families, who met me when I was at my lowest and helped me get back up. Last but certainly not least, my heartfelt gratitude goes to my love, Abby Clery, whose tireless support and belief in me have made all the difference. Your love, kindness, brilliance, patience, and unmatched sense of humor make my life brighter every single day.

Early versions of parts of chapter 1 and chapter 3 were originally published in *iMex México Interdisciplinario/Interdisciplinary Mexico* and *Clepsydra. Revista Internacional de Estudios de Género y Teoría Feminista*, respectively.

Introduction

Toward *Lenchitudes*

In March 2020, I had plans to travel to San Miguel de Allende, Guanajuato, to attend the Ella Lesbian Festival. It was a lucky coincidence that the event was taking place in one of the cities where I had grown up and where my mother still lived. I had become desperate to find events or activist spaces in Mexico that did not promote transphobic and essentialist ideas, which I had encountered in my years of research. I reached out to the festival organizers, who kindly invited me to join. Little did I know that my plans were about to change due to the havoc wreaked on the world by the COVID-19 pandemic. The day before my flight, my institution was forced to switch to online instruction. I texted my department chair to ask a question I knew the answer to, in hopes that I would be wrong. I wanted to know if I could still travel as planned to interview participants and organizers of the festival. "No," he responded, "the university has canceled all research travel." I would spend the next few days packing up my apartment and making arrangements to stay with and care for my mother as we entered the uncertain terrain of a global pandemic. The festival went on despite health concerns and was held again in Mérida in 2021 and in Puerto Vallarta in 2023.

I was disappointed that I couldn't attend the 2020 event, which I had found appealing, in part, due to its organizers' inclusive stances—their website is openly supportive and welcoming of trans and non-binary people. However, I soon realized that this festival was not what I was looking for. Even though local organizers were supportive and generous, the Ella Lesbian Festival is a global network of events with sponsors like Google and IBM ("Ella Festival Partners"). This was a celebration; however, it felt far from a political act and more like a commodification of lesbian culture. While general admission tickets for the 2021 Ella Lesbian Festival in Mérida were 6,800 pesos, or roughly 350 dollars ("Ella Mexico 2021 Program"), according to government sources, as of 2023, the minimum wage in Mexico was approximately 321 dollars per month ("Comunicado Conjunto 102/2022"). This made it immediately clear that the festival was targeted to middle- and upper-class attendees and thus was not the right place for me to think about challenging dominant norms. However, it is worth noting that, since then, the Ella Lesbian Festival has expanded, hosting multiple events that showcase queer women's achievements (including in literature) and becoming a key organization for visibility in Mexico. At the time, my disappointment with the event contributed to my frustration with sapphic spaces and discourses in Mexico. In my experience, what I encountered was either trans-exclusionary and gender essentialist or catered to a neoliberal culture of consumption. Fortunately, shortly after, I came across a different event that became the inspiration behind this book.

In the summer of 2020, due to social distancing requirements, the organizers of the Marcha Lencha in Mexico City decided to hold their first march virtually. A year later, the first in-person event took place on 19 June 2021. Although the media reported "hundreds" in attendance (Salazar), the Instagram account for the march claimed that more than 2,000 people had participated in their inaugural protest. While exact numbers are difficult to pinpoint, the fact that the event was organized in the first place is far more significant and indicative of the social changes occurring within the LGBTQ+ community in Mexico. While the first Marcha del Orgullo Homosexual took the streets of Mexico City on 26 July 1979, other groups with more specific demands and identities sought to form their own spaces. Such was the case of the Comité Organizador de la Marcha Lésbica (COMAL), who in 2003 planned the first Marcha Lésbica de México y América Latina and continued to do so until 2019.

Nonetheless, COMAL positioned itself as deliberately anti-trans—a move followed by other lesbian organizations, such as LesVoz.[1] This standpoint created a rift between those who embraced exclusionary discourses and a newer generation tasked with evolving and changing with the demands of a more diverse community, some of which had been influenced by the advent of queer theory.[2] One of the Marcha Lencha organizers, Sofía J. Poiré, credits COMAL's trans-exclusionary practices with being part of the reason behind the impulse to create a new march that was influenced by the New York Dyke March.[3] However, in a personal interview, she emphasized that the term *dyke* has no direct translation into

Spanish, prompting her and others to search for a word that resonated better in the Mexican context. During a conversation among organizers, Ana de Alejandro, another founder of the march, proposed the term *lenchitudes*, echoing Raquel Medina's—also a founding member—mention of the word *latitudes*, to describe people from diverse backgrounds who share a love for women—individuals from different metaphorical latitudes, yet united by common struggles (Poiré, "Día de la visibilidad").[4] This marked the beginning of the organizers' efforts to embrace a wide range of experiences, as opposed to their predecessors.

My first encounter with the Marcha Lencha through social media during the COVID-19 pandemic was pivotal in shaping the writing of this book. While I knew I wanted to examine literary texts depicting sapphic experiences, I had grown frustrated with what I saw as a narrow view among activists and writers in Mexico, who often seemed to rely heavily on *lesbian* as an identity category. I recognized the significance of the work done by these groups and individuals, which began long before the start of my academic career. Yet I hoped that younger generations would push beyond identity politics and address the sociopolitical changes taking place in contemporary Mexico. My wishful thinking became a reality when I learned about the Marcha Lencha, and even more so when I recognized in the organizers' statements a shared concern with embracing a term that would allow women and others to define themselves while critically challenging normativity and essentialism.

Even though the Marcha Lencha organizers focus on political activism rather than cultural or literary scholarship, I chose to draw from their reflections on *lenchitudes* to establish a framework for analyzing contemporary narrative works in Mexico for two reasons. First, as scholars in Latin America and the Latin American diaspora continue to theorize how *cuir*[5] studies are embodied and developed in the region, the subversive nature of *lenchitudes* serves as a prime example of the efforts occurring in Mexico to name and understand dissident sexualities and genders. Thus, I view *lenchitudes* as potentially operating within the scope of *cuir* studies. Second, the term emerged from a political stance by new generations seeking to understand gender and sexuality in more expansive terms, while rejecting anti-trans positions rooted in essentialism and static notions of sexuality. For these reasons, I found it crucial to develop an approach that aligns with and supports the Marcha Lencha organizers and others challenging patriarchal systems of oppression in Mexico. In this sense, this book advocates for drawing on knowledge produced within Latin America to further build and expand the field of *cuir* studies.

The term *lenchitudes* is derived from *lencha,* a word once used pejoratively in Mexico to describe women perceived as lesbians. Scholars suggest it comes from the character Lencha, a woman from northern Mexico played by actor Lucila Mariscal in the 1990s (Zatarain Olivas and Núñez Noriega 36). Lencha is depicted wearing traditional indigenous clothing, including a headband and two braids, reflecting how Mexican media and beauty standards associate indigeneity and poverty with unattractiveness. The character resembles María Elena Velasco's famous comedic character, La India María, both serving as caricatures of indigeneity. While Lencha is not a lesbian, she is portrayed as lacking conventionally feminine traits, instead being crude and treating men as equals, making her appear unattractive by societal standards.

Thus, the term *lencha* reflects prevailing stereotypes that associate lesbians with vulgarity and lower social classes, while also emphasizing gender transgressions. Women who work in public spaces, like *tortilleras* and *tamaleras,*[6] often embody these transgressions by serving as household providers. Like Mariscal's character, they are sometimes seen as having masculine traits, being quarrelsome, daring, and taking initiative, much like men (Zatarain Olivas and Nuñez Noriega 37). During our conversation, Ana de Alejandro emphasized the importance of reclaiming the derogatory term and infusing it with new meaning. In this way, *lenchitudes* operates similarly to the reappropriation of *queer* in anglophone contexts not only by reclaiming a word once used to demean a community but also by rejecting static identities—as I will explain. Consequently, the Marcha Lencha and its concept of *lenchitudes* offer a lens through which to examine the intersection of gender and sexuality in Mexico.

Defining *Lenchitudes* as a Framework

I began writing this book a few years before the Marcha Lencha first took place, aiming to engage with the ongoing conversations surrounding *cuir* studies in Latin America and, specifically, in Mexico. Some scholars have criticized the use of queer theory—or its translations—in the Latin American context as lacking conceptual force due to linguistic and contextual differences (Epps 898–99), or as perpetuating colonialism (Mogrovejo, "Lo queer" 238). However, for many others, engaging with queerness and its possibilities beyond anglophone countries opens up new articulations that disrupt established understandings of gender and sexuality, while also acknowledging its localized intersections with race, class, and citizenship (Domínguez Ruvalcaba, *Latinoamérica Queer* 21–23). Thus, refusing to engage with queerness as a theoretical tool "basically erases the efforts of complicating the nature of concepts, a practice that is at the core of queer theory" (Dennstedt 32). For Sayak Valencia, shifting from queer to *cuir*—arguably the most common transposition of the term—functions not merely as a translation but as a geopolitical deviation that fosters the construction of agency through language from a Latin American viewpoint ("Del *queer* al cuir" 31–34). I position this book within the continuous efforts to recognize Latin America as a significant site of knowledge production on *lo cuir*.

Numerous scholars and activists have made meaningful contributions to a genealogy of *lo cuir* in the region. José Maristany calls this a *genealogía diferencial*, which he identifies as a theory and practice of *lo cuir* seen in the work of authors like Pedro Lemebel and Néstor Perlongher. Maristany explains that a deeper exploration of this genealogy transcends viewing the Latin American version of *queer* merely as a translation or a gap to be filled. Instead, he argues, it involves mapping different approaches to the representation of minorities in both the Global North and South, allowing for connections or divergences based on shared or distinct experiences (24). For example, before queer/*cuir* studies were formally recognized in Latin America, Lemebel wrote about his visit to the Stonewall Inn during a trip to New York City. His Chilean identity immediately set him apart from the majority of white, masculine, and muscular patrons, making him wonder if gayness was inherently linked to whiteness (64). These types of differences have prompted Latin American scholars of *lo cuir* to reflect on terms like *marica*—which can be roughly translated as *faggot*, although its meaning is more complex than can be conveyed by a direct translation.

Diego Falconí Travéz notes the word's limitations, such as its frequent use in Spain, which creates the false impression of a unified Hispanic solidarity, thereby ignoring issues of racism and classism that affect Latin Americans in Spain. As a result, Falconí suggests moving away from identity labels and instead embracing a gesture or movement: *mariquismo*—perhaps most easily translated as *faggotry*. He contends that the term does not aim to erase gayness, which is still productive in sexual contexts for some, though it may be insufficient for other aspects of life in the Global South. Instead, he explains that *mariquismo* seeks to reshape gayness, reducing its influence without severing global connections; limiting its hedonism without sacrificing pleasure; and reducing camp while preserving wit. Falconí Travéz concludes that *mariquismo* must also address the contradictions among *maricas*, such as the cisnormative limits of the people it names, and should forge alliances with feminists, queer theorists, decolonial thinkers, and anti-racist, body-positive, and disability movements (27). Contributions such as these showcase the multiple possibilities of a *cuir* genealogy that is always in flux, adapting to new societal changes and realities.

Another pioneering thinker of *lo cuir*, Néstor Perlongher, explored the distinction between becoming and identity in relation to minorities, explaining that becoming "is not turning into another person, but entering into an alliance (aberrant), by contagion, an intermingling with difference" (68). Accordingly, he emphasized the perils of fixed identities and how they may become integrated into capitalist frameworks. Perlongher argued that minority politics should not be limited to identity affirmation or shallow calls for solidarity. Although he acknowledged that legal battles and personal identification remained relevant, for him, the fatigue caused by identity movements signaled a need for a move toward greater freedom through expanding differences across minority groups and the wider social spectrum (74–75). Writers like Perlongher reveal that what we now define as queer theory or queer studies is not solely an anglophone creation; rather, those in the Global South have long been theorizing and mobilizing to describe and defend diverse gender expressions and sexual desires.

Other significant contributions highlighting the need for local knowledge production on *lo cuir* are the ongoing conversations in the Southern Cone concerning the experiences of *travesti* subjects. In this context, *travesti* refers to individuals assigned male at birth who identify with feminine bodies, attire, and behaviors but, unlike trans people, may not necessarily consider themselves women, problematizing the gender binary (Pierce, "I Monster" 306). For Argentine activist and intellectual Lohana Berkins, the refusal to align with a particular gender identity is a political stance that underscores the contextual differences distinguishing *travesti* experiences from those of trans people in places like the United States ("Travestis. Una identidad política"). This distinction is evident when we consider the racial and class implications for *travestis* in the Southern Cone. As Cole Rizki explains, "[w]hile in English, *transgender* often needs to be modified in order to respond to local hierarchies of race, class, ability, and other forms of difference, *travesti* underscores instead the impossibility of such disarticulation in the first place" (148). In this way, *travesti* theory and activism not only contest binary concepts of gender in the region but also bring to light the complex intersections specific to this community, along with the challenges they face and their role in driving social and political change.[7]

Also writing from Argentina, activist and thinker Marlene Wayar has proposed a "living"—constantly evolving—theoretical approach that centers the *travesti* community. In *Travesti: una teoría lo suficientemente buena* (2019), Wayar introduces the concept of *nostredad,* a reinterpretation of *otredad* (otherness), aiming to move beyond the binary of "us" versus "them." For Wayar, childhood represents an ideal time for questioning such dichotomies; she sees infancy as a period rich with potential for inquiry and transformation, capable of breaking paradigms (18). The work of thinkers like her and Berkins not only demonstrates the potential of a localized approach to *lo cuir,* but also highlights the strong connection between theory and activism, addressing the specific needs of *cuir* individuals in particular regions.

Building on these examples, this book aims to join the ongoing conversations on *lo cuir* in Latin America, examining how activism and literature can provide insight into the diversity and complexity of gender and sexuality. I envision *lenchitudes*—in plural form, because there is no single way to embody them—as aligning with *lo cuir* by rejecting essentialist identities and challenging patriarchal, heteronormative systems. This connection is inspired by the organizers of the Marcha Lencha, who have circulated their political positions and definition of *lenchitudes* on social media. In the lead-up to the first in-person march in 2021, their Instagram account outlined key points on the matter. Their post described *lenchitudes* as representing desire among women or feminized bodies—those not perceived as cisgender heterosexual men—but also pointed to how individuals who identify with this word are viewed by society. They emphasized that the term is flexible, explaining:

> The concept of *lenchitudes* is vague and fluid because the stigma that we live manifests itself in different ways in different contexts and, above all, because we are very diverse. We can be feminine, androgynous or *machorras*; we can be in a relationship with a woman or not; but we know that our existence and our way of being, our desires, our affections, and our sexuality are uncomfortable for cis-hetero-patriarchy and because of that we want to reclaim *lenchitudes*.[8]

> ("El concepto de lenchitudes es difuso y fluido, porque el estigma que vivimos se manifiesta de distintas maneras en distintos

> contextos, y sobre todo, porque somos muy diversas. Podemos
> ser femeninas, andróginas o machorras; podemos o no estar en
> relación con una mujer; pero sabemos que nuestra existencia,
> nuestra manera de ser, nuestros deseos, nuestros afectos y nues-
> tra sexualidad son incómodos para el cis-hetero-patriarcado y
> por ello queremos reivindicar a las lenchitudes.")[9]

Although *lenchitudes* inherently involve attraction and desire, they are expressed in a variety of ways and carry the potential to disrupt and expose the underlying structures of heteronormative and patriarchal oppression. As the organizers note, this diversity is deliberate: "we take responsibility for our own privileges and openly support our trans sisters/siblings, our racialized sisters/siblings, our disabled sisters/siblings who have been relegated" ("nos responsabilizamos de nuestros privilegios y abiertamente apoyamos a nuestras hermanas trans, a nuestraes hermanaes racializadaes, a nuestraes hermanaes discas [discapacitadaes] que han sido relegadaes"; "¿Quiénes son las lenchitudes?"). Moreover, this definition highlights how diverse forms of violence and discrimination disproportionately affect those seen as deviating from heteronormativity, particularly women and trans and non-binary people.

This mention of violence is especially significant in Mexico, a country where, as of 2023, an average of eleven women were victims of feminicide[10] every day (Santillán Ramírez 27) and where, between 2007 and 2018, the Centro de Apoyo a las Identidades Trans, AC, reported nearly five hundred trans women murdered (Burgueño Duarte and Sánchez González 117). Thus, the Marcha Lencha is not merely a celebration of *lenchitudes*, but also an act of protest. In our conversation, Poiré shared that another reason she collaborated with her co-organizers to establish a new march was her disillusionment with the 2019 Mexico City Pride celebration. She explained that the growing popularity of LGBTQ+ pride celebrations may be connected to their depoliticization, especially in the relationship between these events and corporations. For Poiré, many companies often appear more focused on performing for public approval to gain customers or employees than on advocating for structural changes for the community. Similarly, a number of people attend pride events, not to participate politically, but as a form of entertainment or to perform for social media.

Hence, I borrow the term from the organizers of the Marcha Lencha to advance *lenchitudes* into a framework centered on women—not as a static category, but as an expansive term that includes cisgender and trans women, as well as those who see themselves reflected by it—[11] who feel romantic or erotic attraction toward other women. It seeks to break away from binary constructions of gender and sexuality by making visible their contradictions and challenging hegemonic culture, whether directly or indirectly. As such, *lenchitudes* are conceived not as an endpoint, but as an extension of what scholars have proposed and continue to develop regarding *lo cuir* in Latin America.[12] During our interview, Marcha Lencha organizer Raquel Medina noted that *lenchitudes* are in a constant state of evolution, adapting and changing as they are discussed and reconfigured. I view my adoption of the term as part of this ongoing evolution, in line with how *lo cuir* continues to be adapted, resignified, and deconstructed across Latin America and its diaspora (Pierce et al. 4). In this way, I aim to center *lenchitudes* as a theoretical tool that advances conversations about the contributions of Latin American social movements to knowledge production, challenging the idea that the Global North is the primary site of theory-making.

At the same time, this book examines how *lenchitudes* arise from the context of *cuir* activism in Mexico. While the literary works analyzed are grounded in Mexico, they generally do not emphasize themes of nationalism or national identity. Instead, they delve into the particularities of individual and collective experiences surrounding gender and sexuality. Moreover, my approach to these narrative texts is framed within what Ignacio Sánchez Prado, José Ramón Ruisánchez, and Anna Nogar identify as a decline in national identity as a central subject of analysis in Mexican literary studies. In their introductory chapter to *A History of Mexican Literature* (2016), they explain that this shift has allowed for new perspectives, such as those emerging from gender studies and intellectual history (3). For them, the "critical framework defining national Mexican literature cannot be overlooked, but the picture of Mexican literature that emerges from today's scholarship is far more complex than it ever was under the hegemony of identity-based scholarship" (3). Thus, this project does not seek to define what makes these novels and short stories distinctly Mexican. Instead, it aims to show how *cuir* studies can draw on the knowledge produced by activist efforts in the Mexican context to offer a framework for interpreting and understanding texts written in Mexico.

Nevertheless, it is vital to acknowledge that these narrative works are rooted in unique cultural and historical circumstances. Therefore, I find a contextual analysis necessary to fully grasp how these texts articulate ideas of gender and sexuality. Given the ongoing debates around *lo cuir* and its fraught relationship with national identity, it is essential to acknowledge how "compulsory heterosexuality in the production of gendered colonial, bourgeois, and religious nationalist subjects has been central to post-colonial nation building" (Dhawan 57). In the case of Mexico, as Sofía Ruiz-Alfaro explains, the search for *lo mexicano* and Mexican identity that began in the 1920s and 1930s emphasized the role of gender and sexuality in determining who was, and who was not, deemed fit to represent the postrevolutionary "new" nation (42). As a result, non-normative sexual and gender expressions have historically been pushed to the margins of Mexican identity, yet they remain inseparable from their sociohistorical circumstances. Finally, queerness/*lo cuir* cannot be understood in isolation; it must always be understood in relation to normativity, which is inherently shaped by the specific conditions and characteristics of its surrounding context (Domínguez Ruvalcaba, *Latinoamérica Queer* 81). By situating these literary works within their specific sociopolitical landscapes, we can better comprehend how they challenge or perpetuate heteropatriarchal norms and expectations.

Why Not *Lesbian*?

"The lesbian is dead," claims Mairead Sullivan in the opening lines of *Lesbian Death* (2022) (1). For Sullivan, the lesbian who is dead—or perceived as such by those who hold on to the term as an identity—is the one imagined as singular, mourned by trans-exclusionary feminists much like they lament the "erasure of women." This perspective "has the effect of freezing her in a specific time. In this way she is neither ahistorical nor transhistorical but singular" (43–44). In *Lesbian Death*, the disavowal of lesbian identity is linked to some of the same arguments that led to the rise of the Marcha Lencha—specifically, the increasing association of *lesbian* with transphobia and the rejection of essentialist views associated with 1970s second-wave feminism.[13] To resist identity politics and embrace broader experiences, the organizers of the Marcha Lencha consciously avoid using the word *lesbiana*.

Poiré explains that, while many who see themselves as part of *lenchitudes* may have experiences or desires that align with the label *lesbian*—meaning erotic or romantic relationships between women—not all of them identify with the socially constructed category of *woman*. As a result, *lenchitudes* challenge essentialist notions of gender, extending beyond the experiences of cisgender women to include those of trans and non-binary people ("Día de la visibilidad"). The event organizers' decision to create their own march and disassociate from the term *lesbiana* reflects how this word has been used by certain groups to justify violence against trans people and reinforce a gender binary that has become increasingly restrictive.

Another significant point made by Sullivan, which is relevant to understanding *lenchitudes*, is the assumption by those who uphold lesbian identity that this category is under threat of being replaced by queerness (17). Although Sullivan writes from the US, similar views are evident in some of the arguments made by lesbian feminists in Mexico. For example, Norma Mogrovejo asserts how "by dismantling the subject of feminism," poststructuralist approaches to feminism and queer theory "disavow the social action of women and lesbians who resist misogyny, exclusion, discrimination, and feminicide" ("al desestructurar el sujeto del feminismo, desconocen la acción social de mujeres y lesbianas que resisten a la misoginia, la exclusion, la discriminación y el feminicidio"; "Lo queer" 242–43). This line of thought implies the existence of a singular subject of feminism and contrasts it directly with other approaches, failing to recognize their shared demands.

These views have become more and more widespread in Mexico, as evidenced in March of 2022, when the Centro de Investigaciones Interdisciplinarias en Ciencias y Humanidades (CEIICH) at the Universidad Nacional Autónoma de México (UNAM) hosted a virtual forum titled "Aclaraciones necesarias sobre las categorías sexo y género" ("Necessary Clarifications About the Categories of Sex and Gender"). The event, which included feminist thinkers Marcela Lagarde, Amelia Valcárcel, Alda Facio, and Andrea Medina, relied heavily on this discourse, advancing claims of the alleged "erasure of women." Activists, human rights organizations, and journalists were quick to condemn the event for its transphobic positions, leading to a protest at the university (Cázares). Lagarde has been notably outspoken in excluding trans people from feminism. In an interview, she stated that during the 1990s, some lesbians distanced themselves from feminist organizations, choosing instead to align with LGBTQ+ groups with no links to feminism, concluding that they were "orphans of feminism, generations of very committed women who did not recognize their own political tradition. There is only one step from that to queer" ("mujeres huérfanas del feminismo, generaciones de mujeres muy comprometidas que no reconocieron su tradición política. De ahí a lo queer solo hay un paso"; "Marcela Lagarde"). Lagarde concludes the interview by asserting that *lo queer* seeks to erase women and that it is the responsibility of feminists like herself to fight for their legal recognition and protection.

While Lagarde's focus is on the category of *woman* rather than *lesbian*, her arguments function similarly to claims of the disappearance of the lesbian, as both suggest an erasure or displacement of an identity category, with queerness or queer theory positioned as the culprit. As Mexican trans activist Láurel Miranda explains, these viewpoints "are against gender and in favour of revindicating the material reality of sex as the single deciding factor to determine who is and isn't a woman. So, it's about taking an essentialist stance which feminism has in fact spent years fighting against." Consequently, this approach relies on a universal concept of *woman* that excludes intersecting components of identity such as race, class, or sexual orientation (Miranda). The backlash the UNAM forum received reflects the same ideological clashes that prompted the organizers of the Marcha Lencha to create their own space. As Sullivan indicates, the declarations made by groups echoing arguments like those of Lagarde and Mogrovejo suggest that *queer theory* and *lesbian*—and I would add *woman*—"are well-defined and discrete categories. The idea that queer theory has a rigid boundary is expressed most forcefully in the claim that the lesbian has been excluded from this boundary" (43). In contrast, this book aligns with the rejection of rigid categories, a stance central to both *cuir* epistemologies and the conceptualization of *lenchitudes* by the Marcha Lencha organizers.

Throughout my writing process, I contemplated whether to use the term *lesbian*. While I recognized its practicality due to its recognition and widespread use, I often found it too restrictive, conflicting with the essence I sought to capture by embracing *lenchitudes*. However, while researching the origins of the Marcha Lencha, I noticed the prevalence of the term *sapphic*.[14] For Poiré, this term is useful when thinking of women—in a broad sense of the word—who experience attraction to other women without the limitations that *lesbian* conveys ("Día de la visibilidad"). In her 2009 book, *Sapphistries*, Leila J. Rupp is similarly intentional in her use of the term, which originates from the sixth-century BCE poet Sappho of Lesbos and has a longer, more widespread history than the word *lesbian* (1).[15] For Rupp, the broad use of *lesbian* "downplays the difference among women, especially when the concept and identity of lesbian is available and women choose not to embrace it" (3). Given its malleability, I have chosen to use the term *sapphic* to describe love or erotic desire between women, rather than *lesbian*, which excludes those who may feel attraction to more than one gender.

At the same time, given the considerable critical attention that male gay literature in Mexico has received over the past few decades—as a quick search for academic studies on Luis Zapata's *El vampiro de la colonia Roma* (1979) would confirm—using terms like *queer desire* or *cuir desire* in the title of this book would have risked being interpreted by those unfamiliar with *lenchitudes* as broad enough to include depictions that fall outside its scope. Throughout this project, I also use *lenchitudes* as a framework to approach literary texts and analyze how they either subvert or reinforce heteronormativity, dispelling the assumption that all texts depicting sapphic relationships are inherently subversive. Additionally, when referring to romantic or erotic desire among women, I employ the term *sapphic* to offer a more nuanced understanding of gender and sexuality, free from the limitations and trans-exclusionary implications that the term *lesbian* has come to signify.

The Scope of This Book

In crafting this project, I have deliberately chosen to focus on sapphic representation in literature. With the growing interest in contemporary Latin American women writers and a renewed attention to those historically overlooked, it is imperative that *cuir* women's literature be similarly recognized. In 2024, writer Artemisa Téllez compiled an anthology of Mexican lesbian short stories titled *Hasta que comienza a brillar*. In the prologue, she underscores the importance of including lesbian texts in the current movement reclaiming women's literature. For Téllez, *cuir* women "are also part of the history and evolution of Mexican literature; we want and should have a seat at the table, to converse and be in dialogue with the rest of its productions, to be equally represented, not as a whim or an accident, but as an intellectual, emotional, and erotic possibility for liberation for all women and their writing" ("también formamos parte de la historia y la evolución de la literatura mexicana, queremos y debemos sentarnos a su mesa, departir, compartir y dialogar con el resto de sus producciones, figurar en la misma medida, no como capricho, ni como accidente, sino como una posibilidad intelectual, afectiva y erótica emancipadora para todas las mujeres y para su escritura"; 11–12). Furthermore, my decision to focus solely on literary texts stems from the significant role that literature has played for *cuir* women in Mexico.

As Adriana Fuentes Ponce explains in her study on Mexican lesbian social movements, the first publications by women that directly addressed same-sex desire were literary texts, primarily published in the 1980s and 90s, such as Rosamaría Roffiel's *Amora* (1989) (*Decidir sobre el propio cuerpo* 30). Unlike other forms of media, literature has uniquely captured the nuanced and gradual progress that lesbians have made in Mexican society, reflecting their struggles and triumphs in ways that other art forms have not. While film and television have slowly begun to incorporate more sapphic characters, literature—particularly texts that have historically lacked visibility—has provided women a platform to share their perspectives on *cuir* stories, which often differ significantly from more conventional representations. In this regard, I see sapphic literature in Mexico as having the potential to contribute to what Ann Cvetkovich defines as an *archive of feelings*. According to Cvetkovich, documenting LGBTQ+ history allows us to understand "cultural texts as repositories of feelings and emotions, which are encoded not only in the content of the texts themselves but in the practices that surround their production and reception" (7). With this in mind, I intend for this book to serve as a repository of sapphic narratives, aiming, in part, to highlight texts that might otherwise have limited circulation.

At the same time, despite social changes leading to increased sapphic representation in Mexican film and television, progress has been slow and often lacks voices from within the community. In the 1990s, the rise of neoliberalism in Mexico caused cinema to shift away from the nationalist values that had defined it since its early years, focusing instead on emerging social and economic groups (Sánchez Prado 5). These changes also reflected a desire to use cinema as a tool to present Mexico as a modern, cosmopolitan, and diverse country (Blanco-Cano 68).[16] Although mainstream films over the past two decades have included some depictions of lesbian or bisexual women, these characters are often relegated to the status of secondary characters. This can be seen in films such as *Así del precipicio* (2006, dir. Teresa Suárez), *Niñas mal* (2007, dir. Fernando Sariñana), Gustavo Moheno's remake of Carlos Enrique Taboada's *Hasta el viento tiene miedo* (2007), *Todo incluido* (2009, dir. Rodrigo Ortúzar), and *La otra familia* (2011, dir. Gustavo Loza), among others.

Moreover, much of contemporary Mexican cinema frequently portrays sapphic characters as young, stereotypically beautiful, upper middle class, and living in urban settings (Castro Ricalde 204). As Maricruz Castro Ricalde explains, these depictions often reinforce stereotypes shaped by the male gaze that are non-threatening to heterosexuality (204, 216). These characters are typically played by well-known *telenovela* actresses, and the plots tend to be simple to appeal to "a public that could appreciate these films in movie theaters, television broadcasts, or thanks to their DVD sales" (204). Therefore, despite the growing presence of sapphic characters in Mexican film, until very recently, they have been included for commercial reasons and consequently failed to authentically represent *cuir* women's perspectives.

One of the most notable examples of sapphic representation in audiovisual media is *Las Aparicio* (2010–2011). Produced by the independent company Argos and aired on Cadena 3, a competitor to Televisa and TV Azteca,[17] the series garnered significant popularity. This outsider status contributed to its success, with media reports suggesting that Televisa had blacklisted certain actors for collaborating with a rival network (Smith 135). The freedom provided by being outside mainstream television allowed *Las Aparicio* to explore topics that were considered taboo in Mexico at the time. The series not only portrayed same-sex relationships between women but also delved into issues such as polyamory, women's sexuality and sexual pleasure, workplace sexism, and the consequences of then-President Felipe Calderon's war on drugs. While the show continued the common *telenovela* trend of focusing on the wealthy—and therefore predominantly white—sectors of society, its groundbreaking critique of gender roles contributed to its immediate success (Smith 138). Unlike other sapphic portrayals in Mexican television, *Las Aparicio* became a cultural phenomenon beyond the small screen.

The show's website featured a popular forum where viewers shared how they, like the Aparicio sisters, challenged traditional gender roles. However, the most visited discussion was titled "Cómo salí del closet" ("How I came out of the closet") (Smith 143). The popularity of this topic highlights the need among *cuir* women to express their experiences and underscores the role *Las Aparicio* played in fostering a sense of community and acceptance. As Smith notes, "[t]he moving testimony on these forums shows that women viewers, passionate in their attachment to the characters, clearly feel themselves to be participants and not observers in this drama" (143–44). The lesbian and bisexual communities embraced both the characters and actresses who portrayed Mariana (played by Eréndira Ibarra, Epigmenio Ibarra's daughter) and Julia (played by Liz Gallardo), the sapphic couple on the series. By giving them as much screen time as the other characters, *Las Aparicio* achieved a historic first in Mexican television.

At the same time, one of the show's writers, Natassja Ibarra (the other daughter of Epigmenio Ibarra), was publicly out as a lesbian. Her involvement lent authenticity to the script, as many viewers felt it reflected a genuine understanding of the lesbian experience in Mexico at the time—albeit within the confines of the upper middle class. For many *cuir* women—myself included—*Las Aparicio* represented a crucial, if rare, moment when national television seemed to take us seriously. Although sapphic visibility did not become widespread following the show, the rise and expansion of online streaming platforms present promising prospects. Increasingly, more Mexican shows—and some *telenovelas*, such as *Nadie como tú* (2023)—are including LGBTQ+ characters who transcend traditional stereotypes. Despite these developments in television and streaming, I believe it is still too early to include a thorough analysis in this book.

Moreover, since *Lenchitudes* is written in English, I find it crucial to acknowledge that while I engage with the important works of Chicana lesbian thinkers like Gloria Anzaldúa and Cherríe Moraga, narrative texts by and about Chicanx writers are beyond the scope of my project. I view this as a meaningful distinction, as US readers—including those in academia—often conflate Mexican and Chicanx identities. Chicana feminist lesbians have made significant contributions to literary and cultural studies.[18] For example, Sergio de la Mora argues that much of the work of Chicana feminists has been shaped by the early contributions of Chicana lesbians, whose discussions on sexuality's impact on social structures and the broader Chicano civil rights movement proved groundbreaking (179).[19] However, grouping narratives written by Chicanas with those written by Mexicans or from Mexico (as in the case of Cuban-born Mexican writer Odette Alonso's work) risks erasing the differences between them. Some of these distinctions are outlined by Catrióna Rueda Esquibel, who notes that Chicana lesbians in the United States often face conflicts such as "[b]eing the only Chicana in a white lesbian community, being part of a larger Latina lesbian or lesbian of color community, being the only dyke in a Chicana/o community . . . interracial relationships, Chicana-Chicana relationships" (21). Furthermore, while there are cultural similarities between *lenchitudes* and Chicana lesbians, using a term rooted in activism that responds to specific issues in Mexico would seem, to me, an oversight of the work done by Chicanx writers and thinkers.

As Gabriela F. Arredondo, Aída Hurtado, Norma Klahn, Olga Nájera-Ramírez, and Patricia Zavella explain in *Chicana Feminisms: A Critical Reader* (2003), the unique historical dynamics of Mexico and the United

States and their constant movement across social spaces have led Chicanas to embrace a transnational approach that confronts cultural, political, and economic inequalities (4). These particularities create distinctions between the United States and Mexico that a study like mine would find difficult to bridge. For instance, Chicana feminists theorize the intersections of class, race, and gender, offering crucial insights into *mestizaje*, racial privilege, and decolonial thought. Their work emphasizes resistance to cultural repression and the creation of agency within complex power dynamics (Arredondo et al. 5). Although race and class are interconnected in both countries, their meanings differ significantly between the United States and Mexico.

Taking this into account, I must also note that while only a few of the texts I examine hint at race and class dynamics, they do not engage with these issues deeply enough to support a thorough analysis. I recognize that this reflects a broader issue in Mexican society, where, as Federico Navarrete observes, there is a tendency to deny the existence of racism while admitting to classism, without acknowledging their inherent connection (94). Furthermore, with a few exceptions, the majority of the authors analyzed in this book are based in Mexico City or another major metropolitan area, which affords them greater visibility and makes their texts more accessible to those of us outside of Mexico. Therefore, while I have sought to capture a diverse range of sapphic depictions, racial and class conflicts are underrepresented in these texts. I have addressed and examined these issues when they arise in specific works to ensure they are not overlooked. My hope is that as *cuir* literature continues to expand, future studies will be able to provide more detailed analyses of these critical aspects of Mexican society.

Lenchitudes and Contemporary Mexican Narrative

Literary works offer nuanced and personal insight into sapphic experiences that other forms of media have yet to fully achieve. The connection between literature and the sapphic community is exemplified by *Amora*. As critics have argued, though Roffiel's text has been criticized for its perceived lack of literary merit, it had clear political and social goals at the time of its publication in the late 1980s. First, it featured an openly feminist lesbian as its protagonist during a period when feminists feared being associated with lesbianism (Olivera Córdova, "*Amora*" 133). The novel also portrayed the possibility of women living in community beyond romantic or sexual relationships (Cañedo 68). Second, Roffiel's novel challenged the negative stereotypes of lesbians prevalent at the time and sought to dismantle the heterosexual male fetishization of sapphic relationships (Olivera Córdova, "Amora" 134; Cañedo 63). Lastly, *Amora* aimed to address a gap in Mexican literature by catering to readers who were looking to see their own experiences and sexuality reflected in books (Olivera Córdova, "Amora" 137). This objective underscores the novel's significance; at a time when representation was limited, it played a vital role in forming a small but meaningful network of readers. By connecting individuals through shared experiences and narratives, the book revealed how sapphic literature could foster a sense of community and visibility for *cuir* women.

The network of readers formed around *Amora* has contributed to its status as a cult classic within the lesbian and bisexual communities in Mexico. Despite being one of the best-selling books of its time, it was censored due to its content and remained unavailable for years. However, efforts to suppress the book were unsuccessful, as both critics and the author noted that readers continued to circulate it through photocopies, showing its enduring appeal (Olivera Córdova, *Entre amoras* 105–106). Thus, I consider *Amora* integral to the formation of what Nancy Fraser terms a *subaltern counterpublic*. According to Fraser, these counterpublics are "parallel discursive arenas where members of subordinated social groups invent and circulate counterdiscourses to formulate oppositional interpretations of their identities, interests, and needs" (123). I argue that a counterpublic has been shaped by the readers, writers, and critics of the sapphic literature that Roffiel's novel helped establish in Mexico.

The counterpublic that Fraser describes is evident in the alternative understandings of sapphic love that *Amora* influenced. Roffiel herself has said that her text helped lesbians view their romantic and erotic relationships in a more positive light (quoted in Téllez, "A Chloe le gustaba Olivia" 178). As I previously mentioned, while the author intended to challenge negative stereotypes about lesbians, it was ultimately the readers, through their optimistic interpretation of the text, who gave it significance and established it as a groundbreaking novel for *cuir* women in Mexico (Cañedo 68). Beyond the positive responses *Amora* elicited in the 1990s, its continued readership and impact over the last three decades demonstrate the role that literature can play within a subaltern counterpublic. As Michael Warner explains, a single text or voice alone cannot establish a public (or counterpublic); it is through their circulation and discussion that counterdiscourses are created. For a text to have a public, it must persist over time, and its presence confirmed through a network of citations and references (*Publics and Counterpublics* 90, 97). While I acknowledge that Roffiel's novel is unique in its influence and status as the first lesbian novel in Mexico, I also consider it a powerful example of the potential of sapphic literature. María Elena Olivera Córdova has explained that lesbian literary production in Mexico functions as a form of resistance from a marginalized space, due to the historical exclusion of texts about women's same-sex attraction from the literary canon. Despite this marginalization, Olivera Córdova argues, sapphic texts possess the ability to question dominant norms and stand in contrast to literature considered canonical ("Ni ángeles ni demonios" 277). Therefore, beginning with *Amora*, we can consider sapphic literary texts—and the ongoing efforts to discuss, examine, and circulate them—as part of a subaltern counterpublic.

As I previously mentioned, although male gay literary production in Mexico has been extensively explored by academics, the same cannot be said for literature depicting *cuir* women. As Ernesto Reséndiz Oikión notes, the first scholarly work to focus on lesbian literary representations was published by Elena Madrigal in 2007,[20] followed by the first book-length study on this subject in Mexico, María Elena Olivera Córdova's *Entre amoras* (2009).[21] Critics have traced the origins of lesbian literary representation in Mexico back to characters such as La Gaditana in Federico Gamboa's *Santa* (1903), Rosario in José Revueltas's *Los muros de agua* (1941), the protagonists of Heriberto Frías's "Las inseparables" (1915) (Irwin, "'Las inseparables'" 100–106; Olivera Córdova, *Entre amoras* 9), and Leonor in Juan García Ponce's *Figura de paja* (1964) (Téllez, "A Chole le gustaba Olivia" 176).

These early depictions, shaped by male perspectives, are plagued by negative, misogynist, and often hypersexual stereotypes (Téllez, "A Chloe le gustaba Olivia" 176), reducing women to spectral figures or mere aesthetic objects (Irwin, "'Las inseparables'" 100, 109). Olivera Córdova credits Beatriz Espejo's "Las dulces" (1979) as the first literary text to offer an innovative viewpoint, breaking from earlier portrayals by male authors (*Entre amoras* 67). Nonetheless, it was not until the 1989 publication of *Amora* that contemporary Mexican narrative established a foundational moment for the exploration of lesbian characters. Other literary works soon followed, including Sara Levi-Calderón's *Dos mujeres* (1990), *La muerte alquila un cuarto* (1992) by Gabriela Rábago Palafox, Ethel Krauze's *Infinita* (1992), *Te seguiré buscando* (2003) by Josefina Estrada, *Casa de la magnolia* (2004) by Pedro Ángel Palou, and *¿Y qué fue de Bonita Malacón?* (2007) by José Dimayuga, to name a few.[22]

I have begun this section by discussing lesbian representation because literary criticism thus far has labeled it as such. In fact, critical attention has been devoted to defining the category of lesbian literature, or *lesboliteratura*, in Mexico. For instance, Olivera Córdova defines the *lesbian novel* as one in which the protagonists fictionalize the experiences of women whose sexuality, sensuality, or feelings are directed toward those of the same gender, regardless of the author's gender identity or sexual orientation. Inmaculada Pertusa, meanwhile, identifies lesbian literature as part of the broader fight for equality. According to her, these texts establish deep emotional and/or physical bonds between female characters while simultaneously working to validate these relationships in a hostile environment (quoted in *Entre amoras* 27–28). Olivera Córdova adds that lesbian narrative texts also aim to subvert patriarchy and heterosexuality (27). While this categorization is useful for highlighting specific literary works, I find that, as with the term *lesbian*, this category is limiting because it excludes certain texts.

For example, as I argue in my first chapter, sapphic desire is also present in texts where it may not be the central focus, yet it plays a significant role in the narrative's progression. Artemisa Téllez has highlighted the challenges of relying on a single category to refer to a wide range of works. For Téllez, "[t]o say 'lesbian literature' is in itself something very complicated to speak of: voices, lesbian voices in literature, voices that name and that name us, and that yet, do not define us . . . Complicated, yes, very complicated" ("A Chloe le gustaba Olivia," 173; "Decir 'literatura lésbica' es de por sí algo muy complicado de lo cual hablar: Voces, voces lésbicas en la literatura, voces que nombran y que nos nombran y que, sin embargo, no nos definen . . . Complicado, sí, muy complicado"). To solve some of these problems, she establishes a division between what she terms *lesbofeminist* and *post-feminist* texts.

The former, she contends, represents a type of literature that aims to construct an idealized image of "good lesbians" and that is influenced by feminist thought, as seen in *Amora*. In contrast, when describing *post-feminist* texts, Téllez refers to works produced from the 2000s onward, whose primary objective is to question stereotypical representations (182). She therefore stresses the need to move beyond positive, idealized sapphic depictions in favor of more complex, disruptive characters (184). While I find Téllez's categories useful for examining sapphic literature chronologically, I have chosen not to adopt these labels. This is because even the so-called "good lesbians" can exhibit subversive elements, just as some contemporary, disruptive texts may still reinforce traditional ideas of gender and sexuality.

Whether romanticized or subversive, the portrayal of sapphic characters has been challenging for authors in a male-dominated literary sphere. In *Dude Lit: Mexican Men Writing and Performing Competence, 1955–2012* (2019), Emily Hind draws attention to the gendered nature of the unequal treatment and recognition that women writers have received in Mexico. This issue relates to the term *editopatriarcado* (editorial patriarchy), a term coined by Alma Karla Sandoval and Denisse Buendía to refer to the prejudices and assumptions that literature written by women inherently lacks quality, leading to editorial policies and literary criticism that prioritize works by men and dismiss the literary production of women, particularly those with feminist perspectives (quoted in Damián Miravete).[23]

The gap created in Mexican literature by the marginalization of women writers has been acknowledged by Socorro Venegas and Ave Barrera, who, in 2019, launched the Vindictas project through the Dirección General de Publicaciones at the Universidad Nacional Autónoma de México. This initiative seeks to publish new editions of literary works authored by women throughout twentieth-century Latin America that, at the time of their original publication, were overlooked and forgotten due to the biases of a male-centered literary sphere. While one might expect that, given the discourses on inclusion surrounding the LGBTQ+ movement, these circumstances would be different for women writing within this community, the reality is that the *editopatriarcado* remains alive and well.

This is partly reflected in the absence of sapphic representation in Mexican literature. In a personal communication, Téllez discussed with me the lack of interest in this type of work, arguing that while heterosexual critics do not regard it as "good literature," gay men in the publishing world tend to prioritize texts by other gay men, often including a lesbian author or two to fill quotas. She recounted how a well-known writer—then the editor of a now-defunct LGBTQ+ press and whose name is often linked with LGBTQ+ literature in Mexico—rejected her novel *Crema de vainilla* on the grounds that it featured "too many vaginas." In 2021, this same author led a virtual workshop on Mexican queer literature sponsored by UNAM, during which he claimed that women do not write about women writers—a statement that many of my colleagues, particularly women, would likely find both amusing and false. I joined the workshop out of interest in how queer studies were being framed in Mexico but was disappointed by the lack of discussion on queer theory or its relevance to Latin America. Additionally, I witnessed the instructor repeatedly misgender a non-binary participant, despite their voicing concerns to no avail. Later, he made a post on social media mocking the use of inclusive language.

These attitudes demonstrate that the LGBTQ+ literary sphere in Mexico remains not only male-centered but also influenced by conservative ideas that fail to critically engage with the possibilities of *lo cuir*. For Olivera Córdova, this reflects how what she terms *lesbian literature* has faced more hostility and censorship than gay male literature ("Narrativa lésbica mexicana" 134). Given these circumstances, it is unsurprising that, after its publication, *Amora* was censored for years, pulled from circulation, and heavily criticized—a subject I discuss in chapter 4. Despite growing interest in women's *cuir* literature in Mexico, many of the obstacles that authors like Roffiel faced nearly four decades ago still persist.

This project seeks to join other scholarly works that have brought attention to these often-overlooked narratives in Mexico, such as Olivera Córdova's extensive research and Elena Madrigal and Leticia Romero's *Un juego que cabe entre nosotras* (2014), along with works by Adriana Fuentes Ponce, Artemisa Téllez, Alicia Ramírez Olivares, Jorge Luis Gallegos Vargas, Deborah Shaw, Cynthia Duncan, Francesca Dennstedt, and others. Despite the significant contribution of these scholars, there remains a shortage of studies focusing on literature depicting *cuir* women in Mexico. As a result, there is limited engagement with issues of sexuality and gender beyond binary frameworks. For instance, I have yet to encounter Mexican critics who approach the question of what it means to be a woman or who address the problematic nature of categories such as *lesbian* beyond the transphobic stances that I have discussed.

When asked in an interview about whether a tradition of lesbian literature exists in Mexico, Téllez points out the difficulties posed by essentialism, emphasizing that this topic can be explored from many different perspectives. She adds, "For me, that would be the way to start a tradition, that lesbian literature might tell us about 'other ways to be human and free' and not just two (or more) characters with pussy and tits who love, marry, and/or leave each other. Nobody—including myself—has done that in our country" ("An Interview with Artemisa Téllez" 15). For the author, sapphic literature being written in Mexico is "mostly stories of love and/or sex between women. And they're stories that don't question conventional notions of 'love,' 'sex' or 'women' at all" ("An Interview with Artemisa

Téllez" 16). I agree with Téllez's assertion that many literary texts addressing sapphic desire in Mexico do not necessarily subvert conventional norms. In some instances, I find that they replicate what Lisa Duggan has termed *new homonormativity*, or "a privatized, depoliticized gay culture anchored in domesticity and consumption" (179). Nonetheless, I find the issue is more nuanced than it appears. It is important to acknowledge the complexities and subtleties within these texts, which may challenge or reframe traditional narratives in ways that are less overt but equally significant.

Consequently, I contend that a closer examination of several novels and short stories—including Téllez's own—through the lens of *lenchitudes* reveals that they do, in fact, destabilize normative ideas. This book, therefore, views *lenchitudes* as a point of departure to explore sapphic portrayals in Mexican literature, following Stuart Hall's assertion that although representations do not directly reflect reality, meaning is constructed through representation (3). In this context, I analyze how practices of representation, understood as "the embodying of concepts, ideas and emotions in a symbolic form which can be transmitted and meaningfully interpreted" (Hall 10), can be examined to uncover their dissident possibilities or their compliance with normative ideologies.

To analyze these representations, I have selected and organized my corpus thematically to highlight the recurrence of certain archetypes and themes that lend themselves to examining each text's relation to normativity. As I have noted, while literary production about sapphic relationships is scarce in Mexico, I have broadened the scope of my study beyond what might traditionally be considered *lesbian literature*, allowing for the inclusion of a wider range of authors and texts. Although an approach through the lens of *lenchitudes* expands sapphic representation to include more than just cisgender women, I was unable to find narrative works that address the themes that I seek to highlight in this book while also centering trans or non-binary characters. However, I am hopeful that as more writers create inclusive spaces and collaboration among *cuir* authors continues to grow, this will change in the future.

The works I examine are not in chronological order. My earliest example is Rosamaría Roffiel's *Amora* from 1989, while the most recent text is Odette Alonso's short story "Un puñado de cenizas" from 2018. I selected this timeline because I wanted to explore how the approach to various issues in narrative sapphic characters has changed since *Amora*, given its significance as a foundational text. Simultaneously, the issues discussed throughout this book are reflected in the selected narratives in a way that reveals their relationship to normativity across three decades. Some of the research questions guiding *Lenchitudes* include: How does sapphic representation in contemporary Mexican literature challenge or perpetuate binary understandings of gender and sexuality? In what ways do these often-overlooked narrative texts contribute to new representations that defy compulsory heterosexuality and monogamy? What kinds of archetypes are being created by authors of sapphic literature, and how do they deviate from or reinforce stereotypical representations?

I begin to address these inquiries in chapter 1, "Points of Departure: Traces of Sapphic Desire," by employing José Esteban Muñoz's concept of queerness as potentiality. I examine how sapphic desire is implied in novels and short stories to temporarily destabilize heteronormativity and, in certain cases, challenge masculinity and men's control over women's bodies. This chapter seeks to break free from the restrictive category of *lesbian literature* by illustrating the widespread presence of sapphic representation in contemporary Mexican narrative. Shifting beyond this classification, I turn to Cristina Rivera Garza's *La cresta de Ilión* (2002), which indirectly critiques compulsory heterosexuality and demonstrates how sapphic desire can dislocate both gender and sexuality, albeit temporarily. Similarly, I analyze Ana Clavel's *Cuerpo náufrago* (2005), arguing that while it directly challenges gender norms and uses traces of sapphic desire to further the protagonist's sexual development, it struggles to fully escape the constraints of the gender binary. I then examine Valeria Luiselli's novel *Los ingrávidos* (2011), which I contend presents traces of sapphic desire through an intimacy that never becomes sexual yet undermines the protagonist's husband, who functions as a representation of patriarchal authority. I continue my examination through an analysis of Iliana Godoy's short story "Baños de pureza" (2005), where an erotic encounter between two friends reveals the repercussions of not following society's expectations of heterosexuality. Finally, I analyze Mónica Lavín's "Ladies Bar" (2012), where the strip club serves as a space for the protagonist to challenge heteronormativity by momentarily desiring other women. However, she is ultimately punished for this transgression.

Chapter 2, "*La más macha de las machas: Lencha* masculinities," highlights the limited representation of female masculinity in sapphic narratives. Drawing on Jack Halberstam's *Female Masculinity* (1998) alongside the work of Mexican critics like Olivera Córdova, I explore how female masculinity is portrayed. I propose the concept of *lencha* masculinities to describe various expressions of sapphic gender identity that challenge or render visible the violence associated with hegemonic masculinities and therefore contribute to new perspectives on gender identity. I begin by examining the negative stereotyping of masculine women as inherently reproducing male-perpetrated violence, as seen in Reyna Barrera's novel *Sandra, secreto amor* (2001), and the rejection of masculinity in Ana Klein's *No hay princesa sin dragón* (2004).

To counterbalance these negative representations, I examine the work of two writers who offer a more nuanced understanding of female masculinity. One such example is Victoria Enríquez's 1997 short story "De un pestañazo," loosely based on transgender revolutionary colonel Amelio Robles. Rather than focusing on transgender identity, Enríquez portrays her protagonist as a masculine woman who, in contrast to negative depictions of female masculinity, is a complex figure who respects women and rejects *macho*[24] violence. Similarly, in her short story "A dos, de tres caídas" (2010), Elena Madrigal explores the feminine side of an otherwise masculine protagonist who works as a professional wrestler. Both depictions problematize essentialist representations of female masculinity, offering diverse characters that exemplify the subversive potential of *lencha* masculinities.

In chapter 3, I explore how narratives representing sapphic relationships tend to reject female masculinity and idealize stereotypical femininity, often portraying the latter as dangerous. "The *Fem Fatal:* Femme Representation" traces the prevalence of an archetype I have identified as the *fem fatal*. Drawing on the well-known femme fatale, I propose a Mexican sapphic equivalent that combines the term *fem*—short for *femenina*—and *fatal*, following the Spanish translation. This chapter builds on the work of scholars such as Erika Bornay, Catherine O'Rawe, and Helen Hanson on the femme fatale, as well as those who have studied women's representation in Mexican literature and culture, including Debra A. Castillo and Carlos Monsiváis. I argue that the *fem fatal* is a character who, while portrayed as desirable and feminine, seeks to manipulate and exploit the protagonist's emotions. However, I contend that when the *fem fatal* successfully aligns with the goals of *lenchitudes* by subverting stereotypical representations that vilify female sexuality, she can challenge negative associations and embody an empowered femininity that resists problematic power dynamics.

I argue that this disruption is achieved in Artemisa Téllez's illustrated novel, *Crema de vainilla* (2014), which presents a *fem fatal* who, despite being portrayed as seductive, is not constructed as an antagonist but rather helps the protagonist explore and embrace her sexuality. I then turn to Odette Alonso's "Un puñado de cenizas" (2018), where, although the *fem fatal* is vilified, the use of multiple perspectives adds depth and complexity to the story. Finally, I highlight the relationship between the *fem fatal* and the problematic Lolita archetype, a young woman who is overly sexualized and engages in relationships with older women, as seen in Eve Gil's short story "Arsénico y caramelos" (2005) and Mildred Pérez de la Torre's novel *Lo hice por amor* (2016). By outlining this type of character in narratives depicting sapphic desire, my project emphasizes femme representation while also questioning its simultaneous idealization and vilification.

I conclude with chapter 4, "Queering Heteronormativity or Normalizing Queerness? Monogamy and Motherhood," in which I engage with the tensions between *lo cuir* and the concepts of motherhood and monogamy. I begin by underscoring the contrast between the normalization of male infidelity in Mexico and an approach to non-monogamy that has the potential to subvert heteronormativity. Drawing on Judith Butler's work, I argue that while monogamy and kinship are central to normalizing discourses within the LGBTQ+ community—where access to citizenship and equality is seen as a political goal—a truly *cuir* approach should not reject these outright but rather remain critical of their ties to homonormativity. Thus, while *lenchitudes* is an expansive concept that embraces all sapphic expressions, its objective to question normativity allows it to be both inclusive and critical.

Chapter 4 also returns to the origins of my literary corpus by examining monogamy in Rosamaría Roffiel's *Amora*. While the novel's portrayal of sapphic desire and its feminist perspective were groundbreaking at the time of its publication, I contend that its flawed depiction of non-monogamy contributes to misunderstandings about its subversive potential. However, I also find that the protagonist, Guadalupe, offers a novel approach by rejecting heteronormative family structures and creating her own *cuir* family. In comparison to Roffiel's text, I examine Gilda Salinas's *Del destete al desempance: Cuentos lésbicos y un colado* (2008), which, through a series of short stories, portrays different facets of sapphic life in Mexico City from the 1970s to the 1990s. Although the stories offer a glimpse into the nightlife of gay and lesbian bars in Mexico City, the protagonist, who initially resists commitment, is ultimately redeemed through her acceptance of monogamy. In this sense, the collection upholds heteronormative ideals by positioning monogamy and romantic love as the solution to a chaotic life. I conclude chapter 4 by exploring the portrayal of motherhood in

Rhyme & Reason (2008) by Criseida Santos Guevara. Although sapphic motherhood is largely absent from contemporary Mexican literature, Santos Guevara's novel disrupts heterosexual temporality and traditional expectations of motherhood. By refusing to parent her and her partner's children and ultimately escaping from the relationship, I argue that the protagonist rejects patriarchal expectations and embraces failure.

Despite their many differences, the texts I examine represent various forms of sapphic depictions in contemporary Mexican literature. These contrasts allow for an analysis that, through the lens of *lenchitudes*, demonstrates how sapphic representation is neither monolithic nor inherently dissident. By rejecting static identities such as *lesbian* and theorizing gender and sexuality from a broader perspective, we can better understand how some depictions may be complicit in perpetuating normativity and its associated oppressions, while others create space for subversion. Ultimately, this book seeks to underscore the significance of sociopolitical movements in the development of *lo cuir* in Latin America, while also proposing that academic fields like literary and cultural studies can both draw from and contribute to activist efforts.

Chapter 1

Points of Departure

Traces of Sapphic Desire

When I first embarked on this project years ago, I found it challenging to identify texts that portrayed sapphic desire beyond the works of authors like Roffiel, Levi-Calderón, and Barrera. I was eager to explore these narrative works, which were unfamiliar to me, as my literary education—like that of many of my peers—had predominantly focused on a male, heterosexual canon. Determined to find other examples, I sought guidance from my mentor. "You should go to the library and skim through every book that you think might hold something relevant," he said. I chuckled, assuming he was joking. "I am serious," he replied with a stern look on his face. And so began the journey that led me to the *corpus* for this project.

I relied on my mentor's method to find many of the texts I analyze in this book. Others were recommended to me by scholars like María Elena Olivera Córdova, Elena Madrigal, Artemisa Téllez, and Ernesto Reséndiz Oikión, whose generosity—both through direct conversations and through their work—helped guide my research. After reading as much literary criticism on Mexican lesbian literature as I could find, I recognized, as I noted in my introduction, that using these labels can be valuable, particularly when building an archive or understanding the relationship between literature and societal changes. However, these categories risk excluding certain authors whose contributions to the representation of sexual and gender dissidence can enrich and expand how we view Mexican literature. During my search, I began to identify examples of sapphic desire in texts that had not yet been examined through what I now refer to as the lens of *lenchitudes*. Many of these instances seemed hidden in plain sight or, rather, required a different interpretive approach, as in the case of authors like Lavín or Luiselli.

I begin by examining narratives that, while not exclusively centered on sapphic desire, incorporate it to briefly disrupt heteronormativity. In this chapter, I aim to demonstrate that women's explorations of *lo cuir* are not limited to authors associated with LGBTQ+ representation. I refer to these disruptions as "traces of sapphic desire," drawing from José Esteban Muñoz's conceptualization of queerness as potentiality or utopia. For Muñoz, "[q]ueerness is essentially about the rejection of a here and now and an insistence of potentiality or concrete possibility for another world" (1). Following this perspective of queerness as potentiality, I interpret these moments of desire as instances where heteronormativity is momentarily disrupted, though the longings are not fully realized. Instead, they offer fleeting glimpses of *lo cuir*. I contend that adopting a wider approach, such as *lenchitudes*, allows us to move beyond rigid identities and binaries, enabling us to explore the interstices of gender and sexuality and the insights offered by their literary representations.

In the works I analyze, these instances not only challenge male control over women but also establish intimate spaces between them that exist beyond men's reach. This, I argue, reflects Adrienne Rich's concept of lesbian existence as a form of resistance (24). I use the term *trace* as defined by the *Merriam-Webster* dictionary: "a minute and often barely detectable amount or indication." My word choice stems from the fact that, while the texts I examine may not explicitly focus on *cuir* representation, these moments of desire serve as "cracks through which non-heterosexual realities filter" ("grietas a través de las cuales se filtran realidades ajenas a lo heterosexual"; Fraile Gómez 240). While more evident in some texts than others, I seek to highlight and deconstruct these moments to uncover their significance. These traces of desire embody *lenchitudes*: They transcend categories of identity and reveal how sapphic desire is not only pervasive in Mexican literature but also has the potential to disrupt and expose essentialist and limiting notions of sexuality, along with mechanisms of oppression such as patriarchal control of women. The novels and short stories examined in this chapter approach these moments in various ways. In some cases, sapphic desire opens new avenues for characters to explore their sexuality and gender identity, while, in others, these transgressions lead to punishment.

Despite the differences among these texts, they all reveal the tensions that arise from the queering of women's sexuality. I see these hints of desire as forms of potentiality, following Muñoz's definition as "a certain mode of nonbeing that is eminent, a thing that is present, but not actually existing in the present tense" (9). For Muñoz, potentiality can act as an opening to transformation, and although he cautions against the disappointment that utopian feelings can bring, he argues that they are necessary for imagining change (9). At the same time, I am drawn to these intermittent disruptions because, as Sara Ahmed reminds us, "[i]t is given that the straight world is already in place and that queer moments, where things come out of line, are fleeting"; therefore, instead of searching for permanence, we must "listen to the sound of 'the what' that fleets" (*Queer Phenomenology* 106). This chapter examines these fleeting sounds to reveal their subversive potential within each literary text.

By rejecting essentialist notions of sexuality, this section offers a broader understanding of *lenchitudes* as forms of desire that can evolve and shift, independent of fixed identity categories. In *Queer Phenomenology* (2006), Ahmed dissects the heterosexualization of desire as part of a linear structure that assumes women's sexuality is directed toward men, and vice versa. For Ahmed, lesbian desire[1] follows lines of connection that deviate from this "straight line." She suggests that "[l]esbian desires create spaces, often temporary spaces that come and go with the coming and going of the bodies that inhabit them. The points of this existence don't easily accumulate as lines, or if they do, they might leave different impressions on the ground" (105–106). Therefore, I am less concerned with how the characters define their sexual orientation and more interested in how their desire ebbs and flows, as Ahmed describes, and how it operates within each narrative to momentarily displace patriarchal structures.

I begin by examining the characters Amparo Dávila and La Traicionada in Cristina Rivera Garza's novel *La cresta de Ilión* (2002). I argue that their close and ambiguous relationship leads them to create a language of their own, effectively situating them out of the reach of men. I then explore Antonia/Antón, the protagonist of Ana Clavel's *Cuerpo náufrago* (2005), who one day wakes up in a man's body. I see traces of sapphic desire and the disruptive potential of *lenchitudes* in Antonia/Antón, particularly in moments when, fully conscious of her female identity, she reflects on her attraction to women and questions her sexuality and the boundaries of gender. Nonetheless, I contend, the novel does not fully escape these limits, as it reinforces some of the behaviors and attitudes associated with masculinity and femininity.

My third analysis focuses on Valeria Luiselli's *Los ingrávidos* (2011), particularly the intimate interactions between the nameless protagonist and a friend during her youth in the United States. The novel also explores how, years later, her husband in Mexico becomes obsessed with his wife's possible sapphic desire. I then turn to short stories by Iliana Godoy and Mónica Lavín. In "Baños de pureza" (2005), Godoy narrates a sexual encounter between two friends, followed by the pressure to keep it secret due to heteronormative expectations of women. Similarly, Mónica Lavín's short story "Ladies Bar" (2012) follows a young woman who, after entering a strip club, transitions from wanting to emulate the dancers to experiencing sexual desire for them. This selection of narrative texts offers an opportunity to analyze characters that embody sapphic desire, written by authors not typically associated with such themes. Through the examination of these works, I demonstrate how *lo cuir* subtly, yet significantly, permeates contemporary Mexican literature, revealing a nuanced and often-overlooked dimension of sexuality and gender and problematizing labels such as *lesbian literature*.

The characters I study experience sexuality as fluid, revealing a spectrum of desire that transcends rigid sexual identities. This fluidity offers insight into how women's desire can challenge compulsory heterosexuality, a concept originally coined by Rich in her essay "Compulsory Heterosexuality and Lesbian Existence" (1980). She contends that while heterosexuality is often assumed as a given, lesbianism challenges this restrictive view of sexual orientation. She writes that lesbian existence "comprises both the breaking of a taboo and the rejection of a compulsory way of life. It is also a direct or indirect attack on male right of access to women. But it is more than these, although we may first begin to perceive it as a form of nay-saying to patriarchy, an act of resistance" (24). While Rich emphasizes the potential of sapphic desire to disrupt heterosexual norms, we must not idealize it as a simple alternative.

Romanticizing sapphic relationships presumes they are inherently free from the influences of patriarchy and oppression. This perspective risks oversimplifying *cuir* relationships between women as inherently good, thereby disregarding the diverse and complex experiences that exist. Nevertheless, I am particularly interested in Rich's approach to lesbian desire as an experience that challenges patriarchal control by limiting male access to women. This is especially relevant to this chapter, as in many of the texts I analyze, a clear tension emerges among the men who suspect or witness sapphic desire, which is directly tied to their perceived loss of control over women.

Writing from the Latin American context, Norma Mogrovejo suggests that "[h]eterosexual oppression obstructs and denies love between women to prevent either their individual existential and erotic autonomy or the possibility of forming alliances" ("La opresión heterosexual obstaculiza y niega el amor entre mujeres para impedir o bien su individual autonomía erótica y existencial, o bien la posibilidad de una alianza entre ellas"; *Un amor* 11). She argues that this repression compounds the challenges women already face due to gender hierarchies in various spheres. Therefore, traces of sapphic desire transcend eroticism, offering a glimpse into how female characters form alliances beyond the reach of men—alliances that "are about shared struggles, common grounds, and mutual aspirations, as bonds that are created through the lived experiences of being 'off line' and 'out of line'" (Ahmed, *Queer Phenomenology* 103). This is not to suggest that women are attracted to sameness in these moments of desire. As Ahmed argues, "[t]he very idea of women desiring women because of 'sameness' relies on a fantasy that women are 'the same'" (*Queer Phenomenology* 96). Rather, I propose that these instances temporarily create coalitions among women, allowing them to forego men and experience a sense of freedom, whether physical or emotional.

Before proceeding to my analysis, I find it essential to highlight the relationship between the traces of desire I identify and the concept of *lo cuir*. While one might assume that by discussing sapphic desire we are inherently referring to *lo cuir*, it is crucial to understand that *lo cuir* extends beyond sexual implications. It functions as a broader framework that disrupts traditional gender norms and power structures in various ways. In the ongoing debate about the translatability of *queer* into the Latin American context and Spanish language, Amy Kaminsky has proposed the transposition of the verb *to queer* into *encuirar*. She defines it as follows:

Reminiscent of the verb "to undress" and evoking the act of stripping, *encuirar* means to un-cover reality, to remove the layer of heteronormativity. *Encuirar* seeks to undress not only to show the reality under the misleading clothing—the classic outing—, but also as a form of deconstruction. It questions the stability of the norms. It reveals the instability of identity and, paradoxically, also unveils the need to create and defend alternative identities to survive in a culture ruled by standardized identity.

("Reminiscente del verbo encuerar y evocandor (sic) del acto de desnudar, encuirar significa des-cubrir la realidad, retirar la capa de la heteronormatividad. Encuirar propone desvestir no solamente para mostrar la realidad debajo de la vestidura engañosa–el outing clásico–, sino también como una forma de deconstrucción. Cuestiona la estabilidad de las normas. Revela la inestabilidad de la identidad y, paradójicamente, revela también la necesidad de crear y defender identidades alternativas para sobrevivir en una cultura regida por la identidad normatizada"; 879).

Thus, *encuirar* involves deconstructing normativity and illuminating subversive approaches that expose the fragility of patriarchal and heteronormative structures.

Regarding the translatability of *queer* as a verb, some critics have preferred the term *cuirizar.* This expression serves the same purpose and, on a political level, aims to dismantle the patriarchal order and reveal the mechanisms of oppression embedded in various societies (Domínguez Ruvalcaba, *Latinoamérica Queer* 189). The act of *encuirar/cuirizar* thus enables us to witness the disruption of what Judith Butler has termed *the heterosexualization of desire,* which "requires and institutes the production of discrete and asymmetrical oppositions between 'feminine' and 'masculine' where these are understood as expressive attributes of 'male' and female'" (*Gender Trouble* 23). This challenges the binary constraints imposed on gender expression and sexual orientation.

The works examined in this chapter make these limitations visible, prompting readers to question their normalization. While it would be naïve to assume that experiencing sapphic desire inherently challenges patriarchy, I argue that these moments in the narratives I analyze have direct consequences for both the women who experience them and the men surrounding them. These instances of erotic attraction are not coincidental; rather, they serve a specific function in revealing the complexity of female sexuality while also confronting social norms and the power dynamics that sustain them.

"A Language of Their Own":
La cresta de Ilión (2002) by Cristina Rivera Garza

Cristina Rivera Garza's (b. 1964, Matamoros) oeuvre is among the most widely studied by literary critics in contemporary Mexico. Her writing resists easy categorization due to its diverse themes and structures, making it difficult to situate within any specific movement (Estrada, "Asignaciones de género" 179). Nonetheless, as Oswaldo Estrada argues, Rivera Garza—along with Clavel—belongs to a generation of women writers whose work engages with issues of gender and sexuality, raising critical questions about the construction of subjectivities and combating essentialist modes of representation "not only of themselves as women but of all human beings trapped in intricate labyrinths of social conduct" ("Against Representation" 64–65). Some scholars have referred to this new generation as the *boom femenino*, alluding to the proliferation of women writers throughout Latin America since the 1970s (Finnegan and Lavery 1). This label remains a topic of debate since some writers find it unnecessary and limiting. However, it can be a useful means of approaching literary texts that have long been subject to gatekeeping, as discussed in my introduction regarding the concept of *editopatriarcado*.

Detractors of the term *boom femenino* often argue that it has been used to categorize authors associated with best-sellers and commercialism, such as Laura Esquivel and Ángeles Mastretta. For this reason, scholars Jane E. Lavery and Nuala Finnegan situate those like Rivera Garza and Clavel within a second generation of the *boom femenino*. As they explain, although these writers' literary production is somewhat related to that of their predecessors in its engagement with gender inequality, sexuality, and the body, they deliberately write texts that "are not the best-seller type associated with certain Mexican women's writing of the *boom femenino*" (5–6). At the same time, examining the work of authors like Rivera Garza and Clavel is productive for moving beyond the label of *lesbian literature*. Their writing demonstrates how focusing solely on authors categorized as LGBTQ+ overlooks other contributions that can help us rethink *cuir* representation and its evolution. The generation of women highlighted by Estrada underscores the increasing complexity of Mexican narrative production, particularly as these authors challenge the perception of sexuality and gender as rigidly defined categories.

Due to Rivera Garza's versatility and complexity, I have chosen to analyze her novel *La cresta de Ilión*. The text follows a nameless male protagonist, a doctor at the Granja del Buen Reposo, whose life is permanently altered when a woman identifying herself as Amparo Dávila—referred to as *la Falsa* (the False One) throughout the novel—arrives at his home and decides to stay. This character clearly references Mexican writer Amparo Dávila (b. 1928, Zacatecas; d. 2020), and the novel further complicates her presence by introducing a second, older Amparo Dávila, known as *la Desaparecida* (the Disappeared). This nickname reflects the real Amparo Dávila's situation at the time of *La cresta de Ilión*'s publication, when her work had largely been forgotten by both readers and critics. However, interest in Dávila's work has undergone a dramatic resurgence in the twenty-first century, with fascination for her texts growing significantly over the past two decades (Carrillo Juárez 26).[2] Her fiction is renowned for exploring the boundaries between fantasy and reality, as well as for its engagement with horror and the uncanny. Rivera Garza's inclusion of Dávila as multiple characters in *La cresta de Ilión* serves not only as an homage and a way to enrich her own writing (Carrillo Juárez 36), but also as an exercise in citing one of her literary predecessors, integrating elements from the Zacatecan writer's short stories into her novel.[3]

In *La cresta de Ilión*, the relationship between the younger Amparo and the male protagonist is complicated by her insistence on referring to him as a woman, which eventually causes him to question his gender. The protagonist lives with his former lover, La Traicionada (the Betrayed), who has fallen ill and builds an intimate relationship with Amparo. Throughout the novel, the doctor's insecurities about his gender identity, and eventually his sexuality, lead him to repeatedly assert his masculinity. However, he ultimately fails in this avowal as the two women continue to view him as a woman. Beyond the clear interrogation of gender in Rivera Garza's novel, my focus is on the relationship between La Traicionada and the young Amparo Dávila and its traces of sapphic desire. Their *encuiramiento* (queering) of heteronormativity begins as the characters grow closer, sharing a bed and creating a unique language. This language can be spoken by the doctor only once he embraces his own femininity.

The connection between the women is contrasted with the narrator-protagonist's exclusion and initial inability to understand their language (Breckenridge 153). Their emotional closeness becomes physical when they literally shut him out, creating a space where they can exist in each other's company, free from patriarchal influence. The doctor's initial confusion soon turns to anger as he remarks, "Their closeness bothered me. From the crack in the door, I was able to see the gentleness with which they treated each other, the sweetness in their looks. Their mutual tenderness, developing over the course of only a few days, and with one of them in a semiconscious state, made me suspicious of the whole situation" ("La cercanía entre las dos me molestó. Desde la rendija de la puerta pude observar la delicadeza con la que se trataban, la dulzura con la que se veían la una a la otra. Su mutuo encariñamiento acaecido en unos cuantos días y, además, con una de ellas en estado semi-consciente, me hizo sospechar de toda la situación"; 33, 36).[4] Although he claims to fear "feminine revenge," his anxiety partly arises from recognizing the growing closeness between the women. His preoccupation suggests that, before questioning his gender identity, he constantly asserts his masculinity out of anxiety that their relationship might undermine his power.

There is a contrast between Amparo and La Traicionada's relationship and the doctor's sexual encounters, which is notable for two reasons. First, despite the omnipresence of sapphic desire between the women (Breckenridge 154), readers are kept at a distance from their intimate space, just as the protagonist is. Whether or not sexual acts take place remains unknown to us, as the women choose to preserve their privacy rather than expose their relationship to the male gaze. This lack of sexual depiction reflects what Judith Roof has referred to as "the strategic deployment of a lack of direct image" in sapphic eroticism in film, which avoids representing same-sex sexual acts in heteronormative terms (75). In the context of sapphic literature in Mexico, Cynthia Duncan has observed a similar approach in *Amora*, where "[t]he erotic takes place behind closed doors, between the sheets, and is expressed 'con un lenguaje secreto' ['*with a secret language*'] that limits it to a private space" (79). While themes of secret languages and privacy are present in both novels, in *Amora* it is evident that the characters do engage in sexual encounters, keeping their intimacy just out of reach for the reader. However, in *La cresta de Ilión*, we never learn what Amparo and La Traicionada do. What we do know is that they do not hide their potential physical interactions out of fear or shame—neither do the characters in *Amora*—but rather, because of the presence of the male doctor, they deliberately set boundaries on what both the protagonist and the reader are allowed to know, a choice that serves as a form of agency and power.

On the other hand, we witness the doctor having sex with two women who work in the hospital's archive, whom he derogatorily refers to as *urracas* (magpies). The novel portrays the protagonist's fantasies about them, as well as their sexual encounter. These moments serve to reaffirm his gender identity as a man, as he constantly touches his genitals and emphasizes his sexual prowess (Estrada, "Against Representation" 66). The threesome is described in explicit detail, which Breckenridge interprets as male-centric to the point of parody (154). These descriptions stand in stark contrast to the novel's lack of information regarding the possible physical intimacy between La Traicionada and Amparo.

The second example of how the doctor's sexual encounters differ from the relationship between the two women is evident in his remarks about the tenderness between them, which contrasts sharply with his view of the *urracas*. When describing them, he argues that, "[b]ecause they were women, their rank, so clearly inferior to mine, didn't provoke resentment but spurred a secret desire for upward mobility, which sometimes mixed with strange sexual urges" ("Porque eran mujeres, su rango menor, claramente inferior comparado con el mío, no les provocaba resentimiento alguno sino, por el contrario, secretos deseos arribistas que, a veces, se mezclaban con extrañas urgencias sexuales"; 43, 48). His description underscores his perception of the *urracas* as inferior, not only because of their gender but also due to his higher status as a doctor in comparison to their roles as administrative workers. His depiction of them echoes the sexual division of labor that has historically benefited men and reflects societal structures that restrict women to certain roles or limit their advancement within professional and economic hierarchies (Connell, *Gender and Power* 99). His disdain for the women goes beyond their job roles; calling them *urracas* instead of using their names—or descriptive names, as with La Traicionada—dehumanizes them by likening them to birds. Moreover, he sees them as interchangeable, in contrast to his acknowledgment of male nurses Moisés and Gaspar[5] by name.

Lastly, as the doctor narrates the details of the threesome with the two women, he also expresses his boredom: "Then, improvising, I pulled out and saw how she squirmed on the bed, waiting for more. My boredom, by then, was tremendous" ("Entonces me retiré de improviso y vi cómo se revolcaba sobre la cama esperando más. Mi aburrimiento, para entonces, era mayúsculo"; 58, 49–50).[6] His treatment of women reduces them to sexual objects for his own pleasure, to be discarded once he is finished with them. In contrast, upon discovering the intimate and potentially sexual relationship between La Traicionada and Amparo, he becomes suspicious of their caring behavior. Though the text does not explicitly condemn compulsory heterosexuality (Breckenridge 154), I argue that it critiques the violent and problematic dynamics that arise when men strip women of their subjectivity, in part to assert their own masculinity.

These contrasting interactions demonstrate how sapphic desire and feminine subjects, as encompassed by *lenchitudes,* can challenge compulsory heteronormativity by rendering its worst aspects visible. As Rich reminds us, the very existence of those who desire other women can be read as an attack on the idea that men are entitled to women's bodies (24). At the beginning of the novel, the protagonist perceives his masculinity as dependent on the subjugation of women and the rejection of femininity. As Carlos Monsiváis points out in the context of Mexico, patriarchal ideology turns a biological fact into a goal, where achieving manhood is seen as an accomplishment, attained through one's first sexual act (*recibirse de hombre*). Consequently, its opposite—being a woman—is viewed as a failure to establish subjecthood (*Escenas de pudor* 105). The character expresses his masculinity not only through his sexual behavior but also by rejecting any indication of women's power and his own femininity. While he can affirm his power at work due to his status as a doctor, this changes in the home environment.

Even though the space of the house is stereotypically associated with femininity, it makes the protagonist uneasy as it is taken over by Amparo, rendering him powerless.[7] It is precisely in the home where he begins to feel a sense of inferiority, as he comments, "I felt isolated and weak, like an exile living in an eternally unfamiliar country. And I understood and accepted that, at that very moment, I had become an outcast in my own home" ("Me sentí aislado y débil como el exiliado que vive en un país que nunca le resultará familiar. Y tuve que comprender, y aceptar, en ese justo momento que me había convertido en un apestado en mi propia casa"; 35, 39). While the work sphere offers him the authority that he believes he is entitled to, the privacy of his home becomes unbearable as Amparo Dávila and La Traicionada turn it into a place where they can exert power. In this sense, they display an *encuiramiento* of the domestic space by keeping the doctor from exercising the same type of control that he is granted in the workplace, and by shifting the dynamics in his own house. Although stereotypical views of the home as traditionally led by women might expect men to see it as a refuge from work, instead it becomes an extension of the impenetrable space crafted by Amparo and La Traicionada.

Despite the doctor's claims of superiority, it is Amparo who holds the most power, as she is the one who ignites his doubts about his gender identity. In this way, she subverts typical female gender roles assigned by the patriarchal social order. According to McDowell Carlsen, Amparo fits within the scope of the *loose woman* figure developed by Debra A.

Castillo and defined as not fitting the role of the submissive and pure Mexican woman due to her powerful and sexual transgressions (31–32). Castillo argues that men need these transgressive women to release their sexual desire and to serve as the antithesis of "decent" women (12). She also highlights the well-known essentialist binary that categorizes women as either the Virgin or *La Malinche/Chingada*, a concept emphasized by critics such as Octavio Paz, Luis Leal, and Roger Bartra and one that has been contested by feminist scholars and artists (6). Although this duality is not unique to Mexico, Joanne Hershfield explains that in this specific context, "these binary symbols of woman are tied to specific mythohistorical figures: the Virgin of Guadalupe, Mexico's patron saint, who represents the ambiguous figure of the maternal virgin, and La Malinche, the so-called traitor of Mexico" (13–14). Even though this duality has been challenged and recognized as a patriarchal construct, the Virgin and Malinche are symbols that "reappear in various forms throughout Mexican history in literature, drama, and popular culture" (15). Hence, I will reference this dichotomy throughout the rest of the book.

While Rivera Garza's novel lacks an idealized Virgin figure, I argue that although Amparo shares some qualities with the Chingada/Malinche/loose woman—such as her transgressiveness and refusal to be submissive—she ultimately transcends these archetypes. Both parts of the Virgin/Chingada dichotomy are defined based on their relationship to men, especially regarding sexuality. The Virgin must remain pure and submissive until marriage, after which she becomes a selfless mother and wife, while the Chingada/Malinche/loose woman serves as an outlet for male sexual desire, whether as a prostitute or the "traitor" behind Mexico's conquest. Amparo, however, does not fit either role. She is not submissive, entering and taking control of the male protagonist's home without his consent, placing herself in an active role. This is immediately noticed by the doctor, who remarks, "The woman showed no pity . . . She directed no seductive glances my way, nor did she act with the fragility of a girl in search of 'comfort'" ("la mujer no tuvo piedad alguna . . . No me dirigió miradas seductoras ni actuó con la fragilidad de las muchachas que aparentan andar en busca de cobijo"; 17, 7). This unnerves the doctor, whose initial misogyny makes him believe that all women are alike, making Amparo stand out as an anomaly. At the same time, her attitude shows how she avoids sexual relationships with men—apart from flirtations with another male character, discussed later—and instead forms her ambiguous sapphic relationship with La Traicionada. Through these actions, Amparo defies the Virgin/Chingada dichotomy and rejects male power from the start by challenging hegemonic masculinity.[8]

Amparo's subversive traits are further exemplified by how her relationship with La Traicionada takes place within the doctor's intimate space, forcing him to witness parts of it while excluding him when necessary. His marginalization intensifies when he realizes that they not only share a bedroom but have created a language of their own, symbolizing the intimate space he cannot access. According to Rich, men's fears of exclusion are rooted in the anxiety that women may become indifferent to them, offering sexual, economic, and emotional access only on their own terms and thereby relegating them to marginal roles (17). As such, the traces of sapphic desire in *La cresta de Ilión* extend beyond erotic or romantic attraction, creating a horizontal relationship that excludes those who adhere to patriarchal values and directly confronts the protagonist, who initially embodies these oppressive systems.

Even though the doctor is at first kept out of the world shared by La Traicionada and Amparo, their relationship is altered when he invites another male character, the General Director, to his house to meet the women. The apparent attraction between the man and Amparo does not go unnoticed and even produces anxiety in the doctor. It is important to note that this occurs toward the end of the novel, after the protagonist has undergone a series of transformations and begun to question his gender identity, distancing himself from his earlier patriarchal role and becoming more of an ally to the women. At first, it is La Traicionada who feels uneasy by the attraction between Amparo and the General Director, but eventually, she becomes the one who spends time with him, contributing to how his presence destabilizes the women's relationship.

This is palpable when Amparo confides in the doctor, expressing her distress after witnessing the growing relationship between La Traicionada and the man: " 'You haven't noticed yet, have you?' she asked, lifting her face and looking at me with a combination of alarm and suppressed laughter. 'She spends almost all of her time at the hospital'—she hesitated a moment before gathering her strength—'with the General Director' " ("—¿Pero es que no te has dado cuenta?—me preguntó mientras elevaba el rostro y me veía con una combinación de alarma y de burla contenida—. Se pasa ya casi todo el tiempo en el hospital—se interrumpió un poco, dudó otro tanto en continuar, tomó fuerzas y luego siguió adelante—, con el Director General"; 109, 130). Amparo's sense of betrayal by La Traicionada is clear, adding irony to the character's name, as she becomes the one who betrays others—a detail the protagonist observes. While Amparo helps La Traicionada recover from her illness by establishing a space where she can be cared for without male interference, the doctor's former lover ultimately redirects her attention to the General Director, altering the relationship between the women. Although they once shared a space and language of their own, the presence of a man—and the impact it has on the characters—ultimately shatters their connection.

In "Queering Feminism: Cristina Rivera Garza's *La cresta de Ilión* and the Feminine Sublime" (2010), Rebecca Garonzik examines how the General Director's gender identity can be interpreted as ambiguous, as he is endowed with qualities commonly associated with femininity. This is evident in his concern for his appearance, seen in the doctor's remark about his crimson shirt, which "suggested that there were traces of his personality, of his taste, that I wouldn't have predicted" ("me dio a entender que había rasgos de su personalidad, y de sus gustos, que ni siquiera presentía"; 98, 116). For Garonzik, the General Director's seemingly ambiguous sexuality or femininity is problematized by his apparent attraction to Amparo. In my view, his physical traits and the doctor's suggestions of ambiguity merely illustrate how masculinity can manifest in various forms, regardless of sexual orientation, but can still be used to possess women and exercise power when left unquestioned.

This is particularly evident when the doctor explains, in reference to the General Director, that "[i]t was obvious he had a real desire to meet the False One, whom I had described as beautiful and vulnerable, and he was in pursuit of his prey, making a show of his abilities as a seducer" ("Era obvio que tenía verdaderos deseos de conocer a La Falsa, a quien le había descrito como hermosa y desamparada. Resultaba obvio, pues, que el Director venía en pos de su presa, haciendo gala de sus aptitudes de seductor"; 98, 116–17). It is significant that the doctor describes Amparo as both beautiful and vulnerable—though we know the latter is not true—as those traits ignite the General Director's interest. This reveals that, despite his potentially ambiguous sexuality and gender expression, he views vulnerable women as prey to seduce. Notably, the Spanish edition's use of the adjective *desamparada* contrasts with Amparo's name—meaning *protection* or *shelter*—and character, as she is portrayed as the stronger of the two women. Thus, it is not surprising that, given Amparo's dominance in the novel, the General Director ultimately seduces La Traicionada, who is depicted as ill and susceptible.

Beyond the way the relationship between the two women momentarily allows them to create a space outside of men's reach, I also view these traces of desire as having a profound effect on the doctor. This momentary suspension of compulsory heterosexuality aligns with the potential of *lo cuir* to not only alter sexuality but also disrupt gender dynamics and other mechanisms of oppression. The novel follows the protagonist's transformation, culminating with his acceptance of his "secret." He reflects, "I smiled upon remembering, too, that the pelvis is the most definitive area to determine the sex of an individual. The Emissaries should have known this to be able to discover my secret" ("Sonreí al recordar también que la pelvis es el área más eficaz para determinar el sexo de un individuo. Todas las Emisarias debieron haberlo sabido para poder dar con mi secreto"; 132, 158). He refers to the women who prompted his questioning of his gender as *las Emisarias*, emphasizing that it is the women who possess knowledge he initially lacks and making them the ones who spark the doctor's *encuiramiento*. Despite his frequent attempts to affirm his masculinity by touching his genitals, it is precisely a physical attribute—his pelvic bone—that ultimately exposes his gender. In this sense, there is irony in his reliance on viewing his penis as a marker of gender while, at the same time, possessing a pelvic bone viewed as "feminine." Rivera Garza uses this mechanism to highlight the social construction of sex and gender (Estrada, *Ser mujer* 234). This shift illustrates the novel's broader critique of essentialist gender roles.

While the character's initial misogyny and discomfort with the relationship between La Traicionada and Amparo Dávila position him as an embodiment of patriarchy and hegemonic masculinity, his interaction with the women—especially Amparo—enable him to embrace his femininity and sexuality, ultimately allowing him to speak their language by the novel's end. In doing so, the protagonist enters a female space reminiscent of Rich's lesbian continuum, which encompasses a broad range of histories and experiences shared by women and their connections beyond sexual desire (23). However, as Cristina Rivera Garza demonstrates, this *cuir* space is not exclusive to subjects assigned female at birth and can, in fact, prompt even those with violent masculine traits to question their identity and their relationships with others. Despite the disruption of Amparo and La Traicionada's relationship by the General Director, their traces of sapphic desire reveal the potential of *lo cuir* to challenge strict definitions of gender and sexuality. Lastly, revisiting Téllez's assertion that *lesbian literature* in Mexico lacks deeper interrogations of identity, love, and gender embodiment, it becomes evident that moving beyond strict narrative categories allows us to uncover such explorations in writers like Rivera Garza.

"A Delectable Vértigo":
Cuerpo náufrago (2005) by Ana Clavel

In continuing my analysis of traces of sapphic desire, I turn to Ana Clavel's (b. 1961, Mexico City) novel *Cuerpo náufrago*. While critics like Oswaldo Estrada, Adrienne Erazo, Mariola Pietrak, and Pauline Doucet have explored the text's relationship to gender performativity and sexual desire, I propose a reading that focuses on the protagonist's traces of sapphic desire as a tool that enables her to inhabit a *cuir* state, where gender ceases to matter. As noted in my discussion of Rivera Garza, Clavel is also part of a group of women writers who subvert normativity. Lavery highlights the queerness and transgressive nature of Clavel's work, noting that her texts are tied together by their tendency to queer "certain 'givens,' whether these be religious, moral, sexual, cultural, or historical, and by repeatedly seeking to transgress various 'taboos du jour'" (7). As such, I acknowledge that Clavel and Rivera Garza offer a more multifaceted approach to sexuality than other authors I examine in this chapter.

Cuerpo náufrago follows Antonia/Antón, who, after living her entire life as a woman, suddenly finds herself physically transformed into a man.[9] According to Estrada, this transformation leads her to reflect on the advantages of being perceived as a man in Mexico, while also grappling with the question of whether she remains the same person despite her gender change ("Against Representation" 68). Throughout the novel, Antonia/Antón learns to perform masculinity, drawing on Butler's theory of gender performativity (Estrada, "Against Representation" 69; Lavery 10). Despite her physical changes, she remains aware of her identity as a woman, leading to a fascination with masculinity, sexuality, and objects such as urinals.[10]

Cuerpo náufrago challenges binary frameworks as Antonia/Antón embodies masculine and feminine traits beyond the limits of her own body as understood through purely normative expression. While this provides a compelling exploration of the connection between gender and identity, the novel at times seems deliberately constructed for analysis through the concept of gender performativity. Still, critics have highlighted some of its more intriguing elements. For instance, Pietrak argues that Antonia/Antón's sexuality is not easily definable, as her penis responds to feminine stimuli while her feminine consciousness is drawn to the sensuality of male bodies (40–41). The character transcends gender boundaries, ultimately embracing an androgynous identity defined by desire (Pietrak 41; Estrada, "Against Representation" 70). While my interpretation of this text agrees with critics regarding Antonia/Antón's androgyny, I argue that her exploration of sexuality disrupts gender norms in ways beyond her body's physical responses. As Sara Ahmed contends, heterosexuality is naturalized by portraying women's bodies as "made" for male desire (*Queer Phenomenology* 71). Therefore, although Antonia/Antón is able to explore her attraction to women without fearing social condemnation in her new body, to assume that this desire stems solely from biology is an essentialist perspective that overlooks the character's complexity.

Ahmed's arguments align with Butler's critique of essentialism, which presupposes that the body "preexists the acquisition of its sexed significance," reducing it to a passive medium that precedes discourse (*Gender Trouble* 164). Butler's ideas resonate in the novel as Antonia/Antón navigates societal expectations around gender and sexuality. Though her male body seems to follow a heterosexual path, her feminine psyche complicates matters, leading her to question her sexual orientation. Hoping for her new reality to end, she wishes to return to liking only men. Yet, as she reflects on her relationships with women, "Antonia paused. She could not deceive herself: she had always been attracted to other women's bodies. Then, had she been a lesbian without knowing it? But she liked men too. Carlos, Raimundo, each one in a special way, the same as Malva and Claudia" ("Antonia hizo una pausa. No podía engañarse: siempre le habían atraído los cuerpos de otras mujeres. Entonces, ¿había sido lesbiana sin saberlo? Pero los hombres también le gustaban. Carlos, Raimundo, cada uno de manera especial, lo mismo que Malva y también Claudia"; 93). Though the character navigates her sexuality by interacting with both men and women, the realization that she felt desire for women before her transformation disrupts the assumption that this attraction stems only from her new body. Therefore, this discovery challenges the naturalization of heterosexuality, as described by Ahmed and Butler.

Antonia/Antón's curiosity leads her to explore her sexuality with men. These encounters are characterized by violence and a mutual need for domination, as seen in her interaction with her friend Raimundo:

"everything rushed with an imperious and tyrannical urgency. Subduing, subjugating another man's body can be a matter of strategy but above all of strength . . . She then knew. She knew that sex between men is, above everything else, violent" ("todo se precipitó con una urgencia imperiosa y tiránica. Someter, avasallar el cuerpo de otro hombre puede ser cuestión de estrategia pero sobre todo de fuerza . . . Entonces lo supo. Supo que el sexo entre hombres es, sobre todas las cosas, violento"; 121–22). By portraying these encounters as inherently violent and driven by men's need to subjugate each other, the novel presents a simplistic view of male sexuality. Additionally, it reinforces the outdated active/passive social script, which scholars began questioning in the early 2000s (Russo Garrido 11)—a topic that I discuss more at length in chapter 2.

This superficial characterization continues as Antonia/Antón's male friends guide her in performing masculinity, when they exhibit misogynistic attitudes and frequently objectify women. For example, her friend Francisco dismisses her thoughts on the complexity of male desire, remarking: "All of that, Antón, that story about desire in men, this matter of urinals as something other than urinals, it's all nothing more than women's fantasies. Men are much simpler . . . I would even say rudimentary" ("Todo eso, Antón, esa historia sobre el deseo en los hombres, ese asunto de los mingitorios como otra cosa que mingitorios, todo no son más que fantasías de las mujeres. Los hombres somos mucho más simples . . . Yo diría que hasta rudimentarios"; 151). Francisco's comments are clearly influenced by Mexican constructions of masculinity, which rely on qualities such as the disparagement of femininity (Monsiváis, *Misógino feminista* 51), and show how it is not internal but, rather, determined by the judgment of others (Irwin, *Mexican Masculinities* xviii). For Francisco and Antonia/Antón's male friends, openly discussing male desire as complex and flexible undermines the masculine need to be seen as strong and impenetrable. Although the concept of Mexican masculinity is far from static, evolving with context, race, and class, Héctor Domínguez Ruvalcaba argues that, as a construct of modern colonialism, its sensualizing is seen as disempowerment (*Modernity and the Nation* 3). However, despite its in-depth exploration of gender and sexuality through the protagonist, the novel portrays men as simple-minded and violent, failing to recognize different forms of masculinity.

Moreover, the protagonist's sexual relationships with women, even with a male body, prove to be more insightful for her reflections on sexuality. For instance, it is not until an interaction with a woman that Antonia/Antón consciously feels desired for the first time: "Then I felt observed—Antonia noticed the natural way in which she assumed her new gender and smiled, happy to be able to play with herself—, observed and . . . desired. As if her eyes were a mirror that gave me a pleasant image of myself in return. It had never happened to me before, feeling it and being aware of it at the same time" ("Entonces me sentí observado—Antonia reparó en la naturalidad con que se atribuía su nuevo género y sonrió contenta de poder jugar consigo misma–, observado y . . . deseado. Como si sus ojos fueran un espejo que me devolvía una imagen agradable de mí. Nunca antes me había sucedido, sentirlo y tener conciencia a la vez"; 61). While this scene unfolds, Antonia/Antón is fully aware of her female identity while noticing her growing ability to think of herself as male. Being desired by a woman, however, offers a stark contrast to her previous encounters with men. Yet the text maintains a clear divide between men's and women's expressions of desire. By noticing that the woman's gaze gives her a pleasant self-image—one she had never experienced before—there is a suggestion that men's way of looking at her when she is seen as a woman does not evoke the same positive self-perception.

In her encounter with another woman named Malva, there is a comparable shift in the protagonist's understanding of desire: "And when he held Malva in his arms, trembling like a recently cut bud, he felt that more than master and lord, he was getting lost and abandoned, that all of him melted into a driving force that impelled them to continue forward, throw himself into the sea, strip himself of who he was and was not, of all doubts, of all certainties, and make his way, with an upraised arm, with a broken heart, with a singing sex" ("Y es que cuando tuvo a Malva entre sus brazos, temblorosa como un capullo recién cortado, sintió que, más que dueño y señor, se perdía y se abandonaba, que todo él se fundía en una fuerza de arrastre que los impulsaba a seguir adelante, arrojarse al mar, despojarse de ser quien era y quien no era, de todas las dudas, de todas las certezas, y abrirse paso, a brazo enhiesto, a corazón partido, a sexo cantante"; 81). In this intimate moment, the protagonist realizes that her male friends' insistence on sex as a means of dominating women's bodies is not conducive to true pleasure. Although at first her transformation leads her to fantasize about possessing women as she has been taught, Antonia/Antón ultimately abandons the need for dominance during sexual encounters, instead surrendering to a desire that places her beyond any concerns regarding power structures.

In *Desire/Love* (2012), Lauren Berlant argues against the common idea that desire is purely internal, coming from within us and reflecting who we are. Instead, she contends that desire is also shaped by our encounters with the world, consequently showing how objects of desire are not objective, but rather "things and scenes that you have converted into propping up your world, and so what seems objective and autonomous in them is partly what your desire has created and therefore is a mirage, a shaky anchor" (6). In other words, our desires are unstable as they are both part of us and not part of us. Antonia/Antón outwardly performs heterosexual masculinity in her male body, her female consciousness allows her to achieve an ecstasy that her male peers, fixated on sexual domination, cannot. Although Antonia/Antón is able to attain this state due to her self-awareness as a woman, the novel still grapples with fully escaping binary frameworks. This tension is evident in the portrayal of Malva, who is described as trembling "like a recently cut but." While the protagonist is consumed by desire, Malva remains passive and delicate, reinforcing gender stereotypes.

That Antonia/Antón's meditations on desire and sexuality deepen through her erotic encounters with women reveals that these traces of sapphic desire are essential to her development. While having sex with Paula, a woman she falls in love with and ultimately trusts with her secret, the narrator describes how "Antonia felt disarmed: never before had anyone taken possession of her pleasure like this. Prostrated before her member, on her knees but no less powerful for that, Paula stood to make Antonia doubt the limit where her enjoyment becomes a precipice: who was subjugating whom?" ("Antonia se sintió desarmado: nunca antes nadie se había adueñado así de su placer. Postrada ante su miembro, de rodillas pero no por ello menos poderosa, Paula se erguía para hacer dudar a Antonia en ese límite donde el goce se vuelve precipicio: ¿quién subyugaba a quién?"; 134). On one level, this interaction suggests a subversion of gender roles, with Antonia/Antón in a male body feeling possessed by Paula. However, this scene contradicts the earlier encounter with Malva, where the active/passive roles are somewhat challenged. While this moment blurs the lines between pleasure and loss of control, symbolized by the precipice, Antonia/Antón ultimately reaches climax because she is dominated. Thus, even though sapphic desire offers a form of sexual gratification that she has never experienced before, the dynamic between the two characters replicates the notion that subjugation is necessary for sexual satisfaction.

The protagonist's sense of being disarmed holds particular significance within the context of *Cuerpo náufrago*, as she not only relies on her male friends to learn how to perform masculinity but also turns to books of

chivalry like *Amadís de Gaula* (1508) as guides for complying with masculine roles. Ana Clavel reflects on this choice in her 2008 essay collection,
*A la sombra de los deseos en flor: ensayos sobre la fuerza metafórica del
deseo*, explaining that these books serve to establish clearly delineated and
rigid gender roles (68). This leads Antonia/Antón to perceive masculinity
as an armor that, despite initially offering protection, ultimately weighs
her down. Her metaphor illustrates how the strict rules of masculinity
burden those who try to adhere to them. This perspective sheds light on
her earlier encounter with Raimundo, which she interprets as warlike,
preventing her from fully surrendering to eroticism. This interaction also
contrasts with her experience with Paula, who figuratively disarms her,
lifting the weight of masculinity. In this context, by fully giving herself,
as though standing at the edge of a precipice, Antonia/Antón seemingly
breaks free from the patterns of masculinity she has been taught and
explores new dimensions of her sexuality.

The novel concludes with the protagonist embracing androgyny and
refusing to fit within the confines of binary gender: "He or she—because
there was room for doubt about her gender, although it did not matter to
those who could perceive her beauty" ("Él o ella—porque cabía la duda
sobre su género, aunque poco importaba para aquellos que podían percibir
su belleza"; 181). Antonia/Antón's exploration of her sexuality ultimately
leads to freedom through her encounters with women, allowing her to
embrace traces of sapphic desire and move toward a *cuir* state where
gender and sexuality are no longer bound by binary systems. While the
novel offered a fresh perspective on gender and desire when it was first
published, it still reinforces homogeneous and simplistic representations
of men and masculinity, while also reproducing gendered power dynamics of dominance and submission in sexual relationships. Despite these
limitations, *Cuerpo náufrago* exemplifies the presence of sapphic desire in
contemporary Mexican literature.

"Did You Use to Sleep with Women?":
Los ingrávidos (2011) by Valeria Luiselli

While I have pointed out how some contemporary writers, such as Clavel
and Rivera Garza, problematize gender and sexuality, others, like Valeria
Luiselli (b. 1983, Mexico City), have tended to center their literary production on "issues of belonging, creating homes within global life through

diverse localizing practices that respond to the dissolutions of links between geographical place and human experience" (Raynor 1). The diversity of topics addressed by contemporary Latin American writers shows how they resist narrow definitions. Luiselli's work addresses themes such as travel, language, world literature, and immigration. The translation of her texts into English has granted her access to a wider readership, ultimately leading her to become, as Sarah Booker notes, "something of a literary phenomenon in the United States," as her writing moves fluidly between the local and global, much like her characters' intermediary identities (274). At the same time, her commercial success in the United States has caused a thorough questioning of her identity as a Mexican writer, her position as a global literary figure, and the influence of translation in the US literary market (Samuelson 176). Therefore, although the themes in Luiselli's texts differ from those of authors like Clavel and Rivera Garza, I contend that the presence of sapphic desire in her novel *Los ingrávidos* (2011) illustrates how *lo cuir* permeates Mexican literature, even works that do not directly address gender and sexuality.

Los ingrávidos employs a non-linear narrative, shifting between the nameless protagonist's past as a translator in New York and her present life as a wife and mother in Mexico City and attempt to write a novel as her marriage is falling apart. Even though the novel does not explicitly focus on the subversion of gender or sexuality, in the protagonist's friendship with a woman named Dakota during her time in the United States, I identify moments of sapphic desire rooted in intimacy that offer a *cuir* potential. My analysis is based on intimacy as defined by Lauren Berlant when she explains that "[t]o intimate is to communicate with the sparest of signs and gestures, and at its root intimacy has the quality of eloquence and brevity. But intimacy also involves an aspiration for a narrative about something shared, a story about both oneself and others" ("Intimacy" 281). I contend that this sapphic desire is subversive in part due to the narrator's husband's assumption—and later obsession—that the relationship between them must have been sexual even though it was not. His failure to comprehend their intimacy exposes the limits of his heteronormative views on relationships and sexuality. Therefore, the physical and emotional bond between the two women remains beyond his grasp.

Dakota first appears as the protagonist reflects on her past during the process of writing her novel. Their initial meeting occurs in a bar's restroom: "She was making up her face with a sponge when I went to the sink to wash my hands. I never wash my hands in public toilets, but the woman touching up the future face of Dakota with a sponge seemed to me unsettling and I wanted a closer look. So I washed my hands" ("Ella se estaba maquillando la cara con una esponja cuando me acerqué al tocador para lavarme las manos. Nunca me lavo las manos en los baños públicos, pero la mujer que se estaba repasando el futuro rostro de Dakota con una esponja me pareció inquietante y quise verla de cerca. Así que me lavé las manos"; 15, 24).[11] The women's bathroom, where the narrator first meets Dakota, is traditionally a space meant to reinforce binary gender divisions. However, the narrator's curiosity and desire to interact with Dakota disrupt this, marking the bathroom as a space of *encuiramiento*. Her decision to wash her hands, a deviation from her habit, illustrates her desire to get closer to Dakota. As Halberstam argues, sex-segregated bathrooms "extend a rather outdated notion of a public-private split between male and female society. The bathroom is a domestic space beyond the home that comes to represent domestic order, or a parody of it, out in the world" (*Female Masculinity* 24). The irony of this encounter occurring in a public women's restroom is that it sets the stage for their developing relationship.

Dakota's role as a character who momentarily ignites the protagonist's desire is further highlighted when their connection becomes physical, though not exactly sexual. Dakota moves in with the narrator, who describes how they would often share a bed and "[s]he would get into bed naked and put an arm around my equally bare waist. She had soft, heavy breasts; small nipples" ("Se metía desnuda a la cama y me abrazaba la espalda, también desnuda. Tenía unos senos suaves y abultados; los pezones pequeños"; 38, 46). Though their physical interactions do not become sexual and both women are involved with men—Dakota's boyfriend is mentioned multiple times—they share a unique intimacy when they are alone, beyond the grasp of the men in their lives. This mirrors the relationship between Amparo and la Traicionada in *La cresta de Ilión* and aligns with Adrienne Rich's idea of the lesbian continuum. However, unlike in Rivera Garza's novel, *Los ingrávidos* reveals what occurs between the two women behind closed doors.

In a way, their choice to hold each other naked while sleeping, rather than engage in sex, reveals a deeper connection—one that seems more personal than a fleeting sexual encounter. In discussing intimacy and physical touch, Sara Ahmed explains that "[t]he intimacy of contact shapes bodies as they orientate toward each other doing different kinds of work. In being orientated toward other women, lesbian desires also bring certain objects near, including sexual objects as well as other kinds of objects, *that might not have otherwise been reachable within the body horizon of the social"* (*Queer Phenomenology* 103; emphasis in the original). Thus, it is through this intimacy that the women are drawn to one another, or in Ahmed's terms, orientate toward each other. At the same time, the imperfect tense—*se metía, me abrazaba*—suggests that this was an ongoing action, not a one-time occurrence. This habitual physical closeness does not appear to cause the narrator any internal conflict or lead her to question her sexuality, making it feel like a natural part of her life in New York. At the same time, the reappearance of Dakota in the narrator's memory and her inclusion in her writing highlight the significant role she played in the protagonist's life, particularly during her youth in the United States, which she frequently contrasts with her current role as a wife and mother in Mexico.

When her friend moves out of their apartment and into a new place, they share another intimate moment: "We opened all the windows and stripped down to our panties. We painted the bathroom, the kitchen, but only half of the bedroom because we ran out of paint. We painted each other's nipples cobalt blue. When we'd finished we lay face up on the bedroom floor and lit a cigarette apiece. Dakota suggested we swap panties" ("Abrimos todas las ventanas y nos desnudamos hasta los calzones. Pintamos el baño, la cocina y la mitad del único cuarto. Nos pintamos los pezones de azul cobalto. Cuando se acabó la pintura nos tiramos boca arriba en el piso del cuarto y prendimos un cigarro. Dakota quiso que intercambiáramos calzones"; 56, 63). Just as with their sharing of the bed, their actions evoke an erotic attraction that is always present when the protagonist writes about these memories. The act of stripping down and painting each other's nipples embodies a playfulness and freedom that is afforded by the very knowledge that there is a sexual line that will never be crossed. In Ahmed's definition of queer orientations, she explains that they "might be those that don't line up, which by seeing the world 'slantwise' allow other objects to come into view" (*Queer Phenomenology* 107). In the novel, this alternate perspective provided by queer orientations allows traces of sapphic desire to be expressed, not through overt sexual acts, but rather through moments of intimacy between the narrator and Dakota. Though it is never clear whether they actually swap underwear, the suggestion is erotically charged and reflects a significant degree of closeness.

The narrator's writing about Dakota is frequently scrutinized by her husband—who often reads her novel without her permission—as he fixates on the relationship between the two women. The contrast between her past in New York and her present in Mexico is also clear in the experiences she recounts. When writing about New York, she describes sexual encounters with men and her close friendship with Dakota, but her husband's invasive readings pull the story back to her present in Mexico. He represents heteropatriarchal values, primarily concerned with her sexual freedom. These traces of desire introduce moments of queer temporality, which, as Halberstam explains, arise "once one leaves the temporal frames of bourgeois reproduction and family, longevity, risk/safety, and inheritance" (*In a Queer Time and Place* 7). While the narrator does not fully reject heteronormative time, the potential of a past *cuir* desire disrupts her husband's control and fuels his need to understand her sexuality.

His persistent obsession with his wife's past reveals his urge to control and define her, echoing Rich's argument about men's fear of being excluded or rendered irrelevant by women. While the husband is suspicious of her sexual past in general, it is the potential relationships with other women that cause him the most discomfort. As he continues to read her writing, the narrator tells us, "My husband has started reading some of these pages again. Did you use to sleep with women? he asks" ("Mi marido ha vuelto a leer algunas de estas páginas. ¿Te acostabas con mujeres?, me pregunta"; 39, 46). When she remains silent, he pushes further: "But have you ever slept with a woman? my husband asks again. No, never. I reply. I wouldn't know how" ("¿Pero te has acostado con alguna mujer?, insiste mi marido. Nunca, respondo. No sabría cómo"; 39, 47). Her response illustrates that she must reassert her heterosexuality by claiming to be ignorant about sapphic sexual practices.

At the same time, his obsession with the possibility of these sexual encounters reveals a lack of understanding of the relationship between his wife and Dakota. Though the husband assumes that their connection is sexual, the narrator's traces of sapphic desire are rooted in intimacy. As Berlant notes, "desires for intimacy that bypass the couple or the life narrative it generates have no alternative plots, let alone few laws and stable spaces of culture in which to clarify and to cultivate them" ("Intimacy" 285). Dakota and the protagonist's relationship, therefore, blurs the boundary between the platonic and the erotic, forming a kind of intimacy that the husband cannot comprehend. In this sense, their relationship acts as a form of *encuiramiento*, disrupting heteronormative notions of closeness and connection.

Through the narrator's memories, the novel idealizes the United States as a space of freedom, contrasting it with her current unhappiness and her failing marriage in Mexico. This comparison is further highlighted by the description of the protagonist's *cuir* sister: "Laura lived in Philadelphia with her wife Enea. They still live there. They are active people, pleased with themselves. Enea is Argentinian and teaches at Princeton. Laura and Enea belong to all sorts of groups and organizations; they are academics; they are left-wing; they are vegetarians. This year they're going to climb Kilimanjaro" ("Laura vivía en Filadelfia con su esposa Enea. Todavía viven ahí. Son personas activas, contentas consigo mismas. Enea es argentina, da clases en Princeton. Laura y Enea pertenecen a toda clase de grupos y organizaciones; son académicas; son de izquierda; son vegetarianas. Este año van a subir el Kilimanjaro"; 16, 25). It is significant that the protagonist mentions the women's satisfaction with themselves and their shared activities as a couple, underscoring the kind of connection missing from her relationship with her husband.

Her emphasis on Laura and Enea's active lifestyle contrasts sharply with her own current life, which she appears ashamed of and avoids discussing with her sister: "I don't know what Laura would say now that my only walks are from the kitchen to the living room, from the upstairs bathroom to the children's bedroom. But Laura knows nothing of this, nor will she be told" ("No sé qué diría Laura ahora que mis únicas caminatas son entre la cocina y la sala, entre el baño de arriba y el cuarto del mediano y la bebé. Pero todo eso no lo sabe Laura, ni se lo contaré"; 16, 25). The protagonist appears to regard her life as less fulfilling than her sister's, as her depiction of Laura and Enea highlights their happiness. While this does not suggest that she sees non-heterosexual relationships as a better alternative, there is a yearning for the freedom she last experienced in her youth in New York. This opposition becomes even more evident when considering her husband's fixation on her potential sapphic encounters. While he obsesses over this, her sister and Enea are free to live fulfilling lives in the United States without being questioned. However, the narrative framing the United States as a haven of freedom and opportunity, common in discussions of queer and migrant experiences, conceals the long-standing truth that such opportunities have been achieved by marginalizing many (Luibhéid xxvi). Thus, Laura is able to sustain such a lifestyle by belonging to a privileged minority, just as the protagonist's time in New York City was made possible by the privileges of a certain social class. Although this romanticization is problematic, the protagonist's view of the US as a place free from the social norms represented by her husband allowed her to explore a relationship like the one she had with Dakota.

Los ingrávidos exemplifies how traces of sapphic desire can be found throughout Mexican literature. While not always obvious, these brief disruptions of heteronormativity and their effects on the husband highlight how intimacy between women, even without sexual contact, can challenge patriarchy. Thus, while Luiselli's work would be excluded by rigid labels like *lesbian literature*, approaching gender and sexuality through the lens of *lenchitudes* enables a deeper exploration of sapphic desire across a wider array of texts and its capacity to contest and reveal the limits of normativity.

"A Whim from Time to Time":
"Baños de pureza" (2005) by Iliana Godoy

Iliana Godoy (b. 1952, Mexico City; d. 2017) was a professor, writer, translator, and literary critic. According to poet Beatriz Saavedra Gastélum, who was quoted in a 2020 press release by the Mexican government announcing a posthumous homage to Godoy in the Palacio de Bellas Artes, she conducted a literary workshop for over twenty years and is "one of the great references of Mexican literature" ("uno de los grandes referentes de la literatura mexicana"; "El INBAL"). Godoy published numerous poetry books such as *Mástil en tierra* (1988), *Seducir a la muerte* (1993), and *Coral negro* (2000), along with short story collections and academic monographs on Mesoamerican art. Despite her prolific career as an award-winning poet and academic, no scholarly works have been dedicated to her literary production. The silence surrounding Godoy's work, including the lack of general information about her life, is indicative of an "ongoing context of prejudice in which literary critics live, read, and publish" (Hind, *Dude Lit* 212), contributing to the intentional invisibility of women writers in Mexico and Latin America.

In Godoy's short story "Baños de Pureza," from her collection *Ritual de excesos* (2005), two friends, Ana and Silvia, visit the archeological site known as Los baños de Nezahualcóyotl. Along the way, they stop at the nearby hot springs, where they meet a man named Mauro. Silvia leaves Ana and Mauro alone so that her friend can freely explore her sexuality. After a brief sexual encounter with Mauro, Ana, still aroused, masturbates next to Silvia, leading the two friends to have sex. The story begins with a third-person narrator's reflection that frames the text's open approach to sexuality: "At a closer look, sex is also a thing of warriors; in those fights anything goes" ("Viéndolo bien el sexo es también cosa de guerreros; en esas lides todo se vale"; 43). The ambiguity in the notion that "anything goes" allows for a wide range of interpretations, inviting readers to consider multiple ways to explore sex and sexuality. After Ana's encounter with Mauro, Silvia encourages her to embrace the experience, saying, "What I want is for you to be happy and loosen up" ("Lo que yo quiero es que seas feliz y te quites las telarañas de la cabeza"; 46). It is later revealed that Silvia orchestrated the situation to help Ana regain control of her sexuality after her failed marriage. While sapphic desire is not the story's focus, I argue that, through the moment of *cuir* eroticism, Ana explores her desires and becomes more open to a relationship with Mauro. Despite the liberatory nature of the experience, her inability to accept her sexual encounter with Silvia causes their friendship to unravel.

Silvia's recognition of her friend's sexual anxieties and her struggle with embracing eroticism underscores her desire to help Ana feel free. Yet it is Ana who initiates their sexual contact, exposing her own repressed sexuality. The scene is described as follows:

> The two friends (just how intimate?) sat at the bottom of a deep pool that must have been communal. The hot stools turned Ana on by reminding her of Mauro's skin; without realizing, she slipped her hand down her pants. Feeling the discharge of eroticism in her eyes, Silvia lifted her shirt, released her turgid breasts, lighter than the rest of her skin, and began to caress them; while her nipples perked up a drop of sweat slipped slowly down the middle, Ana collected it and put that unknown salt in her mouth.

> (Las dos amigas (¿qué tan íntimas?) se sentaron al fondo de una poza profunda que debió ser colectiva. Las banquetas calientes excitaron a Ana recordándole la piel de Mauro; sin darse cuenta deslizó su mano bajo el pantalón. Al sentir en sus ojos la descarga del erotismo, Silvia se levantó la playera, liberó sus senos turgentes, más claros que el resto de su piel, y comenzó a acariciarlos; mientras se erguían sus pezones una gota de sudor deslizó despacio por en medio, Ana la recogió y se llevó a la boca aquella sal desconocida; 46–47).

While Ana's arousal originates from her experience with Mauro and her fantasies about him, Lauren Berlant, in conversation with Eve Sedgwick, notes that "even if desire fails to find objects adequate to its aim, its errors can still produce pleasure: desire's fundamental ruthlessness is a source of creativity that produces new optimism, new narratives of possibility, even erotic experimentality" (*Desire/Love* 43). In other words, despite thinking about the man, Ana reaches for Silvia, who, in her eyes, would be inadequate as an object of desire, but she still finds pleasure in their interaction. Even though Ana seems to have no prior sexual experience with women, she is compelled by her desire to initiate contact with Silvia, briefly questioning the boundaries of their friendship. The narrator's question, "¿qué tan íntimas?"/"just how intimate?," functions in two ways. Initially, it serves as a sarcastic remark about the blurring of their friendship as their sexual encounter occurs. Yet, in the context of the full story, it foreshadows their falling out, as their bond is not strong enough to survive the aftermath—a sharp contrast to the portrayal of sapphic intimacy in Luiselli's novel.

The tension in their relationship escalates as Ana's thoughts disrupt their encounter, with the narrator explaining that she "could not come; she suddenly landed on the strangeness of her trance and stopped the rhythmic movement of her body, but Silvia was not going to let her back down after that provocation and kept her hand under her clothes while she managed to arouse her, running her tongue down her neck" ("no lograba venirse; de pronto aterrizó en lo extraño del trance y detuvo el movimiento rítmico de su cuerpo, pero Silvia no iba a dejarla replegarse después de aquella provocación y le mantuvo la mano bajo la ropa mientras se las arreglaba para excitarla, pasándole la lengua por el cuello"; 47;). Ana's perception of herself as being in a state of trance is significant, as a trance suggests a lack of full consciousness, implying that she does not really know what she is doing. Furthermore, describing this state as strange highlights her own limitations and prejudices regarding sexuality. As Ahmed contends, queer desire can become a source of shame because it deviates from normative expectations, which turns it into something that must be hidden from others (*Cultural Politics* 107). Thus, we begin to perceive Ana's sense of shame regarding her fleeting sapphic desire.

On the other hand, Silvia allows herself to embrace the moment, refusing to let social expectations hold her back. She is open to experiencing queer pleasures, which bring bodies together that have been separated by the norms of compulsory heterosexuality, and in doing so, create opportunities for new types of experiences (Ahmed, *Cultural Politics* 165). This openness leads her to reassure Ana by telling her, "Touch yourself more, get aroused, let yourself go, friend. We know that dick is dick, but we can allow ourselves a whim from time to time" ("Tócate más, excítate, déjate ir, amiga. Ya se sabe que la verga es la verga, pero podemos tener un capricho de vez en cuando"; 47). Silvia's remarks allow Ana to refocus on the present moment, downplaying their interaction as a mere whim while simultaneously reaffirming their heterosexuality. This scenario challenges Freud's heterosexist notion of the "contingent invert," someone who "is 'not really' inverted" but rather " 'turns' to 'her own sex' due to the failure to secure a 'normal sexual object.' " (Ahmed, *Queer Phenomenology* 94). Ahmed counters this concept by theorizing "the contingent lesbian," which she views not as an identity category but as someone "shaped by the pull of her desire, which puts her in contact with others and with objects that are off the vertical line" (*Queer Phenomenology* 94). Although Ana's contingent moment is fleeting and ultimately rejected, it underscores how "compulsory heterosexuality doesn't always work" (*Queer Phenomenology* 94), revealing the fragility of its assumptions and illustrating the potential of erotic desire to destabilize normativity.

Afterward, Ana expresses her desire to forget what happened between them, to which Silvia responds, "[I]t doesn't scare me" ("a mí no me asusta"; 47). Her reply reveals the contrast between Silvia's indifference to the meaning of their actions and Ana's firm refusal to engage with them, effectively shutting down any potential challenge to her heterosexual identity. While Silvia is able to view what happened as an action and not something that defines her, Ana is filled with shame. Her request to keep quiet about their sexual encounter corresponds with how feelings of shame arise from how individuals relate to themselves, especially since this is tied to how they are perceived by others (Ahmed, *Cultural Politics* 104). The women's reactions align with their characterizations, with Silvia being depicted as open to new sexual experiences, while Ana is portrayed as so sexually repressed that her friend must devise a plan to help her become sexually active again after her divorce. Nonetheless, their sexual interaction ultimately pushes Ana to engage in a romantic/erotic relationship with Mauro. Although the relationship ultimately ends, Ana's immediate effort to establish a heterosexual connection is indicative of how sometimes shame can be restored only when the person experiencing it can "prove" that their shortcoming in meeting societal expectations is only temporary (Ahmed, *Cultural Politics* 107). Ultimately, Ana's reaction reveals the role that shame and compulsory heterosexuality play in compelling individuals to return to conventional expectations.

Though the women promise to stay lifelong friends after their sexual encounter, their relationship deteriorates due to Ana's fears. In contrast to

Los ingrávidos, which expresses a nostalgic longing for the protagonist's youth and moments of sapphic desire, Godoy's short story illustrates the overpowering force of compulsory heterosexuality. Ana's fear of her own desire and sexuality is central to the text. This is evident in how "Baños de Pureza," unlike the other texts examined in this chapter, does not feature a male figure who is undermined by sapphic desire or seeks to punish it—Mauro is the only male character, and he remains oblivious to Ana and Silvia's interaction. Thus, the narrative demonstrates the deeply ingrained nature of heteronormativity, as Ana herself becomes the one who judges and shames her own desire. The story's title alludes to the Mexican saying *darse baños de pureza*, a phrase describing someone who presents as morally pure while being far from perfect. Despite Silvia offering Ana the possibility of exploring her sexuality without prejudice, her friend's hypocritical adherence to social norms keeps her from exploring other possibilities, culminating in her declaration that "[l]ife is shit" ("La vida es una mierda"; 51).

"Desired and Desirous":
"Ladies Bar" (2012) by Mónica Lavín

Mónica Lavín (b. 1955, Mexico City) is a writer, journalist, screenwriter, and professor at the Universidad Autónoma de la Ciudad de México. Her oeuvre has earned her numerous awards, including the Premio Nacional de Literatura Gilberto Owen for her short story collection *Ruby Tuesday no ha muerto* (1998) and the Premio Iberoamericano de Novela Elena Poniatowska for her historical novel *Yo, la peor* (2009), based on the life of Sor Juana Inés de la Cruz. "Ladies Bar" is part of her collection *Manual para enamorarse* (2012) and follows Mayra and Eduardo, an affluent couple who venture into a strip club in a working-class neighborhood of Mexico City. Mayra becomes fascinated by the dancers and wants to inspire the same desire in Eduardo. After overcoming her inhibitions, she joins them on stage and becomes the center of attention, realizing that the strip club allows her to temporarily step away from her "decent woman" status and feel desire for other women, challenging societal norms. The strip club, typically a heterosexual space, momentarily transforms into a site of *encuiramiento*, where the protagonist's sapphic desire is awakened.

This space, associated with obscurity and hidden desire, plays a pivotal role in Mayra's self-discovery. Early on, the third-person narrator describes its surrounding neighborhood as "[t]he forbidden city within her city; like discovering a secret pleasure in the body that one has inhabited for such a long time" ("La ciudad prohibida de su ciudad; como descubrir un placer secreto en el cuerpo con el que se ha vivido tanto tiempo"; 76). This fragment alludes not only to her journey into an unfamiliar part of the city but also to her awakening to repressed desire. Suddenly, we find ourselves transported to a darker, parallel city where Mayra's behavior contrasts with the expectations of Mexican high society. The narrator emphasizes her social class by describing how the protagonist "[h]as a taste for niceties such as men standing up when she approaches the table, or someone noticing her discreet and tasteful watch, or having her companion choose something good from the menu for both of them and asking for her approval" ("Tiene gusto por delicadezas como que los hombres se pongan de pie cuando ella se acerca a la mesa, o que alguien se fije en su reloj discreto y de buen gusto, que quien la acompañe ordene del menú lo que es bueno para los dos y le pregunte si está de acuerdo"; 75). Her preference for behaviors tied to heteronormative gender roles and capitalist notions of success, like owning expensive clothing and accessories, marks her as a character who conforms to social norms.

In this regard, she embodies what Connell terms *emphasized femininity*, defined as women's compliance with their own subordination to cater to male desires and interests (*Gender and Power* 183). In the context of Mexico, Carlos Monsiváis examines the rise of *sensibilidad femenina* (feminine sensibility) in the nineteenth century, a concept of femininity that relegates women to ornamental roles, justified by the belief that they are delicate and require patriarchal protection. Monsiváis identifies its key aspects, such as "the care of masculine speech in their presence, the submission to the complicated paternalistic hierarchy, the prohibition of going out alone, the impossibility of receiving equal treatment by the law, the obligation to show specific qualities, the whole set of prohibitions and duties" ("el cuidado del habla masculina en su presencia, el sometimiento a la complicada jerarquía paternalista, la prohibición de salir solas, la imposibilidad de recibir trato igualitario de las leyes, la obligación de mostrar cualidades específicas, todo el conjunto de prohibiciones y deberes"; *Misógino feminista* 89). The contrast between Mayra's initial views of her societal role and her encounter with the city's hidden nightlife reveals how, for a brief moment in the strip club, she transgresses the patriarchal norms that view her as an object.

Once in this space, the woman observes the dancers, whom Eduardo refers to as *ficheras*: "Mayra looked at them as she pleased; in a place like that she had permission to look" ("Mayra las miró a su gusto; en un lugar así tenía permiso para mirar"; 78). By describing the bar as "a place like that," it is positioned as part of the "forbidden city"—in other words, lower-class neighborhoods—marking it as a space at the periphery of mainstream society and in a context "in which women's self-expression is contained by the occupational risks of male-dominated spaces" (Price-Glynn 37). Furthermore, Eduardo's labeling of the dancers as *ficheras* establishes a clear connection to the Mexican context. It evokes the popular film genre from the 1970s and 80s, set in cabarets where dancers were given a *ficha*, or token, for each drink consumed by their clients.

Sergio de la Mora traces the origins of this genre of Mexican cinema to the mythologizing of sex workers, beginning with the first film adaptation of Federico Gamboa's novel *Santa* (1903), directed by Luis G. Peredo in 1918 ("Fascinating Machismo" 84). This connection recalls Irwin's analysis of *Santa*, particularly the character of La Gaditana, who embodies nineteenth-century views of the brothel as an ideal space for the proliferation of lesbianism ("Las inseparables" 101). Both the brothel and the *fichera* bar exist within a division of spaces and labor established by heteronormative patriarchy, functioning as sites for male heterosexual pleasure. Yet, as Irwin and de la Mora observe, the sexual permissiveness in these environments allows for an *encuiramiento* of normative sexualities, seen in the sapphic sex worker La Gaditana, or through the queering of male heterosexual desire by *la loca* (loosely equivalent to *queen*) in the case of La Manuela in José Donoso's novel *El lugar sin límites* (1966), adapted into a film by Arturo Ripstein in 1978. While Lavín's short story is set in a more contemporary context, the strip club similarly operates as a space for male pleasure, where social conventions are momentarily suspended. As a patron, Mayra assumes an active role, gazing at the female dancers as objects of sexual consumption.

Upon reflecting on her role, the protagonist continues to see herself as catering to men's desires. However, she begins to shed her social role as a fragile figure and moves toward what Castillo considers a *loose woman*, one who exerts control over her sexuality and how men perceive her. This shift is evident when she imagines herself as one of the dancers: "How would she look in a skirt so tight and short? Just the feeling of the tight garment excited her. Without a doubt, she would get men to look at her" ("¿Cómo se veía ella en una falda así de ceñida y corta? La pura sensación de la prenda ajustada la exaltó. Sin duda conseguiría las miradas de los hombres"; 79). At this point, Mayra's sexuality is defined by the male gaze, illustrating the patriarchal ideology behind what Laura Mulvey, in the context of film, terms *to-be-looked-at-ness*, where female characters are depicted as passive objects to be viewed through an active—male—subject's gaze (19). Simultaneously, as Kim Price-Flynn observes in the context of strip clubs, "[t]he trope of women as sex objects emphasizes the male gaze and spotlights women's desire to be watched" (110). Because the strip club accentuates the objectification of women, by positioning herself alongside the dancers and being fully aware of the privilege her social class grants her, the protagonist performs, imagining herself as one of them, and embraces her status as both sexual object and subject.

Through observing the dancers, Mayra contemplates her own ability to arouse desire in others while also acknowledging the sexual curiosity the women provoke in her: "She saw the woman who had danced for them on the table approach with a charging step and understood that she desired her like Eduardo. And that feeling at the center of those inflamed spirits made her a man and a woman. Desired and desirous. She wanted to touch under that skirt, to find the viscous moisture of that woman who offered herself to her" ("Miró a la mujer que les había bailado en la mesa acercarse con un paso embestidor y comprendió que la deseaba como Eduardo. Y que sentirse el centro de esos ánimos inflamados la volvían hombre y mujer. Deseada y deseosa. Quería tocar bajo esa falda, encontrar la humedad viscosa de esa mujer que se ofrecía a ella"; 81). Mayra's reflection on becoming "a man" underscores the complexities of sapphic desire in a context of compulsory heterosexuality, as it resists easy translation into heterosexual terms, thus posing a radical challenge to gender and sexual hierarchies (Irwin, "Las inseparables" 102).

This moment also illustrates Ahmed's assertion that the naturalization of heterosexuality relies on the belief that women's bodies are made for men, and the idea that women must be "like men" to desire other women serves as a "straightening device" to make sense of such desires (*Queer Phenomenology* 71). Mayra's fantasy, though unrealized, reveals how her social role is shaped by these heterosexual ideals. By entering the bar, she crosses the boundaries of acceptable behavior for women, and she further transgresses gender and sexual norms through an *encuiramiento* of the space, embracing sapphic desire and rejecting the male gaze she once depended on to feel wanted. Like Antonia/Antón in *Cuerpo náufrago*, feeling sought after by women and recognizing her own attraction to them heightens her sexual awareness and provides temporary liberation from societal expectations. Her attraction to the dancer echoes Ahmed's contingent lesbianism, a desire that "comes to be felt 'as if' it were a natural force, which is compelling enough to resist the force of compulsory heterosexuality" (*Queer Phenomenology* 94). It is the dancer's closeness and her ability to make Mayra feel wanted that triggers this attraction.

Nevertheless, Mayra's transgressions are not without consequence, as she is abandoned by Eduardo and led away by a stranger to dance. The narrator describes how "[t]he good girl tried to sneak away[,] seeking protection from Eduardo at the empty table, from the group that forgot her and from the hand that was taking her to a dark place saying no problem, we come here to forget the world" ("La muchacha correcta intentó escabullirse buscando la protección de Eduardo en la mesa vacía, en el corro que la olvidaba y en la mano que la tomaba y se la llevaba a un sitio oscuro diciendo no hay problema, aquí nos venimos a olvidar del mundo"; 81). Even though Mayra temporarily forgets that she is in a male-dominated space during her interaction with the dancer, once she steps off the stage, she is forcefully reminded of her position within the gender hierarchy by being led away by the man who, after seeing her dance, believes he has access to her body as he touches her and presses up against her. Although it is unclear what happens to her after the encounter with the stranger, her sudden awareness of her vulnerability sharply contrasts with the sense of empowerment and desire she experienced during the dance.

She reverts to perceiving herself as needing protection, and since she has crossed the boundaries of what is socially permissible in terms of her sexuality, she becomes a target. While the club allows for momentary transgressions, as Price-Glynn notes, "[i]t is both particular clubs and the broader industry, coupled with men's normative, or conventionally and culturally shared, expectations, that create (and re-create) strip clubs as spaces in which all men can experience themselves as desirable, connected, and powerful" (68). Therefore, in Lavín's story, the protagonist's transgressions allow her to envision the potential of *cuir* desire, but the male-dominated environment ensures that these subversions ultimately lead to her punishment.

All the works examined in this chapter reveal traces of sapphic desire. Despite their differences, these *cuir* moments serve to destabilize male access to and control over women's bodies, while also creating spaces of intimacy and solidarity between women. Moreover, they expose the fragile nature of compulsory heterosexuality by demonstrating the diverse ways in which female desire can manifest. Drawing on Muñoz's definition of potentiality as a pathway for transformation, I view these *cuir* moments as opportunities for readers to rethink binary notions of gender and sexuality. By interpreting desire through the lens of *lenchitudes*, we can better understand the intermittent presence of *lo cuir* in contemporary Mexican literature across a wide range of texts, moving beyond strict categories.

Chapter 2

La más macha de las machas

Lencha Masculinities

In the summer of 2015, a childhood friend reached out to share that she had come out. Although we had not been in contact for years, she knew I had been out for some time and wanted to connect. Like me, she had grown up in Mexico and was living in the United States, navigating being *cuir* across two cultures. She was eager to explore the LGBTQ+ community and frequently bombarded me with questions about my experiences, which I did not mind. Yet one particular conversation has lingered in my mind.

One day, unexpectedly, she asked me if I identified as butch. It was not the first time I had been labeled this way (though previously, it had been more of an assumption than a question). When I said no, she then asked if I thought of myself as femme. Again, I said I did not. Perplexed, she suggested that I was probably "futch," a mix of femme and butch. After what felt like a diagnosis, I could not help but wonder why I needed to fit into a single category. Was my coming out in 2006 not enough? Did I also need to put my gender expression in a box, even if I thought of it as fluid? Could I even identify as butch having grown up in Mexico, where it was not a prevalent category? These questions remained with me for years and, although deeply personal, they were a significant part of what drove me to write this book.

When first envisioning this project, influenced by Adrienne Rich's concept of the lesbian continuum, I considered analyzing sapphic representation as part of various continua: of desire, of gender, and so on. However, the more I reflected on it, the more it seemed that framing these characters' complexities in relation to femininity and masculinity ultimately reinforced binary frameworks. Although we are undeniably influenced and shaped by contextual notions of gender, I find that thinking in terms of a continuum does not necessarily solve the problem of binary notions because for there to be a continuum there must be two opposite ends. Thinking within the confines of these terms runs the risk of reinforcing biological essentialism (Bing and Bergvall 18). This concern became particularly relevant to me as I wrote this chapter, which introduces the concept of *lencha* masculinities. At the core of this section—and the next, on femme representation—lies a contradiction: analyzing gender expression and its potential to challenge the masculine/feminine dichotomy while simultaneously using that very system as a point of departure. Although I could not escape this paradox, it led me to abandon the concept of the continuum.

Instead of evaluating degrees of masculinity based on their proximity to hegemonic masculinity, I propose thinking of *lencha* masculinities in the plural, because they are as diverse as the subjects and characters who embody them. I opted for the term *lencha* to describe these expressions of gender instead of following Halberstam's use of the word *female* for two reasons. First, Halberstam's groundbreaking *Female Masculinity* (1998) examines forms of female masculinity beyond sapphic embodiments, including those found in heterosexual contexts. My focus, however, is on literary representations of sapphic gender expression in Mexico, for which *lencha* offers a more culturally and erotically specific frame. Second, as explained in my introduction, the Marcha Lencha illustrated current efforts in Mexico to name a desire and break away from the word *lesbiana* as a fixed identity. For the event's organizers, *lenchitudes* unites a diverse group of people, including trans women, non-binary individuals, trans men, and *machorras* (a term somewhat similar to *butch*, but with contextual differences), who find themselves reflected in their collective efforts to highlight romantic and sexual attraction to women, regardless of sexual orientation and gender identity ("¿Quiénes son las lenchitudes?"). The event organizers' inclusion of varied experiences, especially those who see themselves or are seen as *machorras*, is crucial in the context of this chapter. This inclusion aligns with their goals and, by extension, the objectives of developing *lenchitudes* as a framework, aiming to critique rigid categories that contribute to binary concepts of gender.

Regarding the term *machorra*, Monsiváis notes that after the Mexican Revolution, the public largely considered lesbians non-existent, with the exception of *machorras*, who were viewed as devoid of sexuality

("Los iguales, los semejantes" 96). Over time, as society was confronted with sapphic existence, those perceived as non-heterosexual were—much like the stereotyping of homosexual men as effeminate—associated with behaviors considered masculine, leading to the equation of *machorras* with lesbians (Bisbey 2). Bisbey further explains that "the *machorra* embodies a masculine/feminine script opposition in which an ontologically female body performs masculinities through stereotypically macho activities like drinking, womanizing, and fighting" (163). However, despite the *machorra*'s performance of a female masculinity inspired by stereotypical Mexican masculinities, heteronormative gender hierarchies prevent her from positioning herself within hegemonic masculinity, and thus she never achieves the same power as male masculinity (Zatarain Olivas and Núñez Noriega 37). While this category falls within the scope of *lenchitudes*, especially as the term has been reappropriated by women as an expression of dissidence and subversion of heteronormativity (Bisbey 183), I propose *lencha* masculinities as a broader category. This category includes *machorras* but also leaves room for different expressions of female masculinity, recognizing that not all *machorras* are necessarily attracted to women.

Therefore, in line with *lo cuir* and its constant shifts, impasses, and reinterpretations from various sites of enunciation, I recognize the impossibility of considering *lencha* masculinities homogeneous. As Manuela Lavinas Picq and María Amelia Viteri write, echoing Bee Scherer and Matthew Ball's arguments: "queer is a predisposition more than a category, focused on defying the foundations of social, intellectual, political, and cultural paradigms in relationship to gender, sexuality, and identity. For this reason, queer defies the frameworks that encompass sexuality as well as concepts such as modernity and the imaginary 'souths' of global political economy" ("lo queer es una predisposición más que una categoría, enfocada en desafiar las fundaciones de paradigmas sociales, intelectuales, políticos, y culturales en relación a género, sexualidad, e identidad. Por esto, lo queer desafía los marcos que encierran tanto a la sexualidad como a conceptos de la modernidad y a los 'sures' imaginarios de la economía política global"; 5). I propose *lencha* masculinities, not as fixed identities, but as disruptions of these paradigms within the works that I analyze. As Francesca Dennstedt points out by engaging with José Esteban Muñoz's work, it is productive to consider "detaching queerness from identity as the first step toward envisioning new models for a Latin American queer future" (31). Given that this project is based on Mexican literature and seeks to understand representations within their context, *lencha* masculinities engage and challenge specific understandings of what is defined as masculine in twentieth- and twenty-first-century Mexico. As Héctor Domínguez Ruvalcaba explains, masculinity is socially produced and therefore offers insights into a nation's cultural peculiarities (*Modernity and the Nation* 1).

At the same time, since *lencha* masculinities strive to align with the *cuir* effort to destabilize systems of oppression rooted in gender essentialism, they must also render visible and, ideally, reject hegemonic masculinity's relationship to power and violence. As Halberstam explains, "[a]s long as masculinity is annexed in our society to power and violence and oppression, we will find some masculine women whose gender expression becomes partially wedded to the worst aspects of a culturally mandated masculinity. However, as the complicated lives of some masculine women show, there are also ways for women to pioneer forms of masculinity that change the meaning of modern gender and sexual identity" (*Female Masculinity* 109). While I do not intend to overlook society's influence on *lencha* masculinities, they must embody the pioneering forms that Halberstam highlights by surpassing or challenging hegemonic masculinity and its oppressive mechanisms to serve as a productive embodiment of *lenchitudes* as an inclusive framework. Furthermore, although this chapter engages with theorists from anglophone regions, it is crucial to remain in conversation with notions of *lo cuir* emerging from Latin America. As Sayak Valencia suggests, *cuir* represents an *ostranienie*, or defamiliarization, of the term *queer* that shifts focus to the Global South and the peripheries to question colonial epistemologies ("Del queer al cuir" 34). To truly align with that shift, it is essential to remain conscious of the context in which the analyzed works are produced.

This chapter examines two novels and two short stories. First, I explore Ana Klein's *No hay princesa sin dragón* (2004), where the protagonist questions gender roles by wishing to be like a boy during her childhood but ultimately discovers her true self in adulthood while coming to terms with her sexuality. Next, I analyze *Sandra, secreto amor* (2001) by Reyna Barrera. Barrera's novel features a masculine antagonist named Ramona, who is portrayed in direct opposition to the feminine protagonists, thus idealizing femininity while stigmatizing masculine traits in women. I then proceed to study Elena Madrigal's short story "A dos, de tres caídas" (2010),[1] where the protagonist is a masculine *luchadora* (wrestler). This character relies on the archetype of the Mexican *luchador* (male wrestler), traditionally associated with masculinity. Nonetheless, Madrigal offers a *luchadora* that is fierce in the ring yet tender in her romantic relationships, showcasing the multifaceted dimensions of *lencha* masculinities. I conclude this chapter by examining Victoria Enríquez's "De un pestañazo" (1997), which is loosely based on Colonel Amelio Robles, often considered Mexico's first famous transgender man and a member of the Zapatista forces during the Revolution. I contend that although each of these works contributes to representations of *lencha* masculinities, Madrigal's and Enríquez's protagonists offer the most productive embodiments of this category through their subversion of essentialist understandings of gender and their depictions of masculine women who confront hegemonic masculinity.

Female Masculinity and Sapphic Desire in Mexico

Women who do not conform to the traditional expectations of selflessness, purity, and passivity have been extensively studied by scholars of Mexico. Starting with Octavio Paz's scapegoating of la Malinche through the archetype of *la Chingada* in his 1950 book *El laberinto de la soledad*, others have reimagined women's roles. Such is the case of Roger Bartra, who, in *La jaula de la melancolía* (1987), builds on Paz's postulates to identify two extremes embodied by what he coins *Chingadalupe*, "an ideal image that the Mexican *macho* must create of his partner, who must fornicate with excessive pleasure and at the same time be virginal and comforting" ("una imagen ideal que el macho mexicano debe formarse de su compañera, la cual debe fornicar con desenfreno gozoso y al mismo tiempo ser virginal y consoladora"; 183).[2] These considerations allow us to return to Castillo's *loose woman*, who is transgressive because she "poses a particular threat to society if she has sex for pleasure because she thus violates both of the stereotypical categories for women: that of the decent woman indifferent to sex and that of the prostitute who accepts money for an unpleasant service" (7). Likewise, in his analysis of transgressive women in Mexican popular culture, Carlos Monsiváis highlights actresses Irma Serrano and María Félix, who embody the liberated woman through what he calls *machificación* (masculinization), taking on dominant roles and displaying an aggressive female sexuality (*Amor perdido* 309).

While all these arguments address either the confinement of women through specific societal expectations or the ways they have attempted to challenge them, they focus exclusively on heterosexual women. In the case of Serrano and Félix, while their alleged masculinization stems from their performance of aggression and their vindication of women's sexuality, they do not abandon heteronormativity. These debates prompted me to explore the subversive potential left out: women who defy traditional femininity by embracing self-defined masculinities while experiencing sapphic sexualities. In this chapter, I aim to highlight these possibilities through the concept of *lencha* masculinities.

If the topic of sapphic desire in contemporary Mexican literature has been scarcely explored, it is safe to say that studies on masculinity in female-identified characters who defy heterosexuality are largely absent. At the turn of the twentieth century, especially after the Ball of the 41,[3] Mexican society became preoccupied with the perceived relationship between male homosexuality and femininity (Irwin, *Mexican Masculinities* xii–xiii). Nonetheless, female masculinity in general, and more specifically as part of sapphic desire in Mexico, is a subject that has not been thoroughly studied. When there are literary representations of this desire, it usually takes places between women who adhere to normative concepts of femininity, in some cases perpetuating the male gaze.[4] Therefore, this chapter examines the possibilities of *lencha* masculinities in Mexican literature. I achieve this by analyzing different depictions of masculinity and their problematization (or lack thereof) of heteropatriarchal structures.

The concept of the *masculine woman* is not new in Mexico. Nonetheless, to delve deeper into its evolution, we must first understand its beginnings. This type of character became common in narratives about the Mexican Revolution. For instance, novels like *La negra Angustias* (1944) by Francisco Rojas González and films such as like *La cucaracha* (1958), directed by Ismael Rodríguez, feature female protagonists who adopt masculine roles and attire to navigate their circumstances (Domínguez Ruvalcaba, *Modernity and the Nation* 40). It is worth noting the first text to associate sapphic desire with female masculinity: Salvador Quevedo y Zubieta's lengthy novel *México marimacho* (1933). The narrative follows two women, Eutimia and Guadalupe, who, in addition to showing traits considered masculine at the time—like an interest in horseback riding and hunting—also maintain a close, sometimes ambiguous relationship. Quevedo y Zubieta's text pathologizes sapphic desire and explicitly identifies the characters as lesbians. Although published a few decades later, the novel shares similarities with *Los cuarenta y uno: una novela crítico-social*, released in 1906 under the pseudonym of Eduardo A. Castrejón. Both works highlight the perceived gender transgression associated with non-heterosexual desire and simultaneously blame the Mexican elite and foreign influences for such behavior.

These portrayals expose the close ties between Mexican nationalism and the homophobia and rigid gender roles prevalent in the first half of the twentieth century. Just as in *Los cuarenta y uno*, *México marimacho* includes a prologue by its author condemning the deterioration of Mexican society. In it, Quevedo y Zubieta recounts an encounter with two young, androgynous women and bemoans "the virile transformation of our former little women" ("la transformación viril de nuestras antiguas mujercitas"; 6). A key difference between the texts is that Castrejón's novel offers one of its characters redemption by having him choose a heterosexual life, while in *México marimacho* both characters die tragically despite their efforts to become conventional wives and mothers. This outcome demonstrates that in Mexico, there is room only for masculinity among men. In her analysis of the novel, Sofía Ruiz-Alfaro explains that despite the fame of the *adelitas* and *coronelas* (women soldiers) during the Mexican Revolution and the supposed social openness brought by the chaos of war, the possibility of female masculinity in the homophobic and heteronormative postrevolutionary era was inconceivable. This fear arose from the belief that it not only threatened the roles of the submissive woman and the macho but also introduced the unimaginable notion of lesbianism (43). Therefore, while masculinity in women was not as socially stigmatized as the perception of effeminacy in men—as exemplified by the Ball of the 41—it was deemed necessary to either dismiss or punish it to prevent its proliferation.

This tendency to disparage female masculinity continued in the 1920s, when upper-class Mexican women, influenced by the flappers in the United States, began to change their style and cut their hair short, earning the nickname *las pelonas* (the bald ones). This group of women faced such significant backlash that in 1928 a group of them was attacked, and their heads were forcefully shaved by a crowd of male students. Regarding the motives behind this hostility, Anne Rubenstein explains that the androgynous style of *las pelonas* threatened to erase visual differences between genders. Furthermore, she notes that Mexican media suggested they could also blur racial and class lines as the trend spread beyond the elites (63). As depicted in *Los cuarenta y uno* and *México marimacho*, the upper classes and foreign influences were accused of corrupting Mexican society.

In response to such transgressions, and in a manner similar to the actions taken against the men at the 1901 ball—albeit on a smaller scale—a conservative group sought to control *las pelonas* because they undermined gender identities and roles. Although the women were not attacked because of their sexual orientation—there is no documentation on this subject—there is an intersection between them and Halberstam's arguments regarding the rejection of female masculinity. This is evident when we consider that many of the jokes and insults hurled at *las pelonas* were based on the idea that they had become less attractive or available to men (Rubenstein 63). Halberstam makes a similar argument, explaining that the butch lesbian poses a threat to heterosexual men by presenting the image of the uncastrated woman who refuses to participate in straight dynamics that portray women as weak and defenseless (*Queer Art* 96). Additionally, masculinity in cisgender women has often been perceived as synonymous with ugliness and undesirability within heterosexual norms (Platero 4). Hence, women are deemed valuable only when they conform to conventional notions of femininity and beauty.

In this context, it is important to recognize that, despite being marked as undesirable, female masculinity can take many forms and varies from individual to individual (Halberstam, *Female Masculinity* 9). These diverse forms arise because when women use masculine attitudes and styles, they produce new meanings by destabilizing not only the visual codes of masculinity, but also the gendered bodies expected to perform them (Rubin 469; Faderman 591). My interest in these characters arises from how their representation can make us reflect on their ability to challenge hegemonic masculinity. Lastly, I highlight how depictions of *lencha* masculinities in the literary works I analyze reveal the ways these characters are stigmatized. The attacks on masculine-presenting women are often less about their same-sex desire and more about the fear that they might become "like men" (Castañeda 110). Therefore, I contend that *lencha* masculinities are effective in challenging this notion by either exposing gender essentialism and violence or, in their most transgressive forms, offering ways to resist them.

In *The Queer Art of Failure* (2011), Halberstam discusses the undesirability linked to being seen as "manly" by examining the butch archetype. He uses the popular television show *The L Word* (2004–2009) as a point of departure, examining how it articulates a new, desirable lesbianism that fits within heterosexual visual models. Developing an appealing lesbian character requires leaving butchness behind, as it symbolizes failed femininity (*Queer Art* 95). Similarly, in her work on media depictions of lesbianism, Ann M. Ciasullo explores how these portrayals produce and reinforce a specific feminine image while simultaneously rejecting the masculine woman. Ciasullo distinguishes between the cultural imagination and the cultural landscape. The former refers to society's collective imagination, while the latter pertains to how characters are portrayed. This implies that although the masculine lesbian exists in the cultural imagination—society is aware of her existence—her representation in the cultural landscape remains precarious (578–79). This occurs because the feminine, or femme, lesbian is an object of media consumption; she is desired by heterosexual men because her appearance does not mark her as queer and is, in turn, relatable for heterosexual women. The butch lesbian, on the other hand, cannot be easily separated from her sexual orientation (Ciasullo 604; Smyth 83), as has historically been the case of the *machorra* in Mexico.

The tendency to represent sapphic desire and gender expression in line with heteronormative aesthetic values operates similarly to Lisa Duggan's concept of new homonormativity, where homosexuality is portrayed as non-threatening in an effort to normalize it (179). Despite contextual differences, Mexico experiences a comparable pattern regarding sapphic representation in literary works. There are few examples of female masculinity in these types of narratives. Notably, well-known texts like Roffiel's *Amora* and Levi-Calderón's *Dos mujeres* avoid depicting such characters.

Olivera Córdova explains that Roffiel avoided including masculine women in her novel to advance a transgressive femininity that challenged the stereotype of the masculine lesbian, prompting readers to wonder how such feminine women could be lesbians (*Entre amoras* 146). In questioning how femininity can be aligned with lesbianism, it becomes evident that there is a generalized association between lesbianism and masculine gender expression. By taking this into account and revisiting Ciasullo's arguments, we can observe that while female masculinity is acknowledged in Mexican society's cultural imagination, it continues to be precariously represented in its cultural landscape. Furthermore, the deliberate exclusion of female masculinities in literary works serves to maintain a palatable lesbian image within the cultural landscape, even when their audience is often limited to readers who actively seek out this type of literature, as demonstrated by the circulation of *Amora* among *cuir* women following its censorship.

Nonetheless, it is important to note that authors like Roffiel, Reyna Barrera, and Gilda Salinas began publishing their work in the 1980s and 1990s. Their literary texts were among the very first to depict sapphic desire and to be written by women (Fuentes Ponce, *Decidir sobre el propio cuerpo* 25). Olivera Córdova argues that the influence of second-wave feminism may have contributed to the rejection of masculinity because of its association with patriarchy ("Masculinidades de mujeres" 139). This connection between second-wave feminism and its influence on early texts depicting sapphic desire is precisely what Téllez refers to when categorizing these works as *lesbofeminist*. One of their main objectives was to portray lesbians positively, which sometimes involved negatively depicting those not aligning with "good lesbian" standards.

This historic exclusion is one of several reasons behind the value of highlighting *lencha* masculinities, since ignoring them obfuscates the multiple ways in which they can undermine heteropatriarchal norms. In his introduction to the Spanish edition of *Female Masculinity*, Halberstam emphasizes how the variety of terms used to describe female masculinity in Spanish-speaking countries not only uncovers the diverse contexts for gender diversity across various national cultures but also suggests the existence of a wide range of possibilities within each category (7–8). By exploring the following texts, I aim to reveal a sample of the numerous opportunities that *lenchitudes* and sapphic literature in Mexico can offer to female masculinities.

"Those Things Are for Men":
No hay princesa sin dragón (2004) by Ana Klein

Ana Klein (b. 1947, Mexico City) is a self-identified lesbian writer who centers sapphic desire in her narrative works by considering that "one cannot write what they have not lived" ("una no puede escribir de lo que no ha vivido"; quoted in Olivera Córdova, *Entre amoras* 145). This is apparent in her three novels: *Si me regreso me muero* (1984), *No hay princesa sin dragón* (2004), and *La princesa en las espirales de la luna* (2008). As opposed to authors like Roffiel, Klein "takes up women's rights to transgress cultural gender, to cross-dress" ("retoma el derecho de las mujeres a transgredir el género cultural, al travestismo"; Olivera Córdova, *Entre amoras* 146). *No hay princesa sin dragón* tells the story of Camila, who, throughout her childhood in 1950s Mexico City, rejects the notion of gender-specific behaviors. The novel follows her into adulthood, detailing her failed relationships with women due to her own fear of her sexuality. Camila's story intertwines with that of her family members, who adhere to heteronormative rules, granting men more freedom and prescribing specific behaviors for women. Although Camila's masculinity does not continue into adulthood, it shapes her as she questions gender roles. While Klein's portrayal of *lencha* masculinities as a phase might be seen as problematic, it is also productive in viewing gender expression as malleable and evolving.

Carlos Monsiváis describes mid-twentieth-century Mexican society as divided between the essentialism of family life and the exaltation of the macho. He argues that machismo reinforces strict family roles and almost mythologizes a historical reality shaped by Judeo-Christian morals and patriarchal ideology.[5] As a result, he points out, submission becomes women's fate, as anatomy marks one's social status (*Amor perdido* 30–31). This traditionally gendered categorization of behaviors is evident from the beginning of Klein's novel, when Camila shares her dream of becoming a sailor with her family. Clearly surprised, they "explained that a girl could not be a sailor; even Justino, the gardener, who was deaf-mute, said no! with all its letters.—Why not?—Camila asked, in a sea of tears.—Because those things are for men—answered the lying maid, in the name of all of humanity" ("explicaron que una niña no podía ser marinera; aun Justino, el jardinero, que era sordomudo, le dijo ¡no!, con todas sus letras.— ¿Por qué no?—preguntó Camila, hecha una mar de lágrimas.—Porque ésas son cosas de hombres—contestó la criada mentirosa, en nombre de la humanidad entera"; 16). The simultaneous response from Camila's family, as well as from the gardener and domestic worker,[6] is conveyed using third-person plural (*explicaron*). This creates the illusion of all members functioning as a collective entity, echoing Monsiváis's arguments about the relationship between the family and the figure of the macho. For Camila, it does not matter who denies her of her dream, as the family collectively gatekeeps traditional gender roles.

This confrontation plays a pivotal role in the protagonist's character development, prompting her to reject feminine attitudes and behaviors in favor of those associated with boys. From childhood, she views femininity as a reminder of gender inequality, and by rejecting it, she aims to rid herself of negative stereotypes like the belief that women are weaker or less competent than men (Craig and LaCroix 452). Therefore, the protagonist defiantly treats these prohibitions as challenges instead of limitations. The image of the sailor, with its connotations of freedom and exploration of unknown territories, acts as a leitmotif throughout the novel. This association is more evident once Camila finds a children's sailor suit that belonged to her father.

When describing the first time she puts it on, the narrator explains that "[i]n the moment of the visionary jump, of the gleaming transformation, plotting with the stars, this sailor of the imagination was completely unaware of the high price she would have to pay in this world for the sacred attempt to be whatever one felt like being" ("En el instante del salto visionario, de la muda luminosa, en complot con las estrellas, esta navegante de la imaginación ignoraba por completo el alto precio que debía pagar en este mundo por el intento sagrado de ser exactamente como a uno se le diera su regalada gana"; 17). This marks a point of no return for her, as she briefly experiences the metaphorical freedom of being a sailor by wearing the suit. However, the narrator reminds us that being a girl with big dreams in a family devoted to maintaining the status quo will present many difficulties. It is then ironic how her last name, Caminos, symbolizes the various paths she can choose, and yet, in order to decide for herself, she must confront the very patriarchal constraints imposed by those sharing her father's family name.

Klein's protagonist differs from other characters analyzed in that her masculinity manifests only during her childhood, when she first begins to question her sexuality. In this sense, it closely resembles the tomboy category, serving as a transient state. However, there is no exact translation of the term or its meanings into Mexican Spanish. The terms *marimacha* or *marimacho* (often used interchangeably) are perhaps the closest equivalents, although they lack the same association with youth and childhood, as one can be a *marimacha* at any age. In English-speaking societies, tomboyism is often considered a form of masculinity that serves as a step toward femininity.[7] It is associated with the "natural" desire of freedom and mobility in children and can even be perceived as a sign of independence in girls. This behavior is encouraged as long as it is temporary. However, when it crosses into masculine identification and threatens to extend beyond childhood, it is often punished (Halberstam, *Female Masculinity* 6). On the other hand, Craig and LaCroix explain that tomboyism is used to give girls limited protection from the negative implications of transgressing gender norms (451). These analyses are significant when we consider Klein's novel from a broader perspective, although it is imperative to highlight contextual differences. The main distinction is that while in the United States tomboyism is often deemed a developmental stage for girls and not inherently negative, in Mexico femininity is expected since childhood and throughout women's lives.

Camila's early exploration of masculinity culminates when, dressed as a boy, she poses as her brother's friend and is not recognized by her own mother: "When Adela asked her name, the girl wished to strip herself of the hat and wash her face to return the memories to her mother's forgetfulness, but she was suddenly overcome with rage and resentfully responded: —Jorgito, *señora*" ("Cuando Adela le preguntó su nombre, la niña quiso despojarse de la gorra y lavarse la cara para devolverle el recuerdo a los olvidos de su madre, pero se le metió de golpe un encabronamiento emputecido y le respondió con rencor:—Jorgito, señora"; 50). Her longing to obtain the freedoms that come with being a boy momentarily comes true, and her mother, who represents the family that has reprimanded her masculinity, is fooled. As is often the case with tomboys, she is briefly granted access to spaces that are typically denied to girls (Craig and LaCroix 456). However, this position is short-lived, and as she faces the reality of her context—where there is no concept of tomboyism—she realizes that it is possible only by "passing" as a boy. Her anger is rooted in the frustration caused by her mother's failure to recognize her. She does not want to be a boy, as that would mean losing her identity. Instead, she wants freedom as a girl. In this sense, *No hay princesa sin dragón* makes for a unique exploration of *lencha* masculinities, as Camila aims not to feel or appear masculine but rather to enjoy the privileges and freedoms afforded to men.

To highlight the protagonist's development, the narrator contrasts her story with those of her parents and grandparents. The plotline that most obviously parallels Camila's is that of her father, Antonio, whose childhood experiences are shaped by his physical beauty, making him insecure about his masculinity. Paradoxically, the same sailor suit that Camila wears years later is what caused her father to be ridiculed as a child for his perceived effeminacy. We first observe this in a flashback, when Antonio's father sees him wearing the suit and tells those around him that they are "going to turn him into a sissy" ("lo van a volver maricón"; 22). He then carries Antonio on horseback, cursing the women who dressed him as a sailor, and takes him to get a buzz cut and then to a tailor to dress him "like a man." Finally, he gives him toy guns and teaches him how to ride a horse to prevent him from becoming "effeminate" (22). As in the case of Camila, his childhood becomes a crucial starting point for his understanding of masculinity.

There is a notable contrast between the women in his family, who dress him in the suit, and his father, who represents patriarchy and seeks to affirm his son's masculinity. The interaction between Antonio and his father is meaningful because, as Michael S. Kimmel explains, it is usually a boy's father who serves as the primary judge of his performance of masculinity, making him the first male figure the boy seeks approval from

(130). Antonio's father reacts immediately to counter his alleged "effeminacy," showing the sense of urgency and alarm that he experiences upon seeing his son wearing something he considers feminine. By pushing the boy into a series of exaggerated behaviors, the father seems to follow the description of the typical macho. This figure, popularized by the golden age of Mexican cinema, transitioned from being viewed as a national threat to a symbol of national pride and identity (Macías-González and Rubenstein 21; Hershfield 27). His father's biggest fear is that wearing the suit will turn Antonio into a "sissy," demonstrating how machismo requires the abjection of homophobia in order to exist (Domínguez Ruvalcaba, *Modernity and the Nation* 109). This underscores the fragility of masculinity, which requires constant validation from others. Monsiváis notes that historically in Mexico, machismo seeks the "social lynching" ("*linchamiento social*") of anything far from what is considered manly, specifically effeminacy ("Crónica de aspectos" 91). Therefore, Antonio's father symbolically eliminates any indication of femininity in his son.

The sailor suit holds different meanings for various characters throughout the novel. Olivera Córdova considers the outfit as representing Camila's rejection of femininity (*Entre amoras* 148). While I agree with this interpretation, I also see the suit as embodying Camila's optimism, allowing her to fantasize about the freedoms afforded to men. On the other hand, her grandfather views the suit as highlighting Antonio's beauty, a quality he equates with femininity and, thus, the possibility of homosexuality. For Antonio, it becomes a reminder of having to reassert his masculinity and sexual power, tormenting him throughout his life. In this sense, the suit is significant because it does not have a stable meaning, functioning as an indication of the precarity of the gender binary. This echoes Butler's explanation of how elements such as acts and gestures associated with gender are performative, meaning that the identities they seem to express are, in fact, fabrications upheld by physical signs and discourse. The implication is that the gendered body's reality is constituted solely by these performative acts (*Gender Trouble* 173). Therefore, if the sailor suit functions as a signifier of masculinity for Camila but symbolizes femininity for Antonio and his father, this paradox reveals the socially constructed and contrived nature of gender.

Antonio's constant preoccupation with proving himself as a man leads him to obsess over his penis, which he considers a symbol of masculinity. This fixation is reminiscent of the doctor in *La cresta de Ilión*, discussed in chapter 1, as both characters consider their genitals to be intrinsically liked to their gender identity and seek validation of their masculinity through sexual encounters with women. This fixation reproduces a phallocentric logic that equates masculinity with penetrative ability and penis size, focusing on the penis as both the material and symbolic center of male sexual identity (Ranea Triviño 42). Driven by his preoccupation with gender, Antonio visits a brothel on his sixteenth birthday to reaffirm his masculinity. As Beatriz Ranea Triviño explains, sexual activity is central in the path to "becoming a man." Sex work, in this context, provides access to women's bodies following patriarchal patterns (83).

The relationship between masculinity and sex exposes a paradox. On one hand, the belief that Antonio must engage in sex with a woman to "become" a man is grounded in heteronormative patriarchal views of masculine behavior. Yet, if masculinity can be attained only by following a specific set of rules, it confirms that it is not natural but socially constructed. In the case of the novel, Antonio's trip to the brothel is applauded by his mother, who interprets his entry into manhood as a marker that she is no longer permitted to question his actions (27). According to Monsiváis, in the Mexican context, victims of machismo frequently become its accomplices ("Crónica de aspectos" 95). This is apparent in the role of women as part of the configuration of national identity in the first half of the twentieth century, which contributed to the belief that mothers were to be "selfless and righteous, dedicated to their family and their Catholic faith, two paramount institutions through which patriarchy was normalized" (Gaytán 25). Hence, Antonio's mother upholds traditional Mexican family values, privileging her son and justifying his behavior, since his transition into manhood brings with it sexual needs that allegedly must be satisfied through his encounters with women.

Even though Antonio checks all the boxes required of masculinity, he remains deeply insecure. His doubts are tied to his father's reaction to him wearing the sailor suit as a child. The narrator tells us that "despite the defiant attitude that Antonio Caminos always showed before life, in a corner of himself lived a boy captive in a sailor suit with a penis the size of his pinky who was very afraid of the possibility of not existing" ("A pesar de la actitud desafiante que Antonio Caminos mostró siempre ante la vida, en un rincón de sí mismo habitaba un niño cautivo en un traje de marinerito con un pene del tamaño de su dedo meñique al que le daba mucho miedo la posibilidad de no existir"; 27). His feelings reiterate the contrast between his experience with the suit and Camila's. For Antonio, the sailor suit is not just a reminder of his potential femininity, but it also holds him captive, unable to shed the fear of failing to uphold masculinity. The fact that part of him still identifies as a boy emphasizes his first encounter with the pressure to be seen as a man. Even though he contemplates this privately, he is unable to forget his father's concerns about his gender identity and sexuality. Simultaneously, the size of his penis becomes the focus of his fear of nonexistence. Viewing the absence of the penis as nonexistence aligns him with the absence and lack historically used to define women in Mexico (Monsiváis, "La mujer en la cultura" 101). This reinforces the patriarchal notion that male sexual experience, epitomized by the penis, signifies sexual potency and is fundamental to his identity as a man.

No hay princesa sin dragón openly questions fixed understandings of gender, and at the same time, it is a bildungsroman where Camila comes to terms with her sexuality and gender expression. While Antonio functions as an example of the multiple contradictions and problems of hegemonic masculinity, Camila represents an exploration of the distinction between gender and sexuality. This is evident as we are told that "[t]his alchemy was not inspired by her sexuality, as *nana* Concepción assumed, but rather by her sailor thinking" ("Esta alquimia no fue inspirada por su sexualidad, como supuso la nana Concepción, sino por su pensamiento marinero"; 17). Whereas her father's relationship to gender is marked by fear and confinement, Camila's is likened to alchemy, symbolizing transformation and exploration. Meanwhile, she remains confident and aware that her gender expression is tied to her desire for freedom, not her sexual orientation. This stands in opposition to the assumption made by her nanny, who has previously chastised her for her gender transgressions. Through her association with the domestic sphere, Concepción acts as an extension of her family and the patriarchal values that sustain it.

As her process of self-discovery takes place, Camila lets go of her rejection of femininity and finds the freedom she searched for in childhood by coming to terms with her sexuality. This is evidenced as we learn that "Camila Caminos forever stopped believing the absurd tale that claimed that a girl could not reach the stars. A smile from Valentina sufficed to jump to the seventh heaven in a heartbeat" ("Camila Caminos dejó de creer, para siempre, en esa absurda patraña que aseguraba que una niña no podía llegar a las estrellas. Una sonrisa de Valentina bastó para brincar al séptimo cielo en un santiamén"; 57). While the novel illustrates the protagonist's newfound confidence after embracing her sexuality, her childhood masculinity is portrayed as a transient phase. Considering that the concept of the tomboy is not directly translatable into the Mexican context, the representation of *lencha* masculinity in childhood in Klein's novel is noteworthy. On one hand, the narrative presents Camila's early rebellion against gender roles as a subversive act that questions male privilege. This depiction highlights *lencha* masculinities as potentially disrupting the gender binary. However, portraying these disruptions as confined to childhood and disappearing with her acceptance of her sexuality could be interpreted as reducing *lencha* masculinities to a transitional phase, which the protagonist must outgrow for complete self-realization.

In her pursuit of freedom, however, Camila must continually contend with her family and those in her domestic sphere, especially her nanny, who acts as a gatekeeper of gender roles. Olivera Córdova describes Nana Concepción as a constant figure in the protagonist's life, representing social rejection of gender transgressions, frightening Camila as a child, and constantly judging her (*Entre amoras* 149). Nana Concepción fits the traditional role of the *madre abnegada* (selfless mother) that contributed to the formation of national identity during the golden age of Mexican cinema—a topic that will be discussed further in chapter 3. She is long-suffering and self-denying (Gaytán 24), and even her name evokes the act of conceiving children. Her unwavering commitment to family and religion is also tied to the nation, as we learn that she gave birth to twenty-seven children and raised them as devout Catholics, some of whom died during the Guerra Cristera.

Despite her associations with motherhood, Concepción's relationship with Camila is always tense, never quite aligning with the stereotype of the nurturing nanny familiar to many middle- and upper-class Mexicans and Latin Americans. This dynamic inevitably came to the forefront after the release of Alfonso Cuarón's *Roma* (2019), loosely inspired by his own relationship with his childhood nanny, Liboria "Libo" Rodríguez. Though the film faced both criticism and praise from scholars and film critics, it contributed to a widespread sense of nostalgia for the image of the nanny. Amid the debates about the movie's portrayal of domestic workers, some critics noted how *Roma* encouraged them to reconnect with their own nannies (De la Mora, "*Roma*" 50). In this regard, Roberto Ortiz notes that "[m]emories of having domestic workers and nannies have been normalized by a certain class and generation" ("Recuerda, Notes on Alfonso Cuarón's *Roma*"). This is arguably one of the most poignant critiques of Cuarón's film, as it forces us—I include myself in this *us*—to face the discomfort of our simultaneous idealization of childhood nannies and complicity in perpetuating this precarious physical and emotional labor. I allow this digression to highlight the nostalgia associated with nannies in Mexico from the comfortable vantage point of the middle and upper classes, precisely because in the novel, Concepción is portrayed as anything but endearing, thus disrupting the familiar sentimental trope and instead positioning her as an antagonistic figure in the reader's eyes.

Even though Concepción is far from typical representations of domestic workers and nannies, her depiction falls into problematic tropes. For example, when contrasted with the Caminos family, her numerous children and strong religious devotion reinforce stereotypically negative portrayals of domestic workers. Demeaning cultural perceptions of household laborers are still common in Mexico and other parts of Latin America. These attitudes, which often have racist undertones, frequently portray them as uneducated, ignorant, unsophisticated, dishonest, and possessing low-level skills (Ríos 224; Thomson 284). While the novel does not directly allude to Concepción's racial identity, Abril Saldaña Tejeda contends that domestic workers in Mexico are invariably racialized, regardless of their ethnicity, because of the enduring colonial imaginary that assigns cleaning and care tasks to indigenous and black women. Moreover, she explains that the physical, and often emotional, proximity involved in domestic work fuels social anxieties, leading to the reinforcement of boundaries to distinguish between workers and employers (74). In *No hay princesa sin dragon*, Concepción's exaggerated traits are used to delineate these boundaries. Furthermore, the details of her life are used to build her up as a representation of conservatism, yet she is ultimately reduced to her interactions with the Caminos family, which fails to critically portray the complexities and problematic aspects of domestic labor in Mexico.

Despite Concepción's role in criticizing Camila's gender expression and sexuality, the protagonist experiences similar hostility from multiple members of her family and household. As she matures, part of her character development involves becoming more self-assured and unafraid to confront those who challenge her. Thus, by the end of the novel, she does not hesitate to get into a heated argument with her uncle Jerónimo, during which she exclaims, "I didn't drop anything along the way, idiot, nor do I need a phallus to get to heaven. And, just so you know, the muses are the patrimony of the imagination, like the Moon, not of your balls, asshole" ("—A mí no se me cayó nada en el camino, pendejo, ni necesito un falo para llegar al cielo. Y para que te enteres, las musas son patrimonio de la imaginación, como la Luna, no de tus cojones, cabrón"; 116–17). Her choice to use the word *patrimonio* is significant given its origin in the

Latin word *pater*, or *father*. In Roman law, the term was used to describe everything that was part of the family, such as women, children, and other property—including enslaved people—which all belonged to the father (Hanisch 11). This allusion to the paternal figure, along with her mention of the phallus, inevitably brings us back to her own father, Antonio.

As Butler reminds us, the phallus, "though clearly not identical with the penis, nevertheless deploys the penis as its naturalized instrument and sign" (*Gender Trouble* 135). Thus, when Camila speaks of the phallus, she refers to both its symbolic power and the body part. By claiming that she does not need a phallus to reach heaven—a metaphor for her discovery of her sexuality—she challenges the very foundation of patriarchal thought that confers power on men. Alternatively, by stating that she did not "drop anything along the way," she alludes to the materiality of the body, specifically the physical penis, which she does not need either. Thus, she turns her back on the physical and symbolic expressions of masculinity that paralyze her father through the image of the sailor suit. Finally, Camila's claim that the muses belong to the realm of the imagination—along with the moon, traditionally linked to femininity—suggests a connection back to that same suit that once initiated her journey of self-discovery.

Even though *No hay princesa sin dragón* does not fully articulate a model of female masculinity, it stresses the fragility of the gender binary through the differing ways Camila and her father relate to the sailor suit. The protagonist's refusal to be constrained by gender roles allows her to break free from societal expectations, while her father remains imprisoned by the pressures of having to prove his masculinity. I categorize Camila within *lencha* masculinities because, even though she ultimately rejects masculinity, she uses it as a transitional state that aids in her growth and acceptance of her sexuality. While seeing *lencha* masculinities as temporary can be problematic if they are reduced to a mere phase to be outgrown, their subversive qualities become evident when understood as demonstrating the fluidity of gender expression, thereby challenging the gender binary.

"An Unbearable Lesbian":
Sandra, secreto amor (2001) by Reyna Barrera

Reyna Barrera (b. 1939, Mexico City) is a prolific writer and scholar who obtained a doctorate in literature from the Universidad Nacional Autónoma de México, where she also worked as a professor specializing in theatre.

She has written poetry, essays, and narrative, and received awards such as the 1987 Premio Plural essay award and the Premio Rubén Bonifaz Nuño for her poetry in 1997 (Olivera Córdova, *Entre amoras* 137). Some of her works include poetry collections such as *Material del olvido* (1993), *Lunario* (2000), and *Luna plena* (2008), as well as the short story book *La Güera Veneno* (2017) and a biographical text on writer Salvador Novo, *Salvador Novo: Navaja de la inteligencia* (1999), among other works.

Barrera's first and only novel, *Sandra, secreto amor* (2001), follows friends Luis, Arcelia, and Eurídice, who work for the Festival Internacional Cervantino in Guanajuato. Through a non-linear narrative, the text transitions from past to present and from Mexico City to Guanajuato. Though it narrates the diverse stories of the group of friends, the novel primarily focuses on Eurídice, who falls in love with a woman named Sandra. Sandra has a possessive ex-girlfriend named Ramona, characterized as masculine. Regarding this character, Olivera Córdova explains how the word *lesbiana* is used exclusively to describe her throughout the novel, which the critic interprets as indicative of an association between the word and the character's negative behavior (*Entre amoras* 141). *Sandra, secreto amor* exemplifies the "transgressive femininity" discussed by Olivera Córdova while demonstrating that love between women does not imply that one of them must be masculine. At the time of the novel's publication, this choice was an attempt to avoid stereotypical associations of sapphic desire with masculinity; however, a more contemporary reading reveals the problematic nature of its negative representation.

The novel creates exclusive categories by referring only to Ramona as *lesbiana* while portraying Eurídice and Sandra positively. Gabriela Cano notes that although the term *lesbiana* is not synonymous with masculinity, it does not exclude masculine identification. She highlights that identity categories are flexible and not hermetically sealed spaces ("Unconcealable Realities" 37–38). The choice to name only Ramona as a *lesbiana* is significant because it links the word to aggression and violence. This likely stems from the association of *lesbiana* with female masculinity and is therefore an attempt to dispel stereotypes in order to depict sapphic desire in a positive, non-threatening manner. However, the oversimplification does more harm than good by assuming all lesbians are masculine and, therefore, violent oppressors. Additionally, it is noteworthy that while the text labels Ramona as a *lesbiana*, she never explicitly refers to herself as such.

From the beginning of the novel, Luis describes her as "Ramona, an unbearable lesbian, especially because she walked like a war tank, hissing"

("Ramona, una lesbiana insoportable, sobre todo porque caminaba como un tanque de guerra, bufando"; 43). This early mention of her in the text stands out for its negative description and comparison of her to an object. Butler's arguments help describe this dehumanization, as they explain that gender differentiation is integral to humanizing individuals in society, and we frequently punish those who fail to represent their assigned gender adequately (*Gender Trouble* 272). While Luis does not explicitly say that Ramona is masculine, he does compare her to an instrument of war, setting the tone for the depiction of her behavior throughout the text.

This warlike quality stands clearly opposed to stereotypical Mexican femininity, which is seen as passive and nurturing. Consequently, Ramona is continuously rejected by other characters throughout the novel. Olivera Córdova explains that Ramona's characterization as a masculine and violent lesbian who reproduces degrading heteronormative roles places her in direct opposition to her rival, Eurídice, who is patient, loving, and respectful of Sandra's freedom (*Entre amoras* 141). Ramona's negative portrayal is a double-edged sword. While it establishes her as the antagonist in the novel, it also embodies a heteronormative frame that considers femininity essential to women and thereby validates patriarchal gender norms. By berating her and portraying her as undesirable, the novel emphasizes the discomfort that characters like her generate in a binary gender system, along with their potential to disrupt it.

While Eurídice is described as loving and tender, Ramona is seen as violent. The narrator provides further insight into this characterization by detailing the latter's childhood, stating that "pride dominated her early character. But her name wasn't Ramón, that name she thought about, repeated it, it was her battle name, her hero name. She dreamed of damsels who smelled of fresh apples and had crystal smiles. Preferable to playing with dolls" ("el orgullo dominaba en ese temprano carácter. Pero no se llamaba Ramón, ese nombre lo pensaba, lo repetía, era su nombre de batalla, su nombre de héroe. Soñaba con doncellas que olieran a manzanas frescas y que tuviesen sonrisa de cristal. Preferible que jugar a las muñecas"; 48). Thus, we learn about Ramona's playful fascination with being a knight and that she chooses a male name for her battle persona. Although she daydreams about rescuing damsels as her alter ego, Ramón, the narrator emphasizes that this is just a fantasy. As I will explain later, there is no indication that she identifies as trans or experiences gender dysphoria. Through this dream, we observe how Ramona idealizes conventional heteronormative gender roles and power dynamics, with this idealization allowing her to assume an active, heroic masculine persona. This portrayal contrasts sharply with Eurídice, whose relationship with Sandra is based on equality, mutual respect, and reciprocity. Consequently, the novel begins by presenting Ramona as complicit in oppressive dynamics.

Her masculinity not only sets her apart from Eurídice and Sandra but also allows her access to male spaces. Barrera writes that, during her youth, she "[a]lmost became antisocial. If she dressed like a boy, teenage girls rejected her; but the men immediately adopted her as one of the guys to complete the baseball team, for example" ("Casi se volvió antisocial. Si vestía como muchacho, las adolescentes la rechazaban; pero ellos la adoptaban de inmediato como un camarada más para completar el equipo de béisbol, por ejemplo"; 53). Despite her not being a man, her masculine expression is validated by cisgender men. This mirrors the construction of male masculinity, as it requires reinforcement from other men through homosociality, which is largely defined by the exclusion of women (Ranea Triviño 45; Gutmann, *Changing Men* 5). Furthermore, this recognition from the men around her is significant within the context of sports, where visible signs of masculinity and the exhibition of so-called "virile" qualities are often prominent (Bourdieu 69). Ramona is rejected by other women for her association with patriarchal violence, as though her masculinity makes her complicit in these mechanisms.

Eurídice hesitates to start a relationship with Sandra due to fear of Ramona's jealousy. The narrator explains that "Romy's character was an obstacle, she was a woman to be reckoned with. She imagined herself being chased by Ramona aboard her car along the interstate, gun in hand, shooting her in broad daylight like she did with Maquis, an alleged love rival" ("El carácter de Romy era un obstáculo, se trataba de una mujer de armas tomar. Se imaginaba perseguida por Ramona a bordo de su automóvil a lo largo del periférico, pistola en mano, disparándole a plena luz del día como hizo con Maquis, una dizque rival de amores"; 77). The fact that Ramona is accepted by men and replicates gender violence adds to her vilification. According to Ranea Triviño, violence or the threat of violence is a way to represent and spectacularize masculinity, as it is performed in the search for recognition. The possibility of committing violence is naturalized as if it were an inherent element of bodies perceived as masculine (64). However, Ramona's relationship to gender is at times portrayed with comedic exaggeration. She performs actions tied to violent masculinity while simultaneously using this violence to reinforce her identity as a woman. For example, when a police officer mistakes her for a man, she is obviously upset: "—Why the hell do you ask me for a draft card, asshole? Can't you see I'm a woman?—while shooting in the air" ("—¡Cómo carajos me pide usted a mí una cartilla de servicio militar, pendejo! ¿No ve que soy mujer?—al tiempo que hacía un disparo al aire"; 63). Ramona's portrayal, which verges on caricature, further establishes her as an extreme cliché of masculine lesbians, whose main function is to accentuate the virtues of Sandra and Eurídice.

By glorifying these two characters who conform to the representation of the desirable lesbian articulated by Halberstam and observed in *lesbofeminist* literature as described by Téllez, the novel fails to recognize the range of gender expressions that are part of *lenchitudes*. Moreover, as Halberstam points out, although female masculinity and lesbian identity are not synonymous, it is crucial to recognize that historically, female masculinity has played an important role in lesbian identification. He explains that, in the anglophone context, butchness has often defined the stereotypical lesbian, making her visible and legible as a confluence of the rupture of both gender norms and heterosexuality (*Female Masculinity* 119). This is also the case in Mexico, as Zatarain Olivas and Núñez Noriega contend that for many *cuir* women, being masculine means that their sexuality is immediately read as sapphic (37). In Barrera's novel, the fact that Ramona's *lencha* masculinity is depicted as analogous to hegemonic masculinity denotes an oversimplified view of power dynamics. Although misogyny and patriarchal violence can certainly be perpetuated among women, equating Ramona to cisgender men is reductive because she does not possess male privilege.

On the other hand, the idealization of femininity in Barrera's novel is not without contradictions, as it adheres to a feminine stereotype rooted in patriarchal concepts of gender. Sandra's attraction to Eurídice occurs precisely because she embodies the opposite of Ramona: "what she was looking for, a kind chest, a soft voice, firm arms" ("lo que ella estaba buscando, un pecho amable, una voz suave, unos brazos firmes"; 57). While it is not problematic for her to be attracted to someone as feminine as herself, since desire is as complex as gender, *Sandra, secreto amor*'s Manichean representation of femininity *vis-à-vis* masculinity reinforces binary gender constructions. Regarding the place of femininity in the context of patriarchy, Margarita Pisano argues that "[d]ialogue from the feminine as a subordinate part of a fixed structure cannot be established outside of masculinity because it lives inside of it, it is its medium, its limit, there it is adjusted time and time again, therefore, it cannot be created independently as an example of itself. We will not be able to dismantle masculinist culture without dismantling femininity" ("El diálogo desde lo femenino como parte subordinada de una estructura fija, no puede entablar un diálogo fuera de la masculinidad, ya que vive dentro de ella, es su medio, su límite, allí se acomoda una y otra vez, por tanto, no puede crearse independientemente como referente a sí misma. No lograremos desmontar la cultura masculinista, sin desmontar la feminidad"; 7). It is then productive to think that if masculinity is defined as contrary to femininity (Domínguez Ruvalcaba, *Modernity and the Nation* 1), the opposite is also true. In the case of the novel, given its binary oppositions, if it were not for female masculinity, the protagonists' positive portrayal through femininity would be lost.

This notion is not new, and in her dialogue with Simone de Beauvoir, Toril Moi contends that the French philosopher's condemnation of femininity as a patriarchal concept serves as a critique of ideology. She explains that this argument remains just as relevant today as when it was first written; whether we subscribe to essentialist notions of gender or see them as products of performativity, using labels to describe them maintains gender stereotypes (107). Although I do not view femininity as a negative trait in the characters I analyze, its glorification should be examined and contextualized. Portraying femininity as aspirational accentuates the heteropatriarchal values that works like Barrera's strive to criticize through depictions of sapphic desire.

In *Sandra, secreto amor*, most characters, as well as the omniscient narrator, lack empathy for Ramona. Despite this, her friend Hellen, the sole person who feels affection for her, embraces her masculinity: "I love her as she is, the most *macha* among *machas*!" ("'Yo la quiero así como es, ¡la más macha de las machas!'"; 63). Calling her friend a *macha* underscores her identity as a woman but inevitably evokes machismo, which Monsiváis characterizes as the always violent and melodramatic embodiment of male supremacy ("Crónica de aspectos" 91). This portrays her masculinity as inseparable from machismo, pointing to how, instead of creating her own gender expression, she replicates a stereotype. For instance, she and her group of friends demonstrate double standards by condemning heterosexual men, yet objectifying women in the same way. The scene is narrated as follows: "Romy's friend group was a compact mass of women who used to bring, every now and then, young women, as if they were a new acquisition. In said meetings, they established a veiled competition, where longstanding rivalry added a ridiculous touch to those women who had been trained in a club tinged with masculinity while they criticized 'The Fellers'" ("El grupo de las amigas de Romy era una masa compacta de mujeres al que solían llevar, de vez en cuando, a jovencitas, como si fuesen una nueva adquisición. En dicha reunión establecían una competencia velada, cuya rivalidad añeja daba un cierto toque ridículo a aquéllas que se habían instruido en un club de tinte varonil al mismo tiempo que criticaban al 'club de Tobi [*sic*]' "; 164).[8] The narrator's observations underscore the connection between Ramona and her friends' objectification of other women and their belonging to a club "tinged with masculinity." Their rivalry and their view of women as "acquisitions" demonstrate how they emulate male masculinity since, as Michael S. Kimmel explains, "[w]omen become a kind of currency that men use to improve their ranking on the masculine social scale" (129). At the same time, referring to the group as a "compact mass" suggests their homogeneity and interchangeability. In this way, like Ramona, her friends who display any masculine traits are portrayed as "ridiculous" clichés.

As I have shown, *Sandra, secreto amor* portrays *lencha* masculinities as occupying the same place as men in a hegemony of gender. Moreover, by depicting Ramona as uncritically repeating patriarchal violence, the novel fails to show female masculinity as a unique type of gender expression created by and for women, portraying it instead as an imitation of hegemonic masculinity (Halberstam, *Female Masculinity* 15). Although Barrera's protagonists undermine compulsory heterosexuality, the novel's one-dimensional portrayal of *lencha* masculinities fails to recognize the multiple possibilities offered by non-traditional gender expressions. Ramona is significant as one of the few masculine women in sapphic narratives in contemporary Mexico. Nevertheless, her representation illustrates that while literature depicting same-sex desire subverts heteronormativity, it is not intrinsically *cuir*.

So far, I have analyzed two works that engage *lencha* masculinities in relation to hegemonic masculinity, yet they do not propose potential models for this gender expression. The following two texts I examine operate differently, providing examples of the potential of *lencha* masculinities. Moreover, they accomplish this by performing an *encuiramiento* of different manifestations of Mexican masculinity: the *luchador* and the revolutionary.

"A Purring Kitten":
"A dos, de tres caídas" (2010) by Elena Madrigal

I begin by exploring the figure of the *luchadora* as presented in the work of Elena Madrigal (Mexico City). In addition to her fiction centered on female desire, Madrigal has significantly contributed to the advancement of LGBTQ+ studies in Mexican literature. As a professor at the Colegio de México, she has authored numerous academic articles on sapphic representation, translation, and Mexican intellectuals such as Alfonso Reyes. She also collaborated with Leticia Romero Chumacero to edit the collection *Un juego que cabe entre nosotras. Acercamientos a la crítica y a la creación de literatura sáfica* (2014). In her short story book *Contarte en lésbico* (2010), Madrigal delves into the multiple possibilities of sapphic desire through the portrayal of diverse and complex characters, from mothers to makeup-selling housewives. A major merit of this collection is Madrigal's skill in crafting complex characters and plots within a brief format—the story I analyze occupies just five pages in this already compact book.

In "A dos, de tres caídas," Madrigal introduces her readers to La Pantera Púrpura, a masculine *luchadora* whose real name is never disclosed—in line with professional *luchadores*, whose real identities should never be revealed. Narrated in the first person from her lover's perspective, the story provides insight into Pantera's personality both in and out of the ring. While the protagonist's masculine traits are comparable to Ramona's, Madrigal's short story avoids portraying them negatively. Unlike the antagonist in *Sandra, secreto amor*, Pantera exhibits a fierce attitude in public but takes on a timid role with her lover, offering a nuanced approach to *lencha* masculinities.

It is particularly relevant that the protagonist is a *luchadora*, given *lucha libre*'s (Mexican professional wrestling) role in Mexican popular culture since the 1930s. During the Golden Age of Mexican Cinema, actors such as Pedro Infante and Jorge Negrete epitomized the ideal Mexican man. However, beginning in the 1950s, films such as *El enmascarado de plata* (1952, dir. René Cardona) sparked a wave of movies featuring popular *luchadores* as heroes (Pereda and Murrieta-Torres 6). The archetype of the macho during the peak of Mexican cinema portrayed machismo—expressed through acts of domination, violence, indifference to danger, and dramatic sentimentalism—as an idealization of masculine behavior. Yet *lucha libre* offered a different space to represent gender (Levi, "Lean Mean" 276). Although *luchador* films typically reinforced traditional gender roles, the 1960s saw a rise in movies featuring *luchadoras* as protagonists. As more women entered the workforce, Mexican cinema began to embrace these characters, whose heroism matched that of their male counterparts and was well received by audiences (Pereda and Murrieta Torres 10), even if not as popular. This acceptance of women protagonists was also reflected in the wrestling ring, though not without resistance.

Ricardo Cárdenas Pérez observes that *lucha libre*, as a spectacle that combines tradition and modernity, offered women the chance to enter a masculine space ("Representaciones y roles" 56). Consequently, the first women's *lucha libre* match took place in 1935 (Cárdenas Pérez, *Género, poder y lucha* 59). The early days of *lucha femenil* (women's wrestling) were difficult, and it took time for promoters, the press, and audiences to take it seriously (Hoechtl 56–57). As women's wrestling gained popularity, its subversive potential became evident, prompting Ernesto P. Uruchurtu, then mayor (*regente*) of Mexico City, to ban women's *luchas* in 1956, a prohibition that remained in place until 1986.[9] This ban reflected conservative fears that *luchadoras* posed a threat to the Mexican family and, by extension, the nation (Van Bavel 22). This concern was partly rooted in the image of the *luchadora* as a symbol of women's growing independence as workers (Cárdenas Pérez, *Género, poder y lucha* 83). However, the issue is more complex than a dichotomous view of Mexican femininity might imply.

In, *Género, poder y lucha libre femenil en el México contemporáneo* (2020), Cárdenas Pérez argues that, despite the categorization of *luchadoras* as *rudas* (villains) or *técnicas* (heroes), this does not necessarily correspond to the binary notion of women as either Virgin or Malinche. He contends that the performance of *lucha libre* transcends this dichotomy, explaining that there are no *luchadoras* who are inherently "good" or those who are purely villains (68). This argument becomes even more significant in light of the ban on women's *lucha libre*, which reflected deeper anxieties about gender roles. In other words, if the ring had not been a space where women could challenge gender essentialism, *lucha femenil* would not have sparked enough outrage to be banned for three decades. In this way, *luchadoras* not only reflected the growing participation of women in the workforce but also carved out a space where they could perform beyond conventional dichotomies.

For instance, *luchadoras* may choose to be *técnicas* or *rudas*, aligning their wrestler persona with certain values. Unlike the Malinche archetype, whose transgressions are often punished, *lucha libre* often allows *rudas* and their villainous performances to emerge victorious and garner a loyal following. For many wrestlers, being a *ruda* affords the flexibility to disregard the rules—as opposed to *técnicas*, who adhere to fair play—and engage with the audience by provoking them (Möbius 169). Whether they opt to be *rudas* or *técnicas*, the ring provides a space where women can choose how they perform as *luchadoras*, emphasizing their agency in crafting their personas.

Not only have women become fixtures in *lucha libre*, but wrestlers known as *exóticos* have also made their mark on the sport. These *luchadores* are known for their flamboyant performances and colorful sequin costumes. While these acts can be criticized for caricaturing feminine gay men, *exóticos* embrace these traits and challenge *luchadores* who exhibit homophobia (Pereda and Murrieta-Torres 11–12). In her analysis of *lucha libre*, Heather Levi draws on Octavio Paz's concepts of the *chingón* versus *la chingada* and the Mexican tradition of *albures*,[10] comparing them to the physical act of immobilizing and humiliating an opponent in the sport (*World* 145). She concludes that *exóticos* undermine patriarchal expectations of gay men as *chingados*, who are penetrated and degraded, thereby empowering themselves by rejecting these stereotypes ("Lean Mean" 276). I have paused to discuss the role of *exóticos* in Mexican wrestling to demonstrate that, although *lucha libre* is often perceived as a masculine and patriarchal sport, it also offers a platform for non-traditional gender expression (Levi, *World* 170). Thus, as a site of performance, it becomes a space for gender exploration.

The flexibility afforded by *lucha libre* is evident in Madrigal's protagonist, who is fluid and unafraid to explore and create her own gender expression. The story opens with Pantera meeting her lover for the first time. Initially, the woman mistakes her for a man, but upon realizing that Pantera is a woman, she is immediately captivated by her masculinity: "but after noticing the sparkle, both cunning and sweet, in her eyes, the luster of her skin, and the cleavage that barely showed her breasts, having calmed down, I just mumbled 'really?'") ("pero al notar el brillo entre dulce y pícaro de sus ojos, el lustre de su piel y el escote en el que sus senos se dibujaban apenas, ya tranquila, sólo farfullé un '¿de veras?'"; 110–11). The protagonist's gender subversion becomes a key factor in her appeal to other women. As Butler explains, masculinity within lesbian contexts is not an attempt to replicate a heterosexual model when paired with a feminine partner. Instead, women redefine masculinity as a new identity, challenging societal perceptions of the female body. Butler argues that this juxtaposition and transgression are part of what makes masculine women desirable (*Gender Trouble* 156). The interactions and ensuing relationship between the characters in Madrigal's short story underscore how female masculinity is depicted as attractive.

Though "A dos, de tres caídas" does not explore Pantera's life as a fighter in detail, the narrator/lover does not reveal her real name, suggesting a certain pleasure in exerting dominance over the *luchadora*, as this emphasizes her wrestler identity. This choice contributes to reversing the roles traditionally associated with feminine- and masculine-presenting sapphic women. Pantera's fighter persona is, of course, performative, coinciding with how most *luchadores* describe the sport as competitive, yet primarily intended to entertain an audience (Levi, "Lean Mean" 277). The spectacle that unfolds in the ring celebrates Pantera's masculinity and puts her in a position of power as she confronts her opponents. At the same time, her sexuality and masculinity outside the sport set her apart from other *luchadoras*. As Levi explains, it is not uncommon for contemporary *luchadoras* to justify their participation in wrestling by framing it as a job. At the same time, they are cautious about how they present themselves, often emphasizing their roles as mothers during interviews. Even *luchadoras* who are not mothers often defend women's participation in the sport by pointing out that many of their peers are (*World* 168–69; Möbius 170). Unlike *exóticos*, whose performance is centered on their perceived *cuiridad* (queerness) and femininity, *luchadoras* do not publicly embrace a *cuir* persona or base their characters on masculinity. Instead, they emphasize motherhood, a central value traditionally tied to Mexican womanhood.

Nonetheless, this was not always the case, as the early *luchadoras* of the 1940s and 1950s embodied transgressive examples of femininity both in and out of the ring. According to Marjolein Van Bavel, this was because they were "independent, combative women who did not comply with a particular political project that cultivated traditional gender notions that construed women as docile, domesticated mothers and wives" (14). Some of these pioneering wrestlers also defied heteronormativity, like Antonia Hinojosa Miguel, known as Toña la Tapatía, who was a lesbian and openly out among her peers (Van Bavel 28). This contrast in the perceptions surrounding *luchadoras* and their place within Mexican femininity points to a difference between what Janina Möbius describes as more traditional variations of the sport that emphasize the *lucha* itself—as seen in the pioneering *luchadoras* of the 1940s and 1950s—and more contemporary versions, which are closely tied to television, influenced by US wrestling, and focused on marketing (172).

The more traditional version of *lucha libre* resonates strongly with working-class audiences, especially women who once saw themselves reflected in the image of *luchadoras* carving out a space in a predominantly male profession (Van Bavel 31; Möbius 174). On the other hand, contemporary *lucha libre* has attracted a more middle-class and bourgeois audience. A visit to Arena México reveals that a significant portion of the audience belongs to the middle and upper classes, alongside a growing number of tourists, primarily from the United States. With the increasing emphasis on show business, contemporary *lucha* has begun to rely more on the spectacularization of wrestlers, contributing in part to the portrayal of *luchadoras* through their associations with male wrestlers (Möbius 174). Despite these changes, the ring continues to serve as a site where gender norms and expectations of women in Mexico can be challenged, as demonstrated by the pioneering women in the sport. Therefore, Pantera is more aligned with traditional representations of *lucha libre*, which offer a broader spectrum for interpreting gender (Möbius 174). In this context, despite her *luchadora* persona being performative, her masculinity remains a vital aspect of how she navigates the world.

While Pantera aims to dominate her rival in the ring to uphold her pride as a *luchadora*,[11] she abandons these expectations of domination when she is with her lover, allowing her to take the lead. The narrator/lover highlights this transformation by saying, "Pantera . . . but she's a kitten purring around my leg. Or might she be a panther that lies down on your bed and waits for you to devour her neck, for you to slide your hand down her shirt, and then finish off her nipples with kisses?" ("Pantera . . . Si es una gatita ronroneando alrededor de mi pierna. ¿O será una pantera que se tira plena en tu cama y espera a que le devores el cuello, a que deslices tu mano bajo su camisa y luego a besos le acabes los pezones?"; 112–13). Using her *luchadora* identity while referring to her as a kitten creates a discrepancy between the expectations of her public/wrestler persona and her sexual role. Simultaneously, her lover's ambiguous assertion that she may be a kitten or a panther demonstrates how Pantera, despite the reversal between them, is capable of embodying both tenderness and fierceness.

Their sexual roles and the complexity of Pantera's eroticism are further exemplified when the narrator reflects:

> Pantera . . . You that put your hands on the back of your neck as I undo your belt buckle and, underneath your men's pants . . . Squirm in pleasure, moan, open up to my tongue that moves your folds and bursts! Explode when my lips that kiss and kiss again the center of your sex and this tiny fingertip that

leaves you exhausted, turned into laughter! Pantera . . . Do you really think that your claws can stop me from biting your waist?

(Pantera . . . Que te llevas las manos a la nuca mientras desato tu cinturón hebillado y bajo tu pantalón de hombre . . . ¡Retuércete de gozo, gime, ábrete a mi lengua que mueve tus pliegues y estalla! ¡Estalla cuando mis labios que besan y rebesan el centro de tu sexo y esta diminuta yema te deja exhausta, vuelta toda una carcajada! Pantera . . . ¿De veras crees que tus zarpazos pueden impedir mis mordiscos en tu cintura?; 113–14).

As a result, the complexity of the power dynamic between the couple becomes apparent. The *luchadora* is depicted as docile yet aroused, highlighting her enjoyment of her partner's assertiveness. By claiming that Pantera's *zarpazos* cannot stop her from biting her waist, the narrator underscores her dominance, revealing that the wrestler's gender expression is malleable and not necessarily linked to her sexual role. In contrast to Ramona in Barrera's novel, Pantera demonstrates that gender expression and identity transcend a binary system.

Earlier, I referenced Levi's discussion of Paz's arguments regarding the *chingón* versus *la chingada* translated into the context of *lucha libre*. From this perspective, the critic's parallelism is fitting in the Mexican cultural setting. However, Paz's essentialist views are apparent when he writes that "[*l*]o *chingado* is passive, inert and open, as opposed to the one who fucks, who is active, aggressive, and closed. The *chingón* is the *macho*, the one who opens the other one up. *La chingada* is the female, pure passivity, defenseless before the exterior" ("Lo chingado es lo pasivo, lo inerte y abierto, por oposición a lo que chinga, que es activo, agresivo y cerrado. El chingón es el macho, el que abre. La chingada, la hembra, la pasividad pura, inerme ante el exterior"; 100). Through these arguments, Paz renders invisible anyone who falls outside of this perceived dichotomy. By categorizing both women and homosexual men as representations of *la chingada* and cisgender heterosexual men as *el chingón*, his arguments disregard the existence of *cuir* women, along with any other gender expressions or potential desires.

While it is important to question and critique Paz's arguments for their essentialist and binary nature, it is equally necessary to recognize how these ideas have permeated culture. Chicana writer Cherríe Moraga echoes the impact of Paz's postulates when she describes her own refusal, as a lesbian, to be penetrated or touched, driven by the fear of becoming *la chingada*. Moraga writes:

> I was forced to confront how, in all my sexual relationships, I had resisted, at all costs, feeling la chingada—which, in effect, meant that I had resisted fully feeling sex at all. *Nobody wants to be made to feel the turtle with its underside all exposed, just pink and folded flesh.* In the effort to avoid embodying la chingada, I became the chingón. In the effort not to feel fucked, I became the fucker, even with women. In the effort not to feel pain or desire, I grew a callous around my heart and imagined I felt nothing at all. (115; emphasis in the original)

Moraga's interpretation of Paz's work in the context of her own experience reveals how, despite being written over seven decades ago, his arguments have influenced both Mexican and Mexican American culture. The concept of impenetrability in masculine women is not unique to Mexico, though it is rooted in its cultural context. The stone butch in the United States, for example, represents a sexual expression partly defined by its untouchability (Halberstam, *Female Masculinity* 123). However, in Moraga's case, even though Paz disregards *cuir* women, it is evident that the *chingón/chingada* dichotomy has, to some extent, embedded itself in the collective imagination even if we no longer find his postulates relevant in the twenty-first century.

This dichotomy has also shaped perceptions regarding dynamics between men, as critics like Domínguez Ruvalcaba have noted with archetypes such as the *mayate*—the active partner who penetrates his sexual counterpart and often refuses to identify as gay, due to the association between masculinity and the role of the penetrator (*Modernity and the Nation* 131). Nonetheless, ethnographers like Guillermo Núñez Noriega and Héctor Carrillo have questioned these arguments and their associations with perceived femininity or masculinity (Russo Garrido 90). As Carrillo argues, this dichotomy "keeps us from giving due consideration to the variety of gay subjectivities, identities, venues, enclaves, groups, and communities that are recognizable throughout Mexico" (39), while simultaneously reinforcing the gender ideologies imposed by the patriarchal system (Núñez Noriega 27). By considering *cuir* sexuality and desire as heterogeneous, we can demonstrate that they offer a rich site for exploring and subverting normative conceptions of sexual and gender roles.

In the case of *cuir* women, this essentialist view perpetuates stereotypical notions of gender and sexuality, obscuring the diverse experiences found in the eroticism of masculine women's experiences (Rubin 471, Morgan 41). The most significant study to challenge this dichotomy in Mexico is Anahi Russo-Garrido's ethnographic work *Tortilleras Negotiating Intimacy: Love, Friendship, and Sex in Queer Mexico City* (2020). She explains that "it appears that such an idea is not applicable between women. How would two passive beings engage in any kind of sexual exchange? However, the fact that the binary is not so common in public imaginaries does not mean it is entirely absent in lesbian circles" (91). Russo-Garrido's research reveals that some women do, in fact, adhere to the active/passive model. However, she has also found that this is not absolute and that it is more often associated with gender roles, such as a more masculine woman paying for a meal or opening the door for a more feminine partner, but does not always translate into sexual practices (96). She explains that "[o]ne of the most common images women shared when asked about sex was the idea that sexual practices produce a fusion of beings for a given moment. This was the most recurring trope" (100). As we would expect given the diversity in *cuir* sexual practices, there are no single truths when it comes to sexual roles. Russo-Garrido's study helps us better understand how Paz's arguments rely on a false narrative rooted in an outdated dichotomy that does not reflect real-life experiences. In this way, *lencha* masculinities also allow for fluid interpretations of sexual pleasure and eroticism.

In Madrigal's story, Pantera's ability to break free from stereotypes makes her a more nuanced character than previous representations of female masculinity. By relinquishing control during sex and letting her partner possess her, she does not invalidate her masculine attributes but instead embraces pleasure and intimacy. "A dos, de tres caídas" provides the kind of representation necessary for *lencha* masculinities to function as a fluid, subversive concept, highlighting their potential to continually challenge binary ideas of gender and sexuality while also rejecting associations with masculine violence that rely on perceptions of feminine passivity.

"You Are Very Pretty, Colonel": "De un pestañazo" (1997) by Victoria Enríquez

Victoria Enríquez (b. 1945, Mexico City) has published three novels: *Linderos* (1989), *Adiós y nunca* (1992), and *Al abrigo del viento* (2008), as well as short stories and essays. She has contributed to various publications, such as *El Nuevo Mal del Siglo*, *Revista de la UAG*, *El Diario de Guerrero*, and the feminist lesbian magazine *Les Voz*, where she has served on the editorial board (Olivera Córdova, *Entre Amoras* 150). I now shift my focus to her short story "De un pestañazo," from the collection *Con fugitivo paso*. Olivera Córdova argues that this story breaks stereotypes, exemplifying the diversity of lesbian women. For her, "De un pestañazo" illustrates how lesbians express their identities in a variety of ways, from dressing in masculine or feminine styles to not concerning themselves with fashion at all. They mirror society, showing that they can be strong or vulnerable, cautious or absent-minded, fall in love or live in the moment, hurt others or choose solitude (*Entre amoras* 152).

The story is inspired by Colonel Amelio Robles, the first known transgender man to be recognized in Mexican history. Robles fought for the Zapatista forces during the Mexican Revolution under his male identity. Gabriela Cano argues that Robles's masculinity was a cultural declaration of the body and how it shapes gender expression, and a political act that problematized socially assigned gender and heterosexual norms ("Unconcealable Realities" 39). Robles's masculinity may have been influenced by the stereotypical values of his social class at the time, but his creation and recreation of gender expression disrupted the belief that such attributes were organic. Therefore, while he reinforced Mexican masculinity, he also served to undermine it (Cano, "Unconcealable Realities" 42).

Even though much can be said about the historical figure of Amelio Robles, my analysis focuses on Enríquez's short story. In this narrative, the protagonist is identified not as transgender but rather as a masculine woman, with the narrator using feminine adjectives to describe her, a characterization that the protagonist does not dispute.[12] In this regard, Olivera Córdova explains that the character merges traditionally feminine traits with those associated with masculinity and disrupts the expectation of androgyny in lesbian characters by presenting a masculine character who cross-dresses (Olivera Córdova, "Narrativa sáfica" 211). While she accurately describes the character as ambiguous, I contend that the masculinity of Enríquez's protagonist is more nuanced and goes beyond cross-dressing, as my analysis will reveal.

"De un pestañazo" tells the story of Colonel Ansiedad Topiltzin de Santiago (referred to as *coronel*/*coronela* interchangeably throughout the text), who later in life is interviewed about their participation in the Revolution. This leads them to reminisce about their youth and the moment they met their lifelong partner, Carmelita. The narration begins by referring to Ansiedad in the masculine form. This is clear when they encounter Carmelita for the first time and are described by the narrator as "[d]ashing, wrapped in his *sarape*; his eyes with long lashes came across the blue, scared eyes of that *güera*, who opened her mouth before the colonel's insane beauty and, for an eternal moment, wished to know everything about him" ("Gallardo, envuelto en su sarape; sus ojos de largas pestañas se toparon con los ojos azules y asustados de aquella güera, que abrió la boca ante la loca belleza del coronel y por un eterno momento, deseó saberlo todo de él"; 70–71). It is not until the colonel takes off their clothes to bathe in the river that the narrator refers to them as a woman by telling us that "she threw the scrunched-up shirt to the edge and dove covering her breasts with her arms" ("lanzó la camisa hecha bola para la orilla y se zambulló cubriéndose los senos con los brazos"; 72). Therefore, Ansiedad must be physically stripped for us to realize that they are a woman, a moment that reveals both physical and emotional vulnerability. Despite their behavior and dress, Enríquez develops the character in a way that makes it clear that everyone around them knows they are a woman (Olivera Córdova, *Narrativa sáfica* 210). Nonetheless, the troops who fight alongside Ansiedad recognize the colonel's bravery and accept them as they are.

Outside of the military context, Enríquez incorporates an element of magic realism by giving the protagonist the power to read minds. This ability, rather than a gift, becomes a burden, as from an early age Ansiedad is forced to bear the weight of knowing how others perceive and judge them, including their mother's rejection. Reaching adulthood and becoming attractive to women only exacerbates Ansiedad's situation, as they are exposed to the negative reactions of women who are uncomfortable with questioning their own sexuality. The protagonist resents this rejection/desire when the narrator explains that "besides always hearing what no one cares about, there was that charm that she exerted over women without trying, and that same thing turned her into a dyke, a butch, and that word that the woman with feathers and a fruit basket hat that showed her legs at the *cantina* thought of: lesnabia" ("aparte de andar siempre oyendo lo que a nadie le importa, estaba ese como encanto que ejercía sin buscarlo, sobre las mujeres, y eso mismo, la convertía en chepe, marimacha y en esa palabra que había pensado esa mujer de plumas y sombrero de frutero que enseñaba las piernas en la cantina: lesnabia"; 74–75). Enríquez creatively misspells the word *lesbiana* as *lesnabia* to underscore Ansiedad's unfamiliarity with the term and their disconnection from it.

Through the misspelling, the narrative illustrates society's projection of an identity onto Ansiedad that the character does not acknowledge or accept. This subtle alteration shows that *lesbiana*, a term often used for self-identification, is not part of Ansiedad's vocabulary or imagination. Therefore, the protagonist refuses to conform to a prescribed identity, showcasing how *lo cuir* can present characters who defy labels. The fact that this is the sole reference to *lesbiana* throughout the story underscores Ansiedad's indifference to conventional identities. The complexity of the character's categorization—or rejection of it—is apparent not just in terms of sexuality, but also in their gender identity. This becomes evident when, after facing multiple rejections, Ansiedad meets Carmelita, who makes them feel desired. Significantly, in nearly all their interactions, Carmelita refers to Ansiedad as a woman. For example, they run into each other by the river and Carmelita compliments them with the words "You are very pretty, colonel" ("Es usted muy bonita, coronel"; 73). While Carmelita uses the masculine word *coronel* for Ansiedad, she describes them with the feminine adjective *bonita*. This choice highlights the complexity of Ansiedad's gender expression, which defies categories. Like with Pantera, it is Ansiedad's challenge to static gender norms that sparks Carmelita's attraction.

While Ansiedad exhibits masculine traits, they do not correct Carmelita's references, showing a non-static approach to their gender expression. This flexibility in their identity, including their displays of masculinity, is elaborated on by Olivera Córdova, who describes them as not fully aligning with the macho behaviors expected during the time of the Revolution. Though they are courageous, tough, and an effective leader who instructs both men and women in war strategies, and have hands hardened by hard work and combat, they also respect women and protect Carmelita from violence. Additionally, in their romantic relationship, it is Carmelita who takes the initiative, exposing how Ansiedad's personality blends seemingly contradictory behaviors (*Narrativa sáfica* 208–209). In contrast to characters like Barrera's, Ansiedad adopts the masculinity of their time but does not use it to perpetuate violence or oppression. Instead, they create their own gender expression, earning respect from their peers while embracing traits typically considered non-masculine, such as tenderness and kindness. Traditional male masculinity in Mexico, particularly during and after the revolution, was inherently unstable, relying on the judgment of others (Irwin, "Mexican Masculinities" xviii). These societal expectations shape some aspects of Ansiedad's own experience of masculinity. However, the character is never portrayed as fearing that their masculinity will be questioned. This confidence illustrates how a *cuir* approach to gender can help problematize the ongoing pressure on men to constantly self-justify. The combination of characteristics in Ansiedad highlights the potential of *lencha* masculinities to question and transform traditional perspectives on gender.

Ansiedad's ability to subvert patriarchal and heterosexual norms is not solely based on their sexuality and masculine appearance. Their significant role in the Revolution and exceptional combat skills provide them with distinct recognition and privileges. Ansiedad is acknowledged by both peers and the government as a skilled combatant—despite their sex assigned at birth being known—without any challenge to their masculinity. This acceptance contradicts the traditional binary constructs essential to state formation (Valencia, "Teoría transfeminista" 72). Ansiedad's case thus challenges this binary system from within the military institution. The government's recognition and the honors bestowed upon both Ansiedad and the real-life Amelio Robles for their contributions to the Revolution underscore a key parallel between the two.

In Robles's case, as Cano explains, not only was he given documents that recognized him as a member of various political and social organizations using his male name, which validated his gender identity, but he was also further legitimized when the national secretary of defense decorated him as a war veteran in 1974. Although this honor was bestowed upon more than three hundred women for their participation in the war, Robles's identity was distinctly acknowledged by being designated as a *veterano* in legal documents, instead of a *veterana* ("Unconcealable Realities" 41). In Enríquez's story, although there is mention of a possible award, Ansiedad shows no interest and dismisses it swiftly.[13] This indifference occurs because the colonel prioritizes their relationship with Carmelita over their military career, even abandoning their role in the war to avoid being separated from her.

This indifference becomes apparent when Carmelita mentions that government representatives, accompanied by the couple's friend, Elena, visited to present Ansiedad with the award. Upon hearing this, the protagonist nonchalantly responds, "Tell her to quit that nonsense that has nothing to do with her and to just come over for lunch on Sunday" ("Dígale que se deje de andar con esas zarandajas, que no le están y que mejor se venga a comer el domingo"; 80–81). Ansiedad's disinterest reveals their rejection of heteropatriarchal institutions, signaling that they no longer seek or require their legitimacy. By opting to invite Elena for lunch, the protagonist clearly favors a peaceful domestic life with Carmelita over their tumultuous military history, setting up a sharp contrast between Ansiedad's past and present.[14]

Halberstam describes his work as seeking to produce a model of masculinity that is conscious of its multiple forms, and he emphasizes the need for new gender taxonomies. He contends that these models should begin not by subverting masculine power or by taking a stance against it, but by ignoring conventional masculinities and refusing to engage with them (*Female Masculinity* 9). Although my approach is based on *lencha* masculinities as representations that indeed subvert patriarchal hegemonies without fully ignoring them, I am interested in this point because Ansiedad abandons the war and chooses to avoid conflict, thereby disengaging from traditional masculinity. This rejection of violence reveals that despite embodying many characteristics of Mexican male behavior at the time, they refuse to participate in hegemonic gender roles.

The protagonist's change in attitude becomes evident through their refusal to engage in violence when General Azoro, Carmelita's former lover and Ansiedad's superior, tries to accuse the colonel of treason upon discovering their relationship. However, one of Ansiedad's peers jumps to their defense by explaining, "You'll have to forgive me, general, you have never been unfair, my colonel might have done something stupid but not treason. It's best if you talk to her as God intended, for she's not one-handed" ("Osté ha de perdonar, mi general, osté nonca ha sido enjusto, puede que mi coronel haya hecho ona tarogada pero no traición. Más mejor hable con ella como Dios manda . . . que pos manca . . . nostá"; 79). By alluding to the possibility of a duel, this phrase brings together what makes the colonel ambiguous: a character referred to as a woman who can confront and fight a man, and not just any man, a revolutionary general (Olivera Córdova, *Narrativa sáfica* 211). While the idea of dueling corresponds to the violence linked to traditional masculinity, the fact that Ansiedad's peers encourage it show that they consider the colonel to be an equal to General Azoro.

Another underlying factor that influences the type of masculinity that Ansiedad is exposed to and draws from is social class. While most *soldaderas* during the Revolution came from rural and lower-class backgrounds, the conflict also saw participation from female soldiers belonging to the middle and upper classes (Reséndez Fuentes 546; Macías 24). This created a distinction where *soldaderas* had no opportunity for social advancement, while affluent female combatants could climb through the ranks if they proved their worth on the battlefield (Reséndez Fuentes 546). Given that Ansiedad fights as a man and comes from a rural setting, their battlefield persona is based on macho notions of masculinity. This exaltation of machismo in the lower classes stems from the vilification of upper-class men, often called *lagartijos* (lizards), who were viewed as excessively vain and effeminate during the Porfirian era.

Thus, Ansiedad, like the real-life Robles, is influenced by a lower-class masculinity that seeks to avoid any association with femininity. Nevertheless, the protagonist, who has used female masculinity to be a part of the state and fight in the Revolution, comes face to face with a man who, through violence, embodies the oppressive qualities of patriarchal hegemony. Ansiedad, an expert in combat, could have won a duel, but instead chooses to walk away, demonstrating that despite being part of the revolutionary forces, they do not use violence to be with Carmelita. They refuse to see her as a prize to be won in a fight, thus avoiding her objectification. While serving in the Zapatista army, Ansiedad engages in the revolutionary conflict. However, after meeting their partner, they forsake the very system that had initially legitimized their masculinity and allowed them to display their prowess as a soldier. The protagonist builds their gender identity by incorporating certain expectations of men from their social class during the revolutionary conflict while also making a choice to leave a patriarchal institution, demonstrating the potential complexity found in *lencha* masculinities. Ansiedad's portrayal in Enríquez's text not only illustrates how women can forge their own masculinities but also shows how these transgressive expressions can confront and reject patriarchal violence.

The characters featured in this chapter contribute to the limited representation of female masculinities in contemporary sapphic literature in Mexico. Even as they negotiate with traditional masculinities in various ways, some of these characters produce models for *lencha* masculinities that do not sustain a hierarchy based on gender. They highlight the diversity that constitutes *lencha* masculinities. By analyzing both the characters and their development within each narrative, we can gain a clearer understanding of whether these literary works, consciously or unconsciously, reinforce heteropatriarchal views of women who defy femininity. Revealing these tensions through the framework of *lenchitudes* illustrates the potential of a localized approach to *lo cuir*. To this effect, *cuir* perspectives aim to disrupt the social order of gender as well as the mandates of femininity and masculinity (Cano, "¿Qué hay detrás? 10). While I do not intend to devalue the significance that some of these novels and short stories have had for readers who see their own desires represented, problematizing their representations of *lencha* masculinities is essential in understanding how sapphic narratives can sometimes reinforce normative and restrictive concepts of gender. By recognizing either their perpetuation or, in some cases, their rejection of heteronormativity, we can appreciate the value of literature as a tool to question or reinforce oppressive structures.

Chapter 3

The *Fem Fatal*

Femme Representation

Years ago, when I was a graduate student still completing my coursework, I took a seminar on gender and sexuality in contemporary Latin American literature. It quickly became my favorite course and steered me toward my area of specialty. To this day, I have fond memories of the thought-provoking discussions encouraged by the professor, who eventually became my advisor and mentor, and the invigorating environment created by my peers. One story in particular comes to mind when I think of that class. We had been discussing Butler's ideas on performativity when our conversation shifted to sexual orientation. The professor mentioned the idea of sexuality as a continuum, particularly in the context of gender being a social construct. While his exact words escape me, I vividly remember one of my classmates—a dear friend of mine to this day—having a knee-jerk reaction. She immediately shouted, "*¡Yo no! ¡Yo soy muy mujer!*" ("Not me! I am very much a woman!"). Within seconds, the entire classroom, including her, erupted in laughter. Once we had all settled down, I interjected with a smirk, "*Entonces ¿yo qué soy?*" ("Then what am I?"). This prompted more laughs, followed by a fascinating discussion. While both her comment and my response were made in good faith and in an environment where we felt safe to do so, her reaction did not surprise me. As I discussed in my last chapter, even though women's sapphic desire is often associated with female masculinity, femininity remains the standard when depicting *cuir* characters in most media. This prompted me to consider the contradictions that come from the exaltation of femininity, particularly when it is coupled with a proudly embodied sexuality.

In this chapter I explore the representation of what I term the *fem fatal*. Building on the archetype of the femme fatale, I examine the frequent depiction of stereotypically feminine characters whose sexuality and assertiveness positions them as antagonists in most of the works analyzed. I coin the term *fem fatal* by shortening *femenina* (feminine) to *fem* and translating *fatale* into Spanish to reference the context and language in which these texts were written. This approach highlights a construction of the femme that considers Mexican notions of femininity rather than adopting the US term as an equivalent. Additionally, the *fem fatal* suggests an *encuiramiento* of the femme fatale, as she is depicted in narrative works focusing on sapphic desire.

Like *lencha* masculinities, the *fem fatal* can be embodied in various ways. As in the case of the masculine archetype, the representation of the *fem fatal* in the novels and short stories I examine often fails to subvert essentialist notions of gender and power. However, this depiction allows for a critique of the representation of femininity. I define the *fem fatal* as having the following characteristics: first, to distinguish herself from the stereotypical heterosexual femme fatale, she must engage in the sexual or romantic seduction of other women; second, her likeness to the femme fatale must be expressed through the exaltation of her femininity and/or an emphasis on her dominant role through her sexuality; and lastly, her femininity and/or sexuality must be used to exert power on others. I consider the *fem fatal* to be a potentially useful category when examining femininity, sexuality, and power. Given that feminist modes of inquiry "are forced to search out symbols from a lexicon that does not yet exist," a reappropriation of the femme fatale as a subversive category "must also and simultaneously involve an understanding and assessment of all the epistemological baggage she carries along with her" (Doane 3). Consequently, in its most transgressive and productive form, the *fem fatal* can disrupt the elements that perpetuate the vilification of women's sexuality, thereby avoiding the reproduction of heteronormative frameworks.

This chapter traces the *fem fatal* as a reinterpretation of the femme fatale in the Mexican context and within sapphic narratives, emphasizing how these texts utilize archetypes to depict femininity. By analyzing these novels and short stories through the framework of *lenchitudes*, I argue that, despite their portrayal of sapphic characters, most of these works do not challenge the notion of femininity—expressed through sexual autonomy—as threatening. Furthermore, by discussing the potential of the *fem fatal* as a tool for *encuiramiento*, I consider how this archetype can be reimagined in opposition to heteronormative and misogynistic renderings of the femme fatale. Thus, this section sets out to answer two questions: How is the *fem fatal* portrayed in the narratives explored in this chapter? And does this portrayal support the objectives of *lenchitudes*, or does it merely transfer the misogyny at the root of the heterosexual femme fatale into the sapphic context?

In examining this archetype, I begin by tracing the characteristics shared by the original femme fatale and the mid-twentieth-century image of the Virgin/Malinche that was prominent in discussions of Mexican identity. By addressing these similarities, my goal is to contextualize this trope and show that the logic behind the femme fatale is similar to the categorization of women by thinkers like Octavio Paz. Although the narratives I examine do not directly address national identity, contextualizing gender and sexuality is important, considering that the texts were written in Mexico. As discussed in my previous chapter, the Virgin/Malinche duality has faced criticism and is considered outdated, especially by feminist critics. In this respect, I align with Castillo, who notes that her interest is not in the accuracy of this duality in representing real women, but in the persistence of these myths in the collective imagination and cultural production (18). Therefore, I examine whether these novels and short stories challenge these antiquated views on women's sexuality and gender expression.

I start my analysis with Artemisa Téllez's illustrated short novel *Crema de vainilla* (2014), arguing that this text provides the most productive and complex representation of the *fem fatal* by eliminating the anxieties around her sexuality and instead developing a nuanced character who is not inherently antagonistic. Next, I examine Odette Alonso's "Un puñado de cenizas" (2018), which, through multiple perspectives, reveals how the *fem fatal* devolves into a character complicit in patriarchal violence, making readers empathize with her victim. My study continues with Mildred Pérez de la Torre's *Lo hice por amor* (2016), which expands the *fem fatal* by exploring the Lolita/nymphet archetype, also present in Eve Gil's "Arsénico y caramelos" (2005). By outlining these depictions of female sexuality and the *fem fatal* archetype, I aim to underscore the trope's presence in contemporary sapphic narratives in Mexico and its potential to align with the objectives of *lenchitudes* as a tool of *encuiramiento*.

From Femme Fatale to *Fem Fatal*

The femme fatale as we have come to know her became clearly defined in art and literature in the nineteenth century (Hanson and O'Rawe 3; Bornay 113). Although frequently associated with Western culture, particularly in the context of noir cinema, the archetype has long existed, exemplified by figures like Lilith or Eve in the Judeo-Christian tradition (Marambio and Rinka 170). Erika Bornay has described her as dominant, cold, and sexual to the point of being animalized (115). Sexuality is consciously wielded by the femme fatale to seduce men and lead them to their downfall (Quinn 2). Although femmes fatales have some recognizable characteristics, they also function as sites of uncertainty. Mary Ann Doane explains how this archetype is "the figure of a certain discursive unease, a potential episte-mological trauma. For her most striking characteristic, perhaps, is the fact that she never really is what she seems to be. She harbors a threat which is not entirely legible, predictable, or manageable" (1). In this sense, her very existence is a testament to male fears about women.

This fear is often visualized through the myth of the *vagina den-tata*. Found in folk myths across different cultures and times, the *vagina dentata*, much like the femme fatale, embodies men's anxieties about the unknowability of women and the perceived threats that this uncertainty might entail, including their castration and the loss of their privileged position (Raitt 423). Therefore, both mythical conceptions of the empowered sexual feminine figure must be neutralized by being killed or punished for their transgressions (Raitt 418; Doane 2).[1] Consequently, the femme fatale archetype is an embodiment of the negation of female sexuality.

While it might be tempting to see the femme fatale as already being *cuir* because she contrasts with the Virgin/good woman archetype, I argue that this is not the case, as it contributes to the same binary notions of femininity and sexuality that *lo cuir* intends to challenge. Even though my study centers on same-sex desire, meaning that male fears are not explicitly present in the texts I analyze, the femme fatale is intrinsically linked to these anxieties about women's sexuality. Additionally, examining the origins of the archetype is crucial to understanding if and how these elements are reflected in literary production depicting sapphic characters. Therefore, in the context of women's same-sex desire, it is more appropriate to speak in terms of misogyny to show how women are not exempt from replicating modes of representation that have been used to castigate them. With this in mind, I will reference these male anxieties in my analyses to show that although the *fem fatal* undermines heterosexuality, it does not always address the patriarchal foundation behind the original archetype. To put it another way, one of the defining qualities of the *fem fatal*—the frequent absence of male characters—does not necessarily prevent male fears from being reconstituted as misogyny.

Although I have presented some of the main attributes and implications of the femme fatale, her depiction varies depending on context. Hence, each portrayal of the archetype must be examined in its specific local and historical context, along with the representational traditions it may have incorporated (Hanson and O'Rawe 3). Consequently, even though the texts that I explore do not focus on national identity or nationalism, it is crucial to first understand the implications of the femme fatale within Mexican culture, particularly in relation to the country's notions of femininity. Since Mexico's consolidation as an independent nation in the nineteenth century and well into the twentieth century, gender roles were rigorously enforced to foster a national identity (Ruiz-Alfaro 42). These roles were imposed and regulated predominantly by men, with bodies—especially those of women—becoming a source of fear when coupled with autonomous desires and impulses (Tuñón 11). In chapter 2, I pointed to the arguments made by critics like Octavio Paz and Roger Bartra regarding the Malinche/*chingada* and the Virgin of Guadalupe as notable archetypes when we consider Mexican femininity. However, I wish to return to the postulates of both Debra A. Castillo and Carlos Monsiváis in my articulation of the *fem fatal* to tie my discussion to the context of Mexico.

As I discussed in my previous chapter, Castillo's *loose woman* is defined as being in control of her own sexuality and engaging in sexual acts for pleasure. Thus, the loose woman challenges conventional portrayals of women: the respectable one who is indifferent to sex and the prostitute who provides a service for money (6). Castillo's categorization differs from the archetypical *femme fatale* because of the former's focus on sexual pleasure and the latter's desire to assert her power through her ability to destroy her victim. Nonetheless, the loose woman is useful when theorizing the *fem fatal*, for she sheds light on how sexuality is often the common denominator in Mexican categorizations of women. Monsiváis returns to the figure of the prostitute by asserting that she serves as a reminder to those who are not that they, too, are defined by their sexuality (or lack of one) ("La mujer en la cultura" 108–109). Consequently, Mexican notions of femininity have been historically linked to their relationship to sexuality and defined through binary opposition.

Despite the unique circumstances shaping understandings of femininity in Mexico, the femme fatale is similarly constructed within the good-versus-evil-woman paradigm. This becomes especially apparent when examined from the perspective of motherhood. In the case of the femme fatale, she is typically depicted as antithetical to the figure of the mother and seen as sterile and barren (Doane 2). Similarly, in the context of Mexico, Castillo argues that the mother is paradoxically valued for her absence or lack, which, by contrast, helps to define and give meaning to maleness. In this way, this absence mirrors the mythical and despised figure of the sexualized woman, who serves as a non-reproductive but endlessly reproducible verifier of masculinity (Castillo 19). Therefore, although the two archetypes are viewed as opposites, they ultimately mirror each other, as "the mother in this masculinist system is 'nothing' precisely to the degree in which she is conceived as pure and unprofaned," while "the profaned female is also 'nothing,' not even a woman, and certainly not *la mujer*" (Castillo 19). The lack observed in the maternal figure is further explained by the emergence of the *madre abnegada* (selfless mother) after the Mexican Revolution.

Modeled after the Virgin archetype, the *madre abnegada*—made famous by actress Sara García during the Golden Age of Mexican Cinema—embodies "a martyr-like feminine form, predisposed to absorb hardship for the sake of her children but always resolute in her religious faith and its ability to safeguard her family" (Gaytán 18). As Marie Sarita Gaytán explains, throughout the twentieth century in Mexico, the concept of motherhood became deeply connected to gender, race, class, spirituality, and patriotism. This national maternal figure included various forms of femininity, some aligning with dominant notions of Mexican identity and others differing. It became prominent as women and progressive leaders questioned rigid patriarchal family norms, emerging during a period of increased social strain and conflict between modern and traditional ways of life (18). The significance of upholding specific beliefs about the role of women in society creates a paradox when we remember that Mexico, as a national project, was based on male-centered relationships, defining the "nation" not by all its residents, but by men of a particular social status and ethnicity (Monsiváis, *Misógino feminista* 81; Pratt, " 'No me interrumpas' " 75). Despite the exclusion of women from the process of nation-building, we are also confronted with exceptions that allow for their idealization (Monsiváis, "La mujer en la cultura" 101), as in the case of the *madre abnegada*.

Therefore, even though women have historically held limited power and authority in the national project, they are frequently represented as the primary producers of the nation's values and principles (Gaytán 21). As explained by Pedro Ángel Palou, the definition of these specific national characters is key to controlling individual bodies and social groups that the state depends on to sustain itself (27). In other words, while women were not given the power to define themselves as citizens during Mexico's nation-building process, they were still essential for cultivating nationalism and disseminating a set of cultural values. These beliefs ultimately defined the standards for what women *should* and *should not* be. When we consider Castillo's conclusions regarding the absence that defines both the *madre abnegada*/Virgin and the sexualized woman/Malinche, it becomes evident that another contradiction arises in characterizing women in Mexico through dichotomous approaches, especially in light of Paz's claims that they are enigmatic and supreme mysteries (89–90). If women are grouped according to a set of characteristics, then depicting them as cryptic and unknowable contradicts these very classifications—a paradox shared by the femme fatale, who is both clearly defined and yet remains a mystery.

As noted by feminist critics, the attempts to define Mexican identity in the twentieth century did not strive to empower or engage with women and other groups excluded from reflections on *mexicanidad* (Mexicanness). Instead, these efforts were aimed at maintaining a traditional male domain of power, with the men behind these studies applying a negative view of women to assert their authority (Hind, *Dude Lit* 148). Essays like Paz's and those written by other Latin American male intellectuals sought to deny women the civic powers that literate men had given themselves (Pratt, " 'No me interrumpas' " 75). By depicting women as silent and mysterious, they dismissed what they had to say about themselves, thus showing that, perhaps, it was not that women were impossible to understand or refused to speak, but that men were not interested in what they had to say. Nonetheless, as Mary Louise Pratt contends, women were, in fact, reflecting on and writing about their place in the world. Pratt refers to these texts as *ensayos de género* (gender essays) and defines them as defiant literature that aims to "interrupt the male monologue," or challenge masculine control over cultural, historical, and intellectual spheres (76).[2] Therefore, in examining femininity and women's experiences in Mexico, we must consider how mythmaking by the male intelligentsia of the twentieth century upheld narrow views on gender and gender roles. This approach is useful when assessing whether sapphic representation avoids reinforcing these outdated perspectives.

While in 1950 Paz described women as mysterious in *El laberinto de la soledad*, that same year a young Rosario Castellanos defended her master's thesis, *Sobre cultura femenina*, at the Universidad Nacional Autónoma de México. Paz's text[3] went on to become one of the most cited studies about Mexican identity. *Sobre cultura femenina*, on the other hand, was published by *América. Revista Antológica* under the direction of Efrén Hernández (Cano, "*Sobre cultura*" 12–13), but was mostly forgotten until 1984, ten years after Castellanos's death (Echenberg 3). Often regarded by critics as a somewhat essentialist reading of women's position in society, *Sobre cultura femenina* is a work from which Castellanos later distanced herself, acknowledging its limitations. However, as Margo Echenberg suggests, the text achieves the denouncement of "authoritarian notions of women and what is written about them, as well as a critique of the limitations of academic philosophy" (5). Despite the weaknesses of Castellanos's thesis, it is crucial to emphasize how she and her contemporaries actively critiqued the portrayals of women by the male intellectuals of their time.[4]

In her later text, *Mujer que sabe latín . . .* (1973), Castellanos criticizes men's tendency to view women as myth and points to how this has contributed to their vilification. She explains how those who create and perpetuate the myth cease to view women as real people with biological, psychological, and physiological qualities as real as theirs. Rather, they are perceived solely as incarnations of a generally malevolent, antagonistic principle (9). I contend that this mythification and denigration of women correspond to fears similar to those that inform the representation of the femme fatale. This is particularly evident in the portrayal of women as unknowable and mysterious, a theme replicated in male-authored Mexican texts that perceive women as enigmas. As Castellanos points out, this dehumanizes them and portrays them as inherently antagonistic.

In the case of sapphic representation in Mexican literature, early depictions dating back to the nineteenth century also relied on stereotypical and negative portrayals, especially when penned by male writers (Reséndiz Oikión 143). Artemisa Téllez has described this period by emphasizing how authors represented women "as vamps who seduced virgins or as beings on the lowest step of degradation who, in addition to being prostitutes, were also depraved and 'deviant.' In these texts we can observe the free flow of their authors' misogynist fantasy and, furthermore, enormous lesbophobia" ("como vampiresas seductoras de vírgenes o bien como seres en el último escalón de la degradación, que además de prostitutas y viciosas eran también 'desviadas.' En estos textos se puede observar el libre flujo de la fantasía misógina de los autores y se trasluce, además, una enorme lesbofobia"; "A Chloe le gustaba Olivia" 175). Even though contemporary Mexican literature has shifted toward more nuanced representations of sapphic characters, moving away from earlier homophobic depictions, the deviant seductress remains a common trope in several narrative works.

Téllez observes that many male writers render sapphism through a stereotypically "deviant" character that is usually shown as "a hypersexual creature, lacking feelings, and pernicious to other women. In many cases she is also a disturbed being that causes pity and wrecks homes. Of course, in all cases she is the recipient of 'poetic justice' and the lesbian of male prose will always have a fatal ending for infringing upon the established order" ("una criatura hipersexual, carente de sentimientos y perniciosa para las demás mujeres. En muchos casos es también un ser perturbado, que genera lástima y que destruye los hogares. Por supuesto que en todos los casos cae sobre ella toda la "justicia poética" y la lesbiana de la prosa masculina tendrá siempre un final fatal por atentar contra el orden establecido"; "A Chloe le gustaba Olivia" 176). Téllez accurately highlights how some male authors perpetuate women's same-sex desire as an anomaly that must be punished to maintain social order. Despite progress from contemporary depictions, this negative portrayal is not limited to male writers and continues in literary representations of sapphic desire. In the narratives I examine, the antagonism of the *fem fatal* often serves to frame the protagonists as victims, contrasting their behavior with that of the seductress. This, I contend, contributes to a simplistic binary classification of characters as good or bad, failing to depict more intricate characterizations. Yet my analysis of Téllez's text shows how more complex approaches to the *fem fatal* can indeed challenge the negative portrayal of sapphic sexuality.

According to Olivera Córdova, starting in the 1990s, novels representing sapphic desire exhibited a series of common characteristics. These included being authored by women, presenting their characters in a positive and humane light, aligning with feminist ideologies, and critiquing prejudiced lesbian stereotypes while challenging expectations rooted in mythical figures like the Virgin of Guadalupe (*Entre amoras* 129–28). While I recognize the necessity of evolving sapphic representation to prevent the perpetuation of harmful stereotypes, I also see the potential for creating imperfect characters who can challenge the mythical figures highlighted by Olivera Córdova. To that effect, only a year after Olivera Córdova's study was published, Téllez posed the following questions: "Why must lesbian characters be exemplary and unblemished beings? Why must we use literature as a vehicle only for positive images if art is, above all things, a relatively reliable representation of human nature that is, in most cases, indeed unfaithful, treacherous, and vile?" ("¿Por qué han de ser los personajes lésbicos seres ejemplares y sin tacha? ¿por qué debemos de utilizar la literatura como vehículo de imágenes solo positivas si el arte es por sobre todas las cosas una representación relativamente fidedigna de la naturaleza humana que en la mayor parte de los casos es, efectivamente, infiel, traicionera y mezquina?"; "A Chloe le gustaba Olivia" 174). By pointing out the tendency to represent sapphic characters as inherently good, Téllez underscores the need for more nuanced portrayals of same-sex desire and experiences. Complex characters are essential for creating rich and diverse narratives; however, this chapter illustrates that transposing the femme fatale—and its accompanying Lolita archetype—into a sapphic context without questioning its patriarchal foundations risks perpetuating misogyny.

As with *lencha* masculinities, my proposal of the *fem fatal* aligns with *lenchitudes* in its potential to expose essentialist and binary understandings of gender and sexuality. My exploration of this archetype has two primary objectives. First, I seek to show that due to its pervasiveness in several texts, it is evident that the authors whose work I analyze are interested in femininity's relationship to power. Although traditionally tied to male fears about women, feminism, and Western conceptions of transgressive femininity, the femme fatale, like any other type of representation, "is not totally under the control of its producers and, once disseminated, comes to take on a life of its own" (Doane 2–3). In transitioning from the femme fatale to the *fem fatal*, there is an opportunity to examine how this character illuminates the conflicting depictions of femininity and sapphic desire in Mexican literature. Although these works portray stereotypically feminine characters as enticing, their antagonistic and problematic behaviors reveal the tensions that they provoke.

My second objective is to show that though the *fem fatal* enables an *encuiramiento* of the femme fatale by stripping the archetype of its heterosexuality, most of the narratives examined tend to replicate the character in the same way it would be depicted in a heterosexual context. In doing so, they miss the chance to overturn the archetype and challenge its misogynistic underpinnings. Even though many of these texts do not subvert the problematic aspects of the original femme fatale, they are useful because they help us understand how taking what has historically been a heterosexual archetype and turning it into a sapphic character does not necessarily align with the objectives of *lo cuir*. These representations illustrate that merely changing the sexual orientation of a character is insufficient to challenge and redefine the underlying gender norms and power structures inherent in the archetype.

"Heaven on Earth's Most Beautiful and Perverse Eve": *Crema de vainilla* (2014) by Artemisa Téllez

Alongside her work as a literary critic, Artemisa Téllez (b. 1979, Mexico City) stands out as one of the most prolific authors delving into sapphic desire and eroticism in Mexico over the past two decades. Although her primary focus has been on poetry, as seen in books such as *Cuerpo de mi soledad* (2010), *Cangrejo* (2016), and *Mujeres de Cromagnon* (2020), she has also written prose. Her short story collections include *Fotografías instantáneas* (2016) and, most recently, *Noche de bruces sobre la tierra* (2022). I have chosen to examine her illustrated short novel, *Crema de vainilla* (2014), for its unique approach to the archetype of the *fem fatal*. What sets this work apart from others analyzed in this chapter is its portrayal of the relationship between the *fem fatal* and the protagonist, which transcends a binary notion of good and bad. By deconstructing normative approaches to same-sex relationships between women and refraining from punishing women's exploration of non-normative sexuality, this complex representation of romantic and erotic desire aligns with the objectives of *lenchitudes* as a framework.

Crema de vainilla stands out as an innovative text, not only for its depiction of sapphic sexuality and the possibilities of BDSM, but also for its incorporation of illustrations by Betsy Romero. It narrates the story of Irene, who is in a perpetual struggle with her attraction to Lala, our *fem fatal*. Their relationship is depicted over several years, highlighting their periods of closeness and separation, ultimately leading them back together. In her prologue to the novel, author Eve Gil describes Lala as an "authentic deadly woman—*femmes fatales*, seems to tell us Lala herself, are *démodé*—who not only seduces those of her same sex and beauty, but does so with an exquisite frivolity that turns makeup, lipstick, perfume, and designer clothes into part of her frantic erotic activity" ("auténtica mujer letal—las femmes fatales, pareciera decirnos la propia Lala, están demodé—la cual no solo seduce a otras jóvenes de su sexo y su belleza, sino también con una exquisita frivolidad que vuelven al maquillaje, al lipstick, al perfume y a las prendas de diseñador parte de su frenética actividad erotica"; 5). While Gil does not clarify why she views Lala as evidence that the femme fatale may be outdated, she does regard the character as a new incarnation of the archetype. Thus, I consider Lala to be a prime example of the *fem fatal*'s potential. Despite possessing some of the defining traits of the original *femme fatale*, her femininity and relationships are much more intricate. This complexity demonstrates how such characters can challenge rigid perceptions of gender and sexuality while also resisting heteronormative narratives where powerful women are punished for their transgressions.

Lala's seductive power is immediately apparent from the initial description of her appearance. When first introduced, Irene, who is also the narrator, portrays her as follows: "Lala is very beautiful. Her long and curly orange hair falls on her too-straight back, over her glaringly white shoulders; her dark green eyes, framed by long eyebrows, make her face the most beautiful I have seen in my life. Her body, narrow up to her waist and with enormous hips and legs, long, very long like a painting by el Greco moves slowly, dragged by the wind" ("Lala es muy hermosa. El pelo largo rizo y anaranjado cae sobre su espalda demasiado derecha, sobre sus hombros deslumbrantemente blancos; sus ojos verde obscuro enmarcados por largas cejas hacen su cara la más bella que haya visto en la vida. El cuerpo, estrecho hasta la cintura y enorme de caderas y pier-nas, largo, larguísimo como una pintura del Greco se mueve lentamente arrastrado por el viento"; 7). This image corresponds, almost verbatim, to Erika Bornay's definition of the femme fatale, for she has long and abundant hair that is often red and notoriously white skin, and is fre-quently described as having green eyes, resulting in a corporality that is synonymous with seduction (114–15).[5] In spite of the emphasis on her corporality, Irene's description also highlights her beauty as belonging in one of El Greco's paintings, the movement of her long body dictated by the wind's direction. In this sense, Lala displays the same conundrum as the femme fatale, for she is reduced to the corporeal while simultaneously displaying an air of mystery and indefinability that puts her out of reach of those who desire her.

The attraction she exudes and the empowerment she inspires are not limited to women. Irene briefly explains how Lala "had been with thousands, first men, then women; however, she was my first" ("había estado con miles, hombres primero, después mujeres; en cambio era mi primera"; 10). The novel refrains from engaging with the negative stereotypes about bisexuals that have become typical in Hollywood depictions of the femme fatale since the revival of noir cinema in the 1980s, where such characters are often shown as flighty, untrustworthy, and designed to appeal to the male gaze (Farrimond 143). Rather, Lala's erotic encounters with both men and women are mentioned to emphasize her comfort with her sexuality and sexual experience, whereas Irene, who has been with only Lala, is just beginning to understand her sexual desire at the start of the novel. Thus, this description serves the purpose of positioning Lala and Irene as opposites in terms of their erotic experiences. Moreover, the novel does not focus on identifying its characters' sexual orientations; for instance, the word *lesbiana* appears only three times in the text and is never used by either character to refer to herself. Instead, *Crema de vainilla* treats sexuality as fluid and focuses on Irene's sexual awakening.

In light of Téllez's reflection on the need to portray lesbian characters that are complex and challenging rather than solely positive representations, I argue that she achieves this through her own work in *Crema de vainilla*. For César Cañedo, the text shatters the idealized image of the "good lesbian" and instead depicts women who live their sexuality as they please. They find pleasure in pain through their explorations of BDSM.[6] Cañedo suggests that this approach reinforces the power of female sexuality as it drives the narrative structure, leading the reader through a highly sensorial experience when engaging with the novel, rather than focusing on a specific conflict or enigma to be resolved (75–76). Just as Lala guides Irene as she explores her sexuality, Téllez directs her audience through this sensory reading experience, enhanced by Romero's illustrations. By choosing to focus on character development instead of on a central conflict, Téllez lays the groundwork for creating transgressive characters and dynamics that deviate from traditional forms of representation without replicating heteronormative tropes that demonize sexually dominant women.

For Irene, Lala becomes an obsession, but beyond her wishes to be with her, the protagonist is moved by a yearning to be sexually dominated by the *fem fatal*, as she explains: "Thinking about her was my delirium, there was no way to get her out of me, of my skin. She's my friend, I understood that, but being before her, on top of her, for her, after her, under her, in her, without her, between her, with her, was becoming an obsession that defined every confine of my universe. Lala could have me whenever she wanted, she could" ("Pensar en ella era mi delirio, no había manera de sacarla de mí, de mi piel. Es mi amiga, lo entendía, pero estar ante ella, sobre ella, para ella, tras ella, bajo ella, en ella, sin ella, entre ella, con ella se convertía en una obsesión que delimitaba todos los confines de mi universo. Lala podía tenerme cuando quisiera, puede"; 17*)*. In this sense, Lala not only guides Irene through self-discovery and acceptance of her sapphic desire, but she also sheds light on the protagonist's longing to be sexually submissive, contributing to Irene's sexual awakening in more than one way.

As Jessica Benjamin explains, the fantasy of erotic domination "embodies the desire for both independence and recognition. However alienated from the original desires, however disturbing or perverse their form, the impulses of erotic violence and submission express deep yearnings for selfhood and transcendence" (281). In Irene's character, these yearnings are the driving force behind the actions in the novel as she slowly discovers and embraces her sexual desires, always being drawn back to her relationship with the *fem fatal* despite the time they spend apart. As the protagonist recounts their story, she reflects on her connection with Lala, stating, "Ideas are dangerous toys and the mind—my mind—a huge toy store. Playing, oh, playing is the only thing that matters and counts, the only thing that transforms, that entertains the hours of our existence" ("Las ideas son juguetes peligrosos y la mente—mi mente—una enorme juguetería. Jugar, ah, jugar es lo único que vale y cuenta, lo único que transforma, que entretiene las horas de nuestra existencia"; 7). Therefore, she looks back at her younger years and sexual awakening with nostalgia and a sense of playfulness, revealing how her sexual submissiveness has provided her with fulfillment.

Returning to Lala's character, I argue that the emphasis placed on her femininity, along with her sexual encounters with other feminine-presenting women, can help us understand how *Crema de vainilla* moves beyond dichotomic understandings of gender roles. In chapter 2, I explained how the construction of *lencha* masculinities often relies on their opposition to femininity. However, although critics have noted a similar reliance on masculine women for femmes to be read as queer (Hemmings 93), Téllez's text—like most of the other works explored in this chapter—positions Lala outside the confines of seemingly binary relationships. Despite the character being dominant and sexually assertive, her power stems from her femininity and sexual appeal, her gender expression does not require a masculine-presenting counterpart to underscore it. Although this might be seen as a lack of representation of female masculinity, it also demonstrates how femininity has the potential to be highlighted independently of masculinity.

In revisiting Olivera Córdova's arguments, we are reminded that earlier authors like Roffiel and Levi-Calderón avoided characters with masculine traits to distance themselves from stereotypes and promote a transgressive femininity (*Entre amoras* 146). These writers sought to break barriers in the early 1990s in the name of positive portrayals of sapphism. However, as society has progressed and become more accepting of the LGBTQ+ community, Téllez's choice to depict *fem* sexuality in relationship to pain and pleasure originates from her desire to write complex and diverse stories ("A Chloe le gustaba Olivia" 184). This shift, as articulated by Téllez when differentiating between *lesbofeminist* and *postfeminist* stages of sapphic literary representation, illustrates the changes occurring within Mexican *cuir* literature. Even though texts like Téllez's do not specifically address Mexican identity, they are valuable as they reveal the evolving possibilities and concerns in sapphic literature over time.

These developing practices of representation are evident in Lala, who, despite being highly sexualized, is empowered by her femininity, as seen in her desire to sexually dominate others. Regarding femme femininity, Laura Harris and Liz Crocker posit that this type of gender expression transcends appearance, taking the form of a set of behaviors related to codes of desire that often place femmes as sexual objects (3). In the case of Téllez's text, however, Lala is depicted not as a sexual object, but rather as a sexual subject who guides others through their erotic fantasies. While her sexual dominance bears some resemblance to that of the stereotypical femme fatale, I contend that Lala renders visible the productive possibilities of the *fem fatal*. This difference lies in how her sexuality is used.

While the femme fatale exerts power by enticing men and eventually causing their downfall, in the case of *Crema de vainilla*, Lala's motivation is driven by pure desire, and Irene's agency reveals the complexity of their relationship. This is evident when Irene discusses the pleasure that she finds in the pain inflicted by Lala: "Every part that I touched was sore. I caressed my body, looking at myself in the mirror; I had never been more beautiful. My mouth, red and swollen, filled with small bleeding fissures, seemed larger, shining like a flower" ("Cada lugar que tocaba estaba adolorido. Acaricié mi cuerpo mirándome en el espejo, nunca había sido tan hermosa. Mi boca, roja e inflamada, llena de pequeñas fisuras sangrantes, parecía más grande; brillaba como una flor"; 26). Just as Lala finds sexual domination empowering, Irene sees beauty in being dominated. This perception extends beyond the sexual encounter, with the bruises and cuts serving as a reminder of Irene's sexual agency and pleasure.

One of the characteristics that sets the novel apart from other works explored in this chapter is, as Cañedo points out, the lack of a conflict to be resolved. Thus, *Crema de vainilla*'s representation of the *fem fatal* does not cast her as an antagonist who is actively trying to seduce Irene to cause her life to spiral out of control. On the contrary, the text revolves around sexual desire and Irene's journey to realizing what she finds sexually gratifying. For Cañedo, the novel allows readers to immerse themselves in the transgression of corporal limits, enabling a reading of the novel that is associated with its consumption as an act of erotic pleasure and enjoyment. He argues that this approach allows us to assimilate the violence inflicted on the body in relation to the potential for sexual pleasure. Although he notes how some readings have viewed the connection between violence and pleasure as problematic (72), the novel's emphasis on the consensual nature of the relationship and Irene's character development as she embraces her desires make *Crema de vainilla* a transgressive text that invites readers to confront their own perspectives and biases on the relationship between pain and pleasure.

The text concludes with Irene accepting Lala's refusal to settle down, as she recognizes their bond as purely sexual. She reflects, "I am her slave and that's the way I want it, for her to want to kill me in order to make me hers; I want to be the fruit that feeds Heaven on Earth's most beautiful and perverse Eve . . ." ("soy su esclava y así lo quiero, que quiera matarme con tal de hacerme suya; quiero ser el fruto del que se alimenta la más bella y perversa Eva del paraíso terrenal . . ."; 52). Unlike the men in heterosexual portrayals of the femme fatale who are destroyed when they try to escape her control, Irene consciously chooses to position herself as Lala's sexual slave, fully aware of the limits of their bond, but also free to leave if she chooses—as she does several times throughout the text. This dynamic, I contend, aligns with the objectives of *lo cuir* and *lenchitudes*, as it lays out forms of intimacy that are not necessarily tied to domestic spaces, heterosexual modes of kinship, normative coupledom, or property (Berlant and Warner 558). As a result, the novel defies heteronormative limitations, emphasizing same-sex desire through the *fem fatal* and refusing to make the triumph of the traditional couple its ultimate aim, as was common in earlier sapphic narratives.

At the same time, Irene's comparison of Lala to Eve further solidifies her lover's alignment with the femme fatale, a connection deepened by the enduring cultural power of Judeo-Christian myths that associate femininity with temptation and downfall. While, in the case of Lilith, Adam's first wife, she refused to obey her husband, and was consequently banished, becoming a demon (Bornay 25–26), Eve serves as the scapegoat who ultimately causes Adam's downfall. Thus, it is significant that Irene views Lala as Eve; however, unlike the biblical tale, she envisions a future where she will continue to be consumed by her without suffering consequences beyond the sacred space they share. In this way, instead of fearing that they will descend into hell as punishment for their perceived sexual transgressions, she views their shared space as heaven on earth. Furthermore, by embracing Eve, who has historically been associated with the disgrace of men—like Malinche in the context of Mexico—she challenges the Judeo-Christian narrative that sustains the dichotomy between the good and bad woman.

Irene's words also point to the thin line separating life and death in her sexual encounters with Lala. Drawing on the postulates of Georges Bataille, Benjamin highlights how the French philosopher relied on Hegel's analysis of the master-slave relationship to explore the link between eroticism and the tension between life and death of the self. According to Bataille, eroticism enables the transgression of the fundamental taboo that separates life from death. While life signifies discontinuity and the isolation of individuals, death represents continuity, uniting individuals into a state of non-differentiation (quoted in Benjamin 285). Consequently, the protagonist wishes for her metaphorical death at the hands of her lover, for this makes her feel as though she belongs to and is consumed by her. By extending beyond the narration of sexual encounters between Lala and Irene, *Crema de vainilla* emphasizes the importance of sexual fantasies and the role of imagination in heightening sexual tension. After all, Irene does remind readers of the limitless potential of her mind in the context of sexual playfulness.

Ultimately, the novel's ending reveals how Téllez's *fem fatal*, unlike the typical femme fatale, is not punished or killed, as is often the case with the latter (Doane 2). Instead, Lala retains her sexual power, as evidenced by Irene's continued submissiveness and the potential for their sexual relationship to persist. In this regard, *Crema de vainilla* contributes to the development of a sapphic version of the deadly woman by incorporating some of the tropes that make her legible as a femme fatale and, at the same time, refusing to perpetuate the misogynistic aspects of this archetype. This leads to an *encuiramiento* of the conventional archetype, as the text rejects the need to contain *fem* sexuality, instead viewing it as fertile ground to explore sapphic experiences. This opens the door to new narrative approaches to *lenchitudes*, where femininity and *fem* eroticism can be empowering without being vilified. Considering how *Crema de vainilla* explores non-traditional relationships instead of writing palatable and non-threatening *lencha* characters, an irony emerges in light of Téllez's assertion mentioned in my introduction. She claims that no Mexican writers of sapphic literature, including herself, are exploring subversive ways to love and be free beyond typical stories of love, marriage, and heartbreak. However, I must disagree with her, as I consider her work to be one of the few examples of women's *cuir* literature that crosses conventional boundaries through a complex and nuanced approach.

"If You Don't Love Me, I Will Be the One to Die": "Un puñado de cenizas" (2006) by Odette Alonso

Despite being born in Cuba, Odette Alonso (b. 1964, Santiago de Cuba) has become one of the best-known writers to depict sapphic desire in Mexico, where she has resided for over thirty years. She has been a vocal advocate for LGBTQ+ literature and works by Latin American women, as evidenced by her efforts to organize the Ciclo de Escritoras Latinoamericanas as part of the Feria Internacional del Libro del Palacio de Minería in Mexico City. Additionally, she participated in the Ciclo Bulevar Arcoíris in 2023, which highlighted literary works on *cuir* representation. Her dedication to supporting LGBTQ+ literature in Mexico is further evident in her collaboration with Paulina Rojas on *Versas y diversas* (2021), a compilation of contemporary sapphic poetry in Mexico. She has published short story collections such as *Con la boca abierta y otros cuentos* (2006) and *Espejo de tres cuerpos* (2009), as well as poetry. Her book of poems *Old Music Island* (2017) was awarded the first Premio Nacional de Narrativa y Poesía LGBTTTI (Ballester Pardo 65–66). While the primary focus of this book is on Mexican authors, it would be an oversight not to include Alonso due to her significant contributions to sapphic literature. Moreover, considering that *lo cuir* seeks to challenge notions of nationalism and citizenship, omitting a Cuban-born writer who has been instrumental in LGBTQ+ literature in Mexico would replicate the same exclusionary practices based on identity politics that this project intends to critique.

Published in the short story collection *Con la boca abierta y otros cuentos*, "Un puñado de cenizas" provides a thought-provoking example of the *fem fatal* for two main reasons. First, despite being primarily portrayed as such, she also acquires characteristics associated with the aggressive lesbian trope, whereby lesbians are depicted as predatory, violent, and pathological (Hart x). In this sense, while she is configured as a *fem fatal*, she is not confined by a single archetype, making for a complex antagonist. Second, while the story is told by an omniscient narrator, there is a shift in the narrative perspective, initially presenting the *fem fatal*'s viewpoint and eventually that of her victim. This approach is innovative compared to the other texts that I examine, which reinforce the *fem fatal*'s characteristic unknowability by primarily presenting the perspective of the woman who falls prey to her seduction. Furthermore, "Un puñado de cenizas" shifts the readers' allegiance through its exploration of revenge, crafting an intricate reading experience that, despite concluding with a good-versus-bad dichotomy, adds depth to the narrative.

Alonso's story takes place in Cuba and follows Yanela, a painter, and Mariana, a married woman who sparks her interest. Although Yanela's femininity is not directly emphasized as in other works examined in this chapter, she uses her feminine sexuality and dominance to seduce Mariana and, much like the original femme fatale would, causes her to lose everything. She stands out for her sharing many of the original archetype's characteristics, such as control over her lovers, her ability to push past their boundaries, her indifference to their suffering, and her use of sexuality to achieve her desires (Bornay 115). While the narrator does not reveal many details about Yanela's appearance that make her physically analogous to the femme fatale, her psychological traits align with the archetype.

For example, the femme fatale's sexuality is often portrayed as feline and lustful, leading to her animalization (Bornay 115). This is immediately evident in Alonso's short story, where Yanela, upon seeing Mariana for the first time, is described as being "[l]ike a cat who stalks, her eyes did not detach from a single one of the girl's movements" ("Como gato que acecha, sus ojos no se desprendieron de uno solo de los movimientos de la muchacha"; 31). Yanela's feline qualities depict her as a hunter stalking her prey, and, as the story advances, she is framed in opposition to Mariana, who is described as innocent and gullible. Yanela's power of seduction drives her relationship with Mariana, as she is the one who pursues her. Mariana's fear of her own *cuir* desire leads her to reject physical contact at first. Undeterred, Yanela ignores Mariana's objections. Her persistence is reminiscent of a major trait of the femme fatale: the deliberate use of her sexual power to compel others into actions that are unwanted or lead them into chaos (Quinn 2). The turmoil Yanela causes stems not only from Mariana's marriage to a man, but from the setting in postrevolutionary Cuba, where Mariana's family and friends are closely tied to Fidel Castro's government, known for its homophobic stances.[7]

Despite Mariana's initial doubts, she is ultimately seduced by Yanela. The character's position as a *fem fatal* is further evidenced by how Mariana views her, as she compares her lover to a virus that has invaded her and filled her with unimaginable pleasure. However, she considers that "with Yanela also came the misfortunes, one after the other" ("con Yanela habían llegado las desgracias, una tras otra"; 51). These adversities begin after the women's relationship is exposed, resulting in Mariana being disowned by her father and ostracized by friends and coworkers. This leads to the women becoming unhoused and living in a park, heightening tensions in their relationship and marking a shift in Yanela's behavior.

The character's depiction as seductive and affectionate ends when Mariana threatens to return to her family. While it is common for the original femme fatale to become crueler as her victim attempts to escape (Quinn 3), Yanela not only grows more perverse but also drops her seductive characteristics, turning overtly violent. When confronted with the possibility of Mariana leaving, Yanela explodes, telling her, "You can't leave me, you will not leave me like this. Don't even think about it. I will follow you wherever you go. And I don't care about your idiot father, or the frigid women in your office, or your mother's tears . . . Or yours, Mar, or yours. I will follow you like a shadow. You will never find someone who loves you like I do" ("No me puedes dejar, no me vas a dejar así. Ni lo pienses. Iré tras de ti adondequiera que te metas. Y no me importa el idiota de tu padre ni las frígidas de tu oficina ni las lágrimas de tu mamá . . . Ni las tuyas, Mar, ni las tuyas. Te voy a perseguir como una sombra. Nunca vas a encontrar quien te quiera como yo"; 49). Among the texts studied in this chapter, Alonso's *fem fatal* inflicts the most harm on the woman she seduces, both by threatening her and by being complicit in her sexual abuse when she takes part in Mariana's rape at the hands of a man. Hence, Yanela's perversity extends beyond her sexual and emotional control to include direct violence. As a result, after causing turmoil in

Mariana's life, Yanela transforms into a violent antagonist, more typically associated with male-inflicted abuse on women's bodies.

In her study on the representation of lesbians as violent, Lynda Hart argues that the portrayal of violent women in media often relies on disrupting the notion of desire between women. For Hart, mainstream lesbian representation has a long-standing history of painting queer women as predatory, dangerous, and deviant (x). Furthermore, she contends that lesbians have been historically positioned both as "not-women" and as inherently violent, becoming useful figures of criminality and operating within a system that supports and enforces heterosexual norms (x–xi). In the context of literature focused on sapphic desire, where heteronormativity is challenged, the violent lesbian trope does not aim to uphold those heterosexual norms. However, it cannot be separated from the homophobic origins highlighted by Hart. Thus, I contend that while Alonso's story constitutes Yanela as a *fem fatal*, she also develops some of the traits of the violent woman described by Hart. Ultimately, the antagonist fails to subvert the problematic characteristics of both archetypes and, instead, uses her body to act as an accomplice to patriarchal violence against women.

This is apparent when Yanela arranges for herself and Mariana to stay with a man named Tony, who demands sexual favors from Mariana in return. When she refuses, Yanela and the man rape her. The transformation in Yanela's behavior distances her from the *fem fatal* not only by her involving a third person instead of using her seductive power on Mariana to continue manipulating her but, most importantly, by her resorting to sexual violence to punish her lover. In this sense, Alonso's short story is complex in the way that it develops a *fem fatal* that steps out of the confines of a single archetype. Furthermore, even though Mariana leaves, Yanela stays and remains in a sexual relationship with Tony. While the story does not offer a reflection on Yanela's sexuality, it is apparent that she is willing to use it to obtain what she wants, regardless of her partner's gender, once again engaging with one of the defining characteristics of the *fem fatal*. Thus, as Katherine Farrimond argues regarding bisexuality in the femme fatale, it "can be read as shorthand for her duplicity and her sexual appeal" (142). Even though Farrimond writes in the context of film noir and the influence of the male gaze, I argue that the dynamic with Tony in "Un puñazo de cenizas" contributes to how Yanela is portrayed as unpredictable and dangerous. This is especially evident as it is through her sexual involvement with a man that she physically and psychologically harms Mariana.

Although Yanela's transformation into a violent woman is triggered by her loss of control over Mariana, her use of sexuality and association with men in the context of sexual violence reinforce negative stereotypes of bisexuality. I interpret this shift in their dynamic as aligning with Hart's argument, where the character's development as a sapphic *fem fatal* temporarily gives way to the image of a violent woman who utilizes patriarchal tools to inflict pain on Mariana. As Rita Segato points out, in the context of heteropatriarchal violence against women, sexual violence is fundamentally about the destruction of the victim's will (20). Hence, Yanela's actions are no longer focused on manipulating her lover to remain with her or to gain something but rather act as punishment for Mariana's resolve to leave her. However, the fact that she grows more unpredictable as the story advances demonstrates how she aligns with heteronormative representations of the bisexual femme fatale, as the archetype "occupies a precarious position in terms of her loyalties and what can be seen of them, and this instability is made still greater in the case of the bisexually active femme fatale" (Farrimond 144). Therefore, the possibility of bisexuality in the text is used to shape Yanela as deceitful, failing to offer a nuanced depiction of women's sexuality.

On the other hand, following Mariana's rejection by her family, the narrator focuses on her point of view. As a result, we as readers are compelled to sympathize with her, not only as we learn what she has suffered at the hands of Yanela, but also because we are shown the suffering through her perspective. "Un puñado de cenizas" is further complicated by Mariana's revenge at the conclusion of the short story. As she watches Tony leave, she returns to the apartment and bludgeons Yanela to death: "The face was disfigured against the table over a pool of blood" ("El rostro se desfiguraba contra la mesa sobre un charco de sangre"; 52). After we have witnessed her suffering, the violence described seems almost justified. This is followed by her setting the apartment on fire, walking away as a turntable continues to play music.

In this sense, Alonso's text engages with the rape-revenge story, introducing a plot twist that is unexpected in the context of the *fem fatal*. As readers, we are tempted to celebrate Mariana's vengeance, since literary depictions of rape-revenge can be represented as powerful and defiant as the survivor seems to enact justice (Pâquet 386). Nonetheless, as Lili Pâquet reminds us, "rape-revenge narratives often establish the necessity of revenge by first showing the trauma of rape," meaning that the survivor's body is depicted as innocent before being assaulted, only to be transformed afterwards (385). These differing approaches underscore the ethical challenges in determining the use and justification of sexual violence as a literary device. Nonetheless, Alonso's text adds depth to sapphic literature by refusing to simplify characters into palatable forms.

Consequently, it is not surprising that Téllez references "Un puñado de cenizas" when discussing the need for more "imperfect" characters in narratives about sapphic desire. She recounts an anecdote from Alonso about a Spanish activist who claimed her text portrayed the LGBTQ+ community negatively, arguing that this could adversely affect the advancement of rights such as adoption for same-sex couples. Téllez finds this criticism amusing, as she distinguishes the artistic value of these texts from their legal implications, stating that "the richness of these texts is precisely their sincerity and ease, it is the ability to narrate to us that public and personal existence that, until today, remained hidden" ("La riqueza de estos textos es precisamente su sinceridad y desenfado, es la habilidad para narrarnos esa existencia pública y personal que hasta hoy había quedado oculta"; A Chloe le gustaba Olivia" 181). I share her opinion that literature depicting LGBTQ+ characters should not strive for a sanitized goodness as an attempt to counteract homophobia. For this reason, Alonso's text stands out for its complex portrayal of sapphic characters and its nuanced use of archetypes, both of which give her protagonists more depth than some of the other works I examine in this chapter.

When returning to the original questions posed at the beginning of this section, I find that "Un puñado de cenizas" does not fully subvert some of the problematic aspects at the root of the femme fatale. Despite Alonso not simply transposing the archetype into a sapphic story, but rather challenging its limits, the narrative still underscores some of the misogyny behind the femme fatale. For example, Mariana killing Yanela as a way for the victim to take control mirrors the conventional punishment of women who wield their sexuality as a tool of manipulation (Doane 2). Moreover, it is significant that Yanela, despite not being the sole perpetrator of Mariana's sexual abuse, is the only one punished, sparing Tony from any repercussions for the crime. Similarly, because *lenchitudes* partly emerge from an activist denunciation of gender violence as a patriarchal tool used against women, the text invites a reading through this lens: Yanela's complicity with Tony can be seen as perpetuating patriarchal abuse in her attempts to control Mariana. Thus, not only is Yanela's sexuality portrayed as threatening, but she also becomes directly implicated in sexual violence against women. Consequently, the narrative reinforces the good-versus-bad-woman dichotomy that *lenchitudes* seek to dismantle.

Other *Fem Fatales*: The Lolita/Nymphet Archetype

I now begin my examination of an archetype that intersects with the femme fatale: the Lolita/nymphet. While there are numerous studies on the deadly woman, the Lolita/nymphet character has not received as much scholarly attention, partly due to ethical concerns surrounding the sexualization of young girls and the taboo surrounding discussions of pedophilia. Nonetheless, as I will show, the shadow of Lolita lingers within the narratives that I analyze. In this section, I will focus on how the young women in these texts are initially seen as innocent. Yet their rebelliousness and aggressive behavior paint them as sexually hostile and manipulative seductresses. I contend that this narrative approach not only sexualizes young girls from the perspective of adults but also shifts blame onto them for their own suffering and the suffering of others. Therefore, the lack of criticism and engagement with these problematic aspects in the texts that I examine indicates a failure to confront and challenge the misogyny underlying these representations.

Before delving into my analysis, I will discuss the Lolita/nymphet archetype and its relationship to the femme fatale. In her examination of the cinematic portrayal of this type of character, Joan Driscoll Lynch attributes its origins to Vladimir Nabokov's novel and explains how she evolves from an "innocent tease" into a "calculating whore" who is trapped in a state of powerlessness and can regain control only by seducing men (45). Traditionally, there are two predominant depictions of the Lolita character. The first is that of a passive, prepubescent girl oblivious to her desirability. The second type portrays her as not only aware of her desirability but also often sexually assertive (Savage 159). The two classifications represent opposing ends on a spectrum, yet characters tend to transition from the first to the second as they evolve.

This development corresponds to what Erika Bornay calls the evolution from an apprentice to a femme fatale (156). Lolita's likeness to this archetype is further highlighted by Marianne Sinclair, who points out that she is always associated with evil. She adds that, even if unwillingly, "[s]he lures, however innocently, grown men into forbidden paths that can lead to eternal damnation in the next world and to jail, disgrace and remorse in this one. She is Lilith, the forbidden fruit, doubly forbidden because unripe; and once tasted she can poison a whole existence" (125). Hence, much like the femme fatale, her attributes can be traced back to biblical figures associated with wicked femininity.

Similarly, Humbert Humbert, the male protagonist in Nabokov's *Lolita* (1955), refers to the young girls that he is sexually attracted to as *nymphets*. He defines them as having a true nature that is not human but, rather, nymphic and consequently, demoniacal (quoted in Torrent Lozano 120). The term is derived from the nymphs in Greek mythology, whose song and beauty enthrall men and drive them mad (Plaza-Morales 62, Calasso 35). Therefore, the concept of the nymphet relies on both the mythification and dehumanization of young girls. Meritxell Torrent Lozano identifies a clear connection between the femme fatale and the nymphet but emphasizes that the main difference lies in the latter's status as a child who is not fully aware of her own power and thus maintains an air of innocence (121). The ethical distinction between the two archetypes is found in their portrayal: While the femme fatale is depicted as a wicked woman who intentionally seduces her victims, she possesses an agency that the Lolita/nymphet lacks. The sexualization of Lolita depends on adults projecting their fantasies onto her.

Although the archetype gained prominence through Nabokov's novel, it has since been popularized. Elizabeth Patnoe argues that the Lolita narrative has evolved as a cultural myth that justifies male sexuality while punishing female sexuality, allowing some individuals to evade accountability for the desires that they impose on others (84). Although Nabokov defined the archetype as being between the ages of nine and fourteen, it has grown to include a broader age range in contemporary culture, as her perceived innocence has become more important than her age. Consequently, in a child, the Lolita type "suggests a feminine coquettishness and a hint of sensuality well beyond one's years. In a grown woman, it hints at a childish coyness, an immaturity of both character and appearance" (Sinclair 5). It is through this combination of innocence and sensuality that, despite her age, the Lolita archetype is framed as awakening desire in adults.

In this section, I demonstrate how the misogynistic nature of the Lolita/nymphet type is not exclusive to heterosexual representation. I agree with Téllez's emphasis on the importance of crafting complex characters that extend beyond an idealized "good lesbian." However, while these texts depict characters on the opposite end of the good/bad dichotomy, they do not offer multifaceted representations. Instead, they adhere to the same Lolita/nymphet trope without advancing it. As a result, they perpetuate the lethal Lolita myth and fail to hold adult women accountable for their problematic desire and the power dynamics that it involves. Moreover, I argue that by presenting the child, rather than the adult, as the one in control of their relationship, these works miss an opportunity to provide a nuanced portrayal of the *fem fatal.*

While I acknowledge the importance of examining teenage desire and its relationship to *lenchitudes*—a topic that requires thoughtful analysis and representation—the adult-centered perspective of both texts I analyze, where the adults are depicted as victims of the girls, perpetuates the same misogynistic logic as heteronormative renderings.[8] They stand in sharp contrast to the readaptations that emerged during the last decade of the twentieth century, such as Nancy J. Jones's *Molly* (2000), Pia Pera's *Lo's Diary* (1995), and Emily Prager's *Roger Fishbite* (1999). Sandra Visser argues that these reinterpretations of Nabokov's novel seek to tell Lolita's story from her perspective, thus giving her the voice she is denied in the original, while also engaging with feminist critiques of the text (28). These changes in perspective demonstrate that, despite the problematic aspects of the Lolita/nymphet archetype, it is possible to challenge its mainstream representation.

"A Mix of Fury and Desire": *Lo hice por amor* (2016) by Mildred Pérez de la Torre

As opposed to the previous authors whose work I have examined, Mildred Pérez de la Torre's (b. 1982, Mexico City) career has focused on her contributions to media outlets such as *Rolling Stone*, *Replicante*, and *Gatopardo*, among others. She serves as editorial director of the web portal Homosensual, which produces LGBTQ+ content in Mexico. Her first and only novel, *Lo hice por amor* (2016), was published by Quimera Ediciones and subsequently won the press's award for *mejor literatura queer* (best queer literature).[9] The novel tells the story of Eugenia, a troubled high school student who finds herself in a close and eventually sexual relationship with the school's principal, Martha.

At the beginning of the text, when Martha sees Eugenia for the first time, she is initially drawn to her out of pity. She criticizes the young woman's disheveled appearance but, after learning that Eugenia's mother died in a car accident, she feels compassion for her: "I felt pity, so much pity for that little girl who was certainly suffering a lot at such an early age" ("sentí pena, mucha pena por esa pequeña que seguramente estaba sufriendo mucho a tan temprana edad"; 10). By referring to her as a little girl and emphasizing her youth, Martha clearly understands that Eugenia is not yet an adult. This initial moment of sympathy sparks the principal's interest in the student and prompts her to offer regular meetings, explaining that she is also a trained psychologist. During their first appointment, Martha learns about Eugenia's difficult home life but also reveals her manipulative interest in her, aware that she is more vulnerable than other girls.

Her sympathy and pity quickly transform into something more perverse as she dismisses the possibility of feeling guilt. She thinks to herself: "The voice in my head told me: Martha, she is a girl. I silently responded that she no longer was" ("La voz en mi mente me decía: Martha, es una niña. Yo, en silencio, le respondía que ya no"; 43). The protagonist, by refusing to acknowledge Eugenia as a child, not only avoids taking responsibility for wanting to act on her desire but also employs a logic like that seen in *Lolita*'s Humbert. This perspective considers nymphets as not being actual children but as merely appearing to be so (Torrent Lozano 120). The allusion to Nabokov's text in *Lo hice por amor* becomes more evident as Martha begins to fantasize about her new student: "Before going to sleep, while I read about nymphets, I thought for the first time—in the back of my mind, in its darkest corner—about the possibility that someday Eugenia and I would be together" ("Antes de dormir, mientras leía sobre nínfulas, pensé por primera vez—muy atrás, en el rinconcito más oscuro de mi mente—en la posibilidad de que algún día Eugenia y yo estuviéramos juntas"; 12). Therefore, Eugenia's portrayal as a nymphet comes not from the girl herself, nor her actions up to this point, but rather from Martha's projections of her desire onto her.

As Liu Ling contends, Lolitas are not nymphets themselves, but they are conceived as such by those—typically men—who wish to possess them (67). This reveals the contradictions in the depiction of the nymphet. They are seen as ruthless and manipulative seductresses, but this perception exists only because of the fantasies projected onto them by their predators. In other words, as Torrent Lozano explains, pedophilia becomes a fundamental element for modern-day nymphets to exert their purported power of seduction (119). By choosing to read about nymphets, Martha sets the stage for her future actions. This reading also allows her to project a mythical construction onto Eugenia, dehumanizing her and making it easier, in her mind, to escalate her obsession.

The main character justifies her interest in Eugenia by attributing it to a protective instinct that she associates with being perceived by others as masculine. She recalls being rejected and taunted with the term *machorra* during her childhood and adolescence. Furthermore, she projects her own experiences onto Eugenia by assuming that the girl is acting out at school to cope with her mother's death. Martha narrates her own teenage rebellion against her mother by cutting her hair "not to look like a brave prince, but like a soldier; I did it because, other than wanting to annoy my mother, I wanted to strip myself of all femininity" ("ya no como príncipe valiente, sino como militar; lo hice porque, además de fastidiar a mi madre, quería despojarme de toda mi feminidad"; 14). Pérez de la Torre's novel is the only one among the works that I explore in relation to the *fem fatal* that addresses depictions of female masculinity. While this chapter does not aim to analyze masculine gender expression, it is important to note that Martha's rejection of her own femininity serves as the basis for her rationalization of what she considers to be protective behaviors, which ultimately leads her to prey on Eugenia. The way Martha characterizes herself and Eugenia creates an oppositional relationship. Martha sees herself as masculine, while Eugenia, by accentuating traits and behaviors perceived as feminine, is directly associated with manipulative actions. As a result, the text creates a dichotomy: Martha is protective, masculine, and good, whereas Eugenia is portrayed as manipulative, feminine, and wicked.

Martha asks the student to move in with her once she is done with high school, when her father will no longer support her financially. This starts a transactional relationship where Eugenia fakes romantic interest to gain financial support. This dynamic aligns with portrayals of the Lolita character, who is often imbued with narcissistic traits that drive her to act in her own self-interest, much like the femme fatale (Sinclair 7). Nonetheless, Eugenia's lack of attraction to the principal is evident, as Martha narrates how the girl is often cruel and seeks to humiliate her. Eugenia's cruelty is tamed as soon as the protagonist asks her to move in with her: "The rage vanished. Eugenia smiled, excited. She seemed to be in love with me" ("La furia se esfumó. Eugenia sonrió, ilusionada. Parecía estar enamorada de mí"; 45). This constant shift in demeanor is typical of Lolitas, who can exhibit immense cruelty while always maintaining a playful and innocent side (Torrent Lozano 121). The nymphet's inconsistency is something that adults who prey on her seek to exploit for their own benefit, as it allows them to see themselves as poor victims who are in love yet also subject to a young girl's whims.

As Eugenia's demands increase and become more expensive, Martha views herself as a victim of her scorn, but her disappointment mainly stems from the girl's perceived loss of innocence. As Martha grows disenchanted yet more obsessed with the student, she associates Eugenia's former untidiness with innocence and sees her growing femininity as threatening. This direct relationship is evident when the principal explains, "Eugenia had lost her tenderness. She was no longer the Eugenia who came into my office sad, dirty, and disheveled. Eugenia now wore her hair up in a tall bun. She now wore eyeliner. She now unbuttoned the top buttons of the uniform's shirt" ("Eugenia había perdido su ternura. Ya no era la Eugenia que entró a mi oficina triste, sucia y desaliñada. Eugenia ahora llevaba el pelo recogido, en un chongo alto. Ahora usaba delineador. Ahora desabrochaba los botones superiores de la camisa del uniforme"; 28). Martha's disillusionment is driven by two main factors: First, she believes the girl has lost her purity, demonstrating how the nymphet begins to disappear as she ages and looks older (Torrent Lozano 122); second, she is upset to learn that she is not the only one Eugenia has been sexually involved with.

Likewise, the physical characteristics that defined Eugenia earlier change significantly as she accentuates her femininity. The connection between Eugenia's transformation and Martha's apparent disenchantment is partially rooted in her perceived loss of innocence. Innocence, then, is understood as something that can be lost as soon as the child or teen approaches the terrain of behavior seen as adult—in this case, Eugenia's feminine and sexual appearance. Thus, to maintain this perception of purity, this transformation must be delayed, as delay is "seen as a friend to the child. Delay is said to be a feature of its growth: children grow by delaying their approach to the realms of sexuality, labor, and harm. The point of delay as a boon to growth is to shelter children from these domains" (Bond Stockton 62). In the context of the novel, however, Martha is both attracted to this innocence and wary of how Eugenia's sexualization might lead to its loss.

This is a common contradiction in works depicting the Lolita archetype (Sinclair 5), as the life of a nymphet is short, and once she gets closer to adulthood, her charm disappears in the eyes of her predators (Torrent Lozano 122). The protagonist rationalizes her obsession with this "innocence" by characterizing it as a wish to protect the girl. She is upset when Eugenia tells her about a sexual encounter with an eighteen-year-old boy, arguing that he is of legal age and Eugenia is a minor; nonetheless, she does not question her own sexual contact with her. The protagonist's attitude exposes her hypocrisy, as she is not only an adult but also an authority figure whose behavior toward the girl is predatory.

To this effect, I now return to the second reason behind Martha's disillusionment, which concerns Eugenia's sexual encounters with other people. This is especially evident when the two have sex, as the protagonist explains:

> She allowed it. She wanted it. But when I kissed her, suffering with every bite, I understood that Eugenia was not the angelic girl that I believed; she was everything but that. It was painful to realize that she had done that before. I was not the first. I was not the only one. I was one more mouth. One more tongue that let itself be forced by hers, without complaining, without asking her to stop, because I didn't want her to; because if she had stopped, my heart would have inevitably stopped one day without having had the slightest idea of what love is.

> ("Ella se dejaba. Ella quería. Pero al besarla, al sufrir con cada mordida, comprendí que Eugenia no era la chica angelical que yo creía; ella era todo menos eso. Fue doloroso darme cuenta de que ella había hecho eso antes. Yo no era la primera. Yo no era la única. Yo era una boca más. Una lengua más que se dejaba violentar por la suya, sin quejarse, sin pedirle que se detuviera, porque no quería que lo hiciera; porque si se hubiera detenido, mi corazón, irremediablemente, se hubiera parado algún día sin haber tenido la más remota idea de lo que es el amor"; 39–40).

I have reproduced this lengthy passage because it contains several points that are worth highlighting. While Martha initially emphasizes how Eugenia welcomes and desires her sexual advances, her view of the power dynamic changes significantly when she considers the girl's perceived lack of innocence. She then sees herself as the one being *violentada*, or subjected to violence, torn between wanting and not wanting Eugenia. Thus, we are confronted with what Roberto Calasso refers to as the paradox of the nymphet: possessing her means being possessed by her (35). This contradiction furthers Martha's self-characterization as innocent, particularly when she emphasizes how Eugenia has "forced" herself onto others before her, portraying herself as just another victim.

The protagonist's disenchantment can be better understood through Bonnie MacLachlan's analysis of the cultural significance of virginity. She contends that although the concept varies according to context, there is a clear relationship between ideas of the Virgin and power, for, historically, "remaining 'intact' before engaging in sexual activity reserved the full force of erotic energy for this anticipated event" (4). Despite never using the term *virginity*, Martha's emphasis on how Eugenia is not innocent accentuates the contradictory nature of her thoughts. She feels no conflict or guilt about her obsession with the girl, yet she reproduces the antiquated patriarchal myth of virginity. Monsiváis notes that this notion was historically considered sacred in Mexico, representing a form of the right to property (*Misógino feminista* 27). Despite its sapphic modern-day context, the concept of the right to property remains present in the novel, as the relationship between the two characters is transactional in nature. The principal agrees to financially support Eugenia on the condition that she does not have sex with anyone else, an agreement that the student blatantly disregards.

Lo hice por amor concludes with Martha discovering the smell of gas in her apartment and finding Eugenia in her bed with another, younger woman. Instead of confronting them, she lies on the couch and cries, choosing death for herself and the two women: "I decided to stay there and share my fate with them" ("Decidí quedarme ahí y compartir suerte con ellas"; 62). Her plans to die by suicide fail, as she eventually wakes to her sister and paramedics finding the two bodies. This ending reveals another similarity between the Lolita archetype and the femme fatale: both are punished for their transgressions. In the case of the former, as Sinclair states, "nymphets who tried using sex as a weapon still ended up as the victims even though they thought they had the winning ticket at first" (125). It is not coincidental that Martha survives due to how the novel configures her as a victim of the Lolita's deception. Therefore, Eugenia must suffer the consequences of her actions while Martha is spared.

Furthermore, Martha's sister, Thelma, looks after the depressed protagonist following Eugenia's death. Although Thelma frequently worries that her sister might take her own life or face legal action from the girl's family, she never expresses disapproval of Martha's relationship with Eugenia. On the contrary, as the principal explains, "She didn't care about the thing with Eugenia. She didn't see it as good or bad. She saw it as it was: a relationship between two women" ("A ella no le importaba lo de Eugenia. Ella no lo veía ni bien ni mal. Lo veía como era: una relación entre dos mujeres"; 24). Even though Thelma acts as the voice of reason throughout the novel for Martha, she does not question the fact that her sister is in a relationship with a minor who is also a student at the school where she works. I consider this a missed opportunity for the novel to explore the ethical implications of the Lolita archetype.

Although *Lo hice por amor* shows the pervasiveness of the *fem fatal* in texts depicting sapphic desire through its exploration of the Lolita myth, it ultimately reproduces the same misogyny present in heteronormative renderings of the nymphet character. While it challenges the stereotypical "good lesbian" highlighted by Téllez, it falls short of offering a complex approach that allows for an *encuiramiento* of the Lolita/nymphet. By not addressing the power dynamics between the characters and victimizing Martha, it reinforces the outdated myth that views women's sexuality, especially in relation to femininity, as dangerous. Additionally, Eugenia's lack of voice enhances her depiction as mysterious and unintelligible, a characteristic she shares with the femme fatale. *Lo hice por amor* is an important contribution to LGBTQ+ representation in contemporary Mexican literature. Nonetheless, it illustrates that not all narratives portraying sapphic relationships are inherently *cuir* when we regard *lo cuir* as inseparable from the need to subvert and challenge hegemonic understandings of gender and sexuality.

"A Small and Helpless Baby":
"Arsénico y caramelos" (2007) by Eve Gil

I conclude this chapter by analyzing "Arsénico y caramelos" by author Eve Gil (Hermosillo, 1968). Gil is a novelist, essayist, and short story writer as well as a journalist and literary critic. Her first novels, *Hombres necios* (1996) and *El suplicio de Adán* (1998), deal with issues such as the student movement of 1971 and criticize religious institutions, which led to backlash in her native state of Sonora (Olivera Córdova, *Entre amoras* 135). "Arsénico y caramelos" is part of the erotic short story collection *La dulce hiel del deseo* (2007), compiled by Ana Clavel and featuring authors such as Cristina Rivera Garza, Brenda Lozano, and Rosa Beltrán. The story revolves around the relationship between high school English teacher Emma and her student Portia. Much like the relationship in *Lo hice por amor*, this relationship is framed by the power dynamics between a young student and an authority figure. Portia, like Eugenia, is initially shown as innocent but later develops into a menacing Lolita type who turns the protagonist's life upside down. Unlike Eugenia, however, it is Portia who actively pursues and seduces the authority figure in "Arsénico y caramelos."

At the start of Gil's short story, Emma describes Portia as "a girl like all the others. Even though she invaded the classroom without apologizing for her considerable delay. Even though she compulsively licked traces of sugar between her fingers. Extravagant mane, yellow pencil behind her ear" ("una niña como todas las demás. Aunque invadiera el aula sin disculparse por su considerable retardo. Aunque lamiera compulsiva restos de azúcar entre sus dedos. Extravagante melena, lápiz amarillo tras la oreja"; 71). The narrator's description of the girl reads as ambiguous, for she is at once sexualized by her teacher's gaze—licking her fingers compulsively and having extravagant hair—while her childlike characteristics are emphasized. In contrast to *Lo hice por amor*, "Arsénico y caramelos" portrays the Lolita character from the start as embodying both innocence and seduction, even if her seduction is presented as naïve—a trait generally present in this archetype.

The school principal's description of Portia when talking to Emma underscores this contradictory portrayal, as she says that the girl "[j]ust turned fourteen . . . I know that she looks more like a woman than the others, but she is a baby, miss . . . a small and helpless baby" ("Acaba de cumplir catorce . . . Sé que hasta parece más mujer que las otras, pero es un bebé, miss . . . un pequeño y desamparado bebé"; 72). Her initially ambivalent description reveals that the adults who sexualize her are conscious of her young age and, more importantly, her vulnerability. Henry Giroux describes this liminal space between childhood and adulthood as contributing to the discourse around "the disappearing child." He contends that if innocence functions as the moral basis separating children from adults, the concept of "the disappearing child" highlights that this distinction is threatened by forces that blur the boundaries between childhood and adulthood (31). Although this rhetoric tends to be used by the right to defend their positions under the guise of "protecting children," the idea of innocence is as much a projection of adult fantasies as sexualization. Therefore, this narrative not only oversimplifies childhood and the diverse experiences of children, but it also allows adults to avoid taking responsibility for the ways in which children are influenced by the social and cultural institutions predominantly managed by adults (Giroux 31). Much like with Eugenia in *Lo hice por amor*, the adults in Gil's short story stress that, although Portia is a child, she appears to be older. This emphasis operates similarly to the idealization of innocence, permitting adults to shift the blame for their sexualization of Portia onto the student herself.

A notable similarity between "Arsénico y caramelos" and Pérez de la Torre's novel is that both reference Nabokov's work, thus situating themselves within the cultural production engaging with the Lolita archetype—a choice that seems too obvious in both cases. After being asked to tutor Portia, Emma finds herself considering the offer "with an open Nabokov book on her lap" ("con un libro de Nabokov abierto sobre el regazo"; 74). For Martha and Emma, reading Nabokov or texts about nymphets marks the moment they start to acknowledge their attraction to their respective students. It also shapes the fantasies they create about them, influenced directly by literature. Although in the case of "Arsénico y caramelos" the protagonist is initially hesitant to get involved with the student, she agrees to help after the girl's mother pleads with her. Emma suggests summer tutoring, as we are told that she felt "eager to be left alone again with Lolita" ("ansiosa de quedar nuevamente a solas con Lolita"; 76). Thus, it becomes evident that her hesitation is rooted not in disinterest but in her recognition of her attraction to the student.

As their tutoring sessions begin, Portia soon feels at ease with her teacher and admits that she did not need tutoring and intentionally failed her English class to get close to Emma. The girl tells the protagonist, "It was precisely what I wanted, dear . . . for you to stay . . . with me. Emma was left petrified, she did not know what to do, what to say, how to react. Portia suddenly said: We sniff each other out like dogs, you should already know that!" ("Era precisamente lo que quería, cariño . . . que te quedaras . . . conmigo . . . Emma quedó petrificada, no sabía qué hacer, qué decir, cómo reaccionar. Portia dijo de golpe: Entre nosotras nos olfateamos como perras, ¡ya deberías saberlo!"; 81). At this point, we witness her transformation from innocent to aggressive, which portrays Emma as never having been in control.

Furthermore, the student mocks the protagonist's apparent inexperience, pointing out that she should be aware of how women who are attracted to other women can easily recognize each other. Her comment inverts their dynamic as it signals that Portia is more familiar with sapphic interactions than Emma is, and her forceful demeanor leaves the teacher speechless. In this sense, I find the failures of "Arsénico y caramelos" to question the misogyny and problematic aspects of the archetype to be like those found in *Lo hice por amor*. Although the texts could, indeed, offer a complex perspective on teenage desire, their uncritical perpetuation of the Lolita myth is closely associated with their depiction of the adults as victims.

In line with this, even though the short story is told in third person by an omniscient narrator, we are privy to Emma's thoughts and feelings throughout the text. By deliberately excluding Portia's perspective, the narrator characterizes her as indecipherable, just like the femme fatale. While the absence of the girl's perspective is found in both Pérez de la Torre's and Gil's works, in *Lo hice por amor*, the protagonist narrates the story, whereas in "Arsénico y caramelos," the omniscient narrator sets a tone that is strongly sympathetic to Emma. This becomes evident when she embraces Portia after the student confides that her mother rejected her because of her sexuality: "The teacher did not intend to squeeze her, she wanted to instill solidarity in her, sincerely, to tell her that she too . . . but Portia molded her pubescent voluptuousness to the teacher's body, who was no longer able to dodge the girl's demanding lips" ("La miss no tenía intención de apretujarla, quería transmitirle solidaridad, sinceramente, decirle que ella también . . . pero Portia amoldó su púber voluptuosidad al cuerpo de la miss quien ya no pudo esquivar los demandantes labios de la niña"; 81–82). This interaction underscores the contradictory nature of Emma's interest in Portia, similar to the dynamics found in men who prey on Lolitas; she desires her, but her vulnerability sparks in her a wish to comfort her. Thus, this paradoxical portrayal reflects one of the main traits of this archetype in the heterosexual context: her ability to incite forbidden desire through "innocent provocation" (Sinclair 5). However, the narrator's tone depicts Portia's advances as aggressive and intentional, casting Emma as her victim.

In a passage that is remarkably similar to the one I examined in *Lo hice por amor*, their erotic interaction reinforces the dichotomous depiction of Emma as innocent and Portia as a seductress: "She was possessed by that young woman who knew exactly where to touch her, where and how. After a quick orgasm, synchronized with a hymn to beauty, miss Emma was left smeared on the brownish carpet. She was recovering from the impact as Portia, naked like an angel, her sex child-like, an open and throbbing peach pit, smoked a cigarette next to her with the elegant impatience of lovers in French films" ("Fue poseída por aquella jovencita que sabía exactamente dónde tocarla, dónde y cómo. Tras un orgasmo rápido, sincronizado con un himno a la belleza, miss Emma quedó untada a la alfombra pardusca. Se recuperaba apenas del impacto cuando ya Portia, desnuda como un ángel, infantil el sexo, abierto y palpitante corazón de durazno, fumaba a su lado con la elegante impaciencia de los amantes de las películas francesas"; 82). This description of Portia possessing Emma maintains the inversion of their power dynamic, emphasizing her dominance, which is often a feature in the representation of nymphets (Torrent Lozano 121). Moreover, the description of her body as childlike and angelic sharply contrasts with her smoking and the comparison of the scene to a French film. By ending the portrayal with images associated with adult behaviors, the narrator attempts to make the reader overlook the problematic reminders that Portia is not an adult. Consequently, this depiction serves as a reminder that, from the perspective of the *nympho-lept*—a term used by Nabokov's Humbert for those who prey on Lolitas to avoid admitting to pedophilia—the nymphet is not a child but only appears to be one (Torrent Lozano 120). By trying to negate her youth, the narrator strips her of one of her defining qualities and relies on the dehumanization inherent in the nymphet trope.

I find the most fascinating and complex aspect of Gil's short story to be its use of motherhood as a device to attempt to redeem Emma. "Arsénico y caramelos" ends with a confrontation between the protagonist and Portia, during which the girl reveals that the school's principal and other female teachers are sexually involved with students in exchange for scholarships and other favors, insinuating that Emma, too, could be part of this group. The narrator tells us that, "faced with the temptation that the girl offered her on a silver platter, the possibility of fornicating with other little girls even younger than Portia, than her own daughter, the mother who inhabited her erupted" ("ante la tentación que aquella niña le brindaba en bandeja de plata, la posibilidad de fornicar a otras niñitas incluso más pequeñas que Portia, que su propia hija, hizo erupción la madre que la habitaba"; 88). Although it is implied that Emma is tempted to partake in such a crime despite knowing the gravity of the situation, the thought of her daughter saves her from succumbing. While the protagonist ultimately flees to avoid the consequences of her encounter with Portia, the emergence of motherhood as an eruptive force within her reflects the traditional notions of selflessness tied to motherhood in Mexico.

In this sense, what sets "Arsénico y caramelos" apart from all the other works examined in this chapter is its configuration of the Lolita/ *fem fatal* in direct contrast with motherhood. Emma is far from the ideal Virgin archetype due to her attraction to women, especially to young girls.

However, throughout the text the narrator reveals that she is in an extra-marital relationship with an adult woman named Carolina, which causes tension with her family after her daughter and husband find out. Despite secretly continuing the affair, Emma does not bring herself to leave her family. Nonetheless, when she decides to flee following her involvement with Portia, she expresses sadness when realizing that she must also leave Carolina. Thus, even though she does not embody the typical *madre abnegada*, she refuses to leave her family to be with Carolina, showing her adherence to the values that prioritize women's dedication to their husbands and children over their own wishes. At the same time, when tempted by Portia's insinuation, Emma's sense of motherhood drives her to reject and condemn it, as well as to decide to leave. This decision, as I have explained, spares her from the direct consequences of her actions but requires her to abandon both her family and her lover, sacrificing any possibility of her own happiness. In her act of self-punishment, Emma achieves an aspiration to selflessness, showing the traditional values of Mexican motherhood as her only path forward.

In the case of Portia, despite not being punished with death, as is common with both the nymphet/Lolita and the femme fatale, she is beaten and rejected by Emma, not only for her seduction but also for her knowledge of and involvement in the sexual abuse of her classmates. Her actions align with the nymphet archetype, which Sinclair describes as frequently portrayed as both an accomplice and victim of unrepressed desires (126). Portia's participation in the exploitation of her classmates, along with the use of her sexuality to get what she wants, exemplifies the Lolita's narcissistic drive (7). Thus, her egotism and self-indulgence contrast with Emma's motherly sacrifice, highlighting how the text ultimately relies on tropes about good versus bad women.

Engaging with a figure as problematic as Lolita is a challenging endeavor because of its ethical implications. Nabokov's famous portrayal has been the subject of multiple debates and studies about its literary value and whether the novel condemns or validates its protagonist's pedophilia and abuse. Although my study takes place in a different context, encountering *Lolita* during the research and writing of these pages felt unavoidable. I found myself continually revisiting Roxane Gay's reflection on Nabokov's work. For Gay, *Lolita* is both devastating and exceptional, because of how the writing makes readers feel complicit in Humbert's obsession. She explains that, as the novel progresses, the protagonist devolves as his predation becomes clearer, and "this narrative fall from grace is what makes *Lolita* a masterpiece instead of a travesty" (54). Seeking to contribute to the debate about the 1950 novel is not the aim of this book and lies beyond my area of study. However, Gay's attention to the aesthetic value of the text aided in my conclusion that the two works I have examined contribute to the varied depiction of sapphic characters by illustrating the presence of the Lolita/nymphet archetype in Mexican narratives. Yet, when they are analyzed through the perspective of *lenchitudes*, it becomes apparent that they do not challenge the archetype's patriarchal and misogynistic foundations because of their lack of nuanced characters.

In this chapter, I have explored the concept of the *fem fatal* to demonstrate how narratives depicting sapphic desire often present femininity as enticing yet imbued with negative qualities that replicate the misogyny behind the original femme fatale. Additionally, I have traced the Lolita/nymphet archetype as part of the *fem fatal* to underscore how these texts, though transgressive in their portrayal of sapphic characters who do not conform to heteronormative standards, still perpetuate the sexualization and objectification of young girls. This section, while focusing on a specific archetype and not encompassing all representations of femininity, seeks to make visible the tensions in its depiction. Finally, I have shown how an analysis from the perspective of *lenchitudes* can uncover that some narratives use the *fem fatal* to portray femininity and female sexuality as dangerous, while others can lead to an *encuiramiento* of this archetype that challenges normativity.

Chapter 4

Queering Heteronormativity or Normalizing Queerness?

Monogamy and Motherhood

If you were to ask someone who grew up in Mexico—at least up until my generation—about the term *casa chica* (small house) or the metaphor of *la catedral* (the cathedral) for a man's wife and *la/s capilla/s* (the chapel/s) for his extramarital affair/s, I believe that most would recognize these concepts. Born in 1928, my grandmother was intimately familiar with this reality. After my mother's passing in 2023, I found myself sifting through old papers. Among letters from distant relatives I did not recognize, I discovered my grandparents' divorce papers. Despite my knowing about their troubled marriage and my grandfather's abuse, reading my grandmother's words—a version of her that I never knew—revealed a palpable sense of exhaustion after twenty years of marriage.

She described how their relationship was marked by a fundamental incompatibility due to their differing views on the institution of marriage, its purpose, and their roles within it. She continued, "Indeed, I believe that fidelity between spouses must be mutual and repeatedly maintained; Mr. Guajardo, on the other hand, believes that it is a woman's duty and a man's option. He has made good on that opinion many times" ("Efectivamente, yo conceptúo que la fidelidad entre los cónyuges debe ser mutua y reiteradamente sostenida; el señor Guajardo, en cambio, opina que es un deber de la mujer y una facultad para el hombre. En multitud de ocasiones ha hecho efectivo su pensamiento"). In 1960s Chihuahua, both her words and her choice to pursue a divorce were rare occurrences.

According to family lore, she was never again invited to events where women's husbands were present, as her status as a divorcée deemed her as untrustworthy to her conservative community. My grandfather, on the other hand, faced no repercussions, social or otherwise.

By the time of their separation, my grandparents, Luz de la Peña and Homero Guajardo, had a marriage marked by two decades of unhappiness and four daughters. Before their divorce, my grandmother, like many women of her era and even today, chose not to speak of her husband's infidelities. This silence is a cultural strategy that renders practices like extramarital affairs "partially acceptable under the condition of their absolute concealment from public view" (Rojas et al. 356). Unlike many others, my grandmother chose to break her silence and start over. A few decades later, my mother's marriage to my father ended under similar circumstances. In contrast, some other women in my family have continued to be cathedrals, while their husbands have sought chapels elsewhere.

Though these personal anecdotes may seem unrelated to this chapter's examination of motherhood, monogamy, and *lo cuir*, they become relevant in discussions of monogamy and heteronormativity in Mexico. They highlight the need to address the culturally accepted practice of male infidelity in heterosexual relationships, particularly marriage. To engage with scholarship on the disruptive potential of non-monogamy, I first examine the normalization of male adultery in Mexican society, contrasting it with a perspective that views non-monogamy as a potentially subversive challenge to heteronormativity. I conclude my study by conceptualizing the relationship between motherhood, monogamy, and *lo cuir*.

Resolving the debate over whether adhering to these values is counterproductive to the goals of *lo cuir* lies beyond the scope of this book, as this conversation is ongoing and includes a wide range of perspectives. In that respect, I concur with Butler's assertion that when it comes to marriage and kinship, "a politics which incorporates a critical understanding is the only one that can maintain a claim to being self-reflective and nondogmatic. To be political does not merely mean to take a single and enduring 'stand'" ("Is Kinship" 20). Thus, this chapter aims to critically examine how these issues are represented without taking an absolute stance. To this end, I bring different theoretical approaches into the conversation to lay the groundwork for my exploration of how monogamy is portrayed in women's *cuir* literature in contemporary Mexico.

I follow my contextualization of these debates with an analysis of three narrative works. I begin with Rosamaría Roffiel's *Amora*, where

Guadalupe, a self-proclaimed feminist, struggles with her love interest's rejection of monogamy, leading to a conflict between her expectations and values. Nonetheless, I contend that *Amora* provides new perspectives on relationship configurations, particularly in its portrayal of Guadalupe's understanding of kinship as one that transcends biological family ties and is instead built on friendship, feminism, and companionship. Next, I examine Gilda Salinas's collection of short texts, *Del destete al desempance. Cuentos lésbicos y un colado*, which follows its protagonist as she explores her sexuality during her youth. However, I argue that the character ultimately succumbs to the idealization of romantic love and monogamy, conforming to heteronormative and capitalist ideals of success and maturity. I conclude with a discussion on the potential and limitations of motherhood in challenging heterosexual notions of reproduction, followed by an analysis of Criseida Santos Guevara's *Rhyme & Reason*. I contend that the novel's protagonist embodies Halberstam's concept of queer temporality by rejecting motherhood and the nuclear family.

Cathedrals and Chapels, or Male Infidelity in Mexico

Even though my work centers on sapphic desire, an analysis of texts situated in Mexico requires recognizing the differences between socially sanctioned male infidelity and *cuir* approaches to non-monogamy. As I mentioned at the beginning of this chapter, it is not uncommon to hear stories about *la casa chica*, *capillas*, and *catedrales* in Mexico. While relationship models have evolved and continue to do so with the reshaping of gender roles,[1] the discrepancies between rigid understandings of marriage and family and the realities of daily life have persisted since colonization and the imposition of Catholic values. In her study of adultery in New Spain, Teresa Armendares Lozano notes that by the eighteenth century, the church's official nuclear family model—framed as "God's law" and condemning transgressors as sinners—had become widely assimilated into society (66). However, church and legal authorities often overlooked irregularities like unreported infidelities or those that did not cause major disturbances, as, despite the law being nominally respected, there was little desire to enforce it (69). These transgressions were, predictably, gendered—an attitude that has mostly endured since then.

Although there is a notable lack of studies on the discourse surrounding male infidelity in Mexico, some of the few existing analyses unanimously agree that while women's adultery is harshly judged or punished, men are not held to the same standard of faithfulness in their marriages or relationships (Tenorio Tovar 27; Espinoza Romo et al. 140; Rodríguez Dorantes 219). Men who commit these infidelities often refuse to take responsibility, instead shifting the blame onto the women they become involved with, arguing that they are the ones who chose to be with a married man (Tenorio Tovar 27). Furthermore, there is a perception that men's sexual urges are natural and uncontrollable (Rojas Martínez 92). Thus, it is not uncommon for women who are cheated on to blame their husband's lover, thereby reinforcing the unwritten norm that grants men the freedom to be non-monogamous while condemning women's sexuality (Rodríguez Dorantes 220). This disparity is not surprising given the historical role of the *madre abnegada*, as discussed in chapters 2 and 3, in shaping the concept of *mexicanidad*.

However, when we consider the potential of non-monogamy as a means of subverting the patriarchal views that underpin these gendered attitudes, it is important to differentiate between adultery and consensual arrangements. Infidelity, as Espinoza Romo explains, is understood as the violation of an implicit or explicit intimate commitment between the members of a couple (139). Thus, it suggests that the person committing infidelity is doing so through deception, with the partner being cheated on lacking any form of consent or knowledge. For Nathan Rambukkana, adultery "exists *within* the logic of heteronormativity; insofar as it functions to define monogamy as a desired norm and non-monogamy as a bracketed exception, it is a breach—but not a break—with this system. Paradigmatically, it belongs to monogamy" (18–19; emphasis in the original). Unlike the normalized cheating in some sectors of Mexican society, polyamory and similar arrangements require the explicit consent and awareness of all partners, setting them apart by their clear agreements and their emphasis on gender egalitarianism—unlike patriarchal forms of polygamy (Schippers 15–16). Consequently, while monogamy and non-monogamy are interdependent, by distinguishing between infidelity and consensual agreements between adults, we can envision possibilities beyond traditional marriage or romantic relationships.

Marriage and Monogamy

The texts I study do not directly address the expansion of marriage rights for same-sex couples, but rather delve into issues of monogamy and family.

Nonetheless, the relationship between marriage and monogamy is intrinsic, as the legal recognition of dyadic relationships has been central to both heteronormativity and LGBTQ+ rights discussions. Therefore, there is a belief deeply embedded within Western ideology that institutionalizes relationships under a patriarchal structure, manifesting as a monogamous, heterosexual system regulated by the state and oriented toward procreation (Herrera Gómez 259). In this vein, Mimi Schippers explains mononormativity as a larger framework referring to "the institutionalized arrangements and cultural narratives that situate the monogamous dyad as the only legitimate, natural, or desirable relationship form, thereby systematically conferring privileges on those who are or appear to be in monogamous couples and disadvantages on those who are not" (14). In light of this, the critiques surrounding monogamy and, more specifically, marriage, have emphasized issues such as homonormativity, meaning "a politics that does not contest dominant heteronormative assumptions and institutions but upholds and sustains them," in order to create a gay culture based on domesticity (Duggan 179) or the erasure of difference (Domínguez Ruvalcaba, *Latinoamérica Queer* 172).

Butler finds these views on marriage problematic because they foster a sense of personhood reliant on state legitimation, which is achieved through exclusionary processes and the perception of illegitimacy for those who do not conform to established norms ("Is Kinship" 17). Butler argues that when recognition is sought and obtained based on norms that legitimize marriage or critique it, the exclusion simply moves from one segment of the queer community to another. This approach changes a broad delegitimization into a more targeted one, which conflicts with the ideas of a truly democratic and sexually progressive movement ("Is Kinship" 26–27). Although Butler's arguments center on marriage as a form of state legitimation, I contend that marriage cannot be separated from the broader narratives of monogamy. Brigitte Vasallo illustrates the connection between sexual exclusivity and social hierarchies, suggesting that monogamy is seen as the only socially acceptable form of relationship-building and, like marriage, serves as a form of control aimed at reproduction and lineage (34). Therefore, it is evident that monogamy sets the foundation for marriage, as heteronormative marriage structures rely on monogamous relationships.

At the same time, any criticism of marriage as an institution must also consider its connection to capitalism. As Eva Illouz explains, until the early twentieth century, marriage was primarily about financial gain rather than romantic feelings, with people from certain social classes using it as a means to merge their fortunes (28). As marriage and the idea of romantic love became intertwined, there was an institutionalization of feelings and close relationships under patriarchal ideology (Herrera Gómez 259). Thus, as A.J. Macfarlane argues, "[r]omantic love is, of course, possible and present outside capitalism, but only in capitalist or capitalist-influenced societies, is it made the cultural pivot of the ideology" (36). As Alyssa Schneebaum explains, the concept of love has been employed in capitalist and patriarchal societies to persuade women to enter into marriage (100). Simultaneously, love has been marketed as a means of fitting into society, as it is tied to the human fear of solitude (383), a fear that is intensified by the media and exploited by capital.

Taking these arguments into account, it is important to also consider the more optimistic views on marriage, monogamy, and family structures, which suggest that incorporating non-heterosexual subjects into these configurations can serve to queer the state and challenge heteronormativity (Domínguez Ruvalcaba, *Latinoamérica Queer* 172). Katrina Kimport argues that while queer couples may fall outside the heteronormative ideal, they often conform to preexisting patterns and do not necessarily change the system by participating in marriage (106). She contends that marriage itself is not inherently heteronormative, despite its history, and that there is potential for resistance and resignification. However, she concludes that this potential depends on how queer subjects interpret marriage and that challenging heteronormativity must include a critique of hegemonic heterosexuality to avoid assimilation (16–17). While from a theoretical perspective this might seem to potentially open spaces of resistance, it is still unclear how it might translate into praxis.

Michael Warner explains that, despite marriage being socially constructed, it is impossible to shed its historical baggage, as recognizing its social construction does not tell us how transformative or regressive it is (*Trouble with Normal* 127–28). Additionally, while the notion that queer individuals can resignify marriage offers hope for those adhering to monogamy, it risks further delegitimizing other forms of relationships (Kimport 128–29; Warner, *Trouble with Normal* 82). I align with Butler, who argues that even within a progressive sexual movement that supports marriage as an option, the notion that it—and by extension, monogamy—"should become the only way to sanction or legitimate sexuality is unacceptably conservative" ("Is Kinship" 21). Consequently, considering both optimistic and critical views on marriage and monogamy—and although state recognition of *cuir* couples can extend rights to disenfranchised individuals—I contend that it is crucial to look beyond normative relationship structures. Thus, while an absolute rejection of marriage risks replicating the conservative discourse that aims to exclude *cuir* individuals from state legitimation, it is important to remain critical of this institution and not regard it—or monogamy—as the sole objective, but as one possibility among a range of choices.

Marriage Equality in Mexico

Alongside the political and social struggles surrounding marriage equality in Mexico, the debates about its implications have also been addressed by LGBTQ+ activists, with many regarding marriage as a violent, patriarchal institution that perpetuates hierarchies. Nonetheless, even those critical of marriage see its extension to same-sex couples as a significant step toward securing broader LGBTQ+ rights (Beltrán y Puga 67). The push for marriage equality in Mexico began in 2009 in Mexico City when the city's congress removed the clause in its civil code that defined marriage as being between a man and a woman for the purpose of procreation. However, some activists have noted that this initiative was led by politicians outside the LGBTQ+ community aiming to implement more inclusive policies (Beltrán y Puga 56). Thus, advocates in Mexico have had to depend on coalitions of socially progressive organizations and politicians as a primary strategy to advance the expansion of rights (Díez 154).

Even though policy changes in Mexico City did not occur until 2009, the goal of marriage equality was first articulated in 1998 during the first Forum on Sexual Diversity and Human Rights, where LGBTQ+ rights supporters gathered to discuss policy priorities (Díez 153–54). This meeting led to reforms in the capital's civil code, including the repeal of a clause that equated homosexuality with child molestation and the introduction of penalties for discriminating against vulnerable groups, including sexual minorities, such as jail time and community service. Mexico City thus became the first jurisdiction to implement antidiscrimination policies (Díez 156–57). These laws created the groundwork for the legal movement toward marriage equality, indicating a link between the institutionalization of same-sex unions and the establishment of other legal protections.

Nonetheless, Mexico's laws are decentralized, meaning that protections are governed by each state. After the reform to Mexico City's civil code and the passing of a national antidiscrimination bill in 2003 that established the National Anti-Discrimination Council (Consejo Nacional para Prevenir la Discriminación, or CONAPRED), Mexico's Supreme Court ruled in 2010 that restricting marriage to heterosexual couples constituted discrimination based on sexual orientation (Beltrán y Puga 57). Given that most states' civil codes continued to define marriage as being between a man and a woman, lawyers and activists outside Mexico City had to file legal protections to secure access to marriage. This effort culminated in the Supreme Court's 2015 decision to issue a *jurisprudencia* (jurisprudence)—a binding legal precedent formed after five consistent court rulings on the same issue—declaring states' definitions of marriage in their civil codes unconstitutional for violating antidiscrimination laws (Beltrán y Puga 61). This legal milestone helped activists and lawyers combat discrimination across states, and, in 2023, Tamaulipas became the last Mexican state to amend its civil code to recognize same-sex marriage, thereby legalizing it nationwide. While many activists and LGBTQ+ community members in Mexico may not see marriage as a productive political goal due to its association with heteronormativity and the state's role in its legitimation, the legal progress made through marriage equality has helped to broaden acceptance of sexual diversity (Beltrán y Puga 64). Nonetheless, as I have argued, when this acceptance stems from an erasure of difference and a process of normalization, it risks sacrificing its critical and subversive potential.

Can Non-monogamy Be a Form of Resistance?

If we return to the idea that *lo cuir* can be a tool for challenging power dynamics and the underlying social, intellectual, political, and cultural paradigms around gender, sexuality, and identity (Viteri and Lavinas Picq 5), then we must also explore subversive possibilities in configurations beyond monogamy. Building on this, queer theory opens up space to examine "the discursive construction of normal, healthy, moral desire and sexual practices not just as a mechanism of disciplinary power, but also as a contested terrain of sexual politics" (Schippers 6). From this perspective, it is productive to expand our understanding of relationships beyond what scholars, building on Rich's concept of compulsory heterosexuality, have termed compulsory monogamy—the institutionalization of dynamics that compel individuals to engage in dyadic monogamous arrangements (Schippers 13). With this in mind, we must consider intimacy beyond the private sphere, as the idea that being part of a couple is the only path to a fulfilling life is heavily influenced by and shaped within the social realm (Berlant, "Intimacy" 286). As Berlant puts it, "[t]o rethink intimacy is to appraise how we have been and how we live and how we might imagine lives that make more sense than the ones so many are living" ("Intimacy" 286). By considering intimacy beyond the confines of the private, we gain a clearer understanding of the influence of compulsory monogamy not just on our sexual or romantic relationships, but also on our interactions with society and on counterhegemonic narratives.

In *Fraught Intimacies: Non/Monogamy in the Public Sphere* (2015), Rambukkana contends that when situating monogamy and non-monogamy within a framework of intimacy that engages with the social, we should resist categorizing all romantic or sexual relationships as belonging to one category or the other and avoid celebrating one while condemning the other as inferior. Instead, he suggests, we should challenge a rigid understanding of these concepts and view them as interconnected, representing only a part of the broad spectrum of intimate relationships. He identifies this dichotomy as a product of heteronormative beliefs, showing how the supposed contradiction between monogamy and non-monogamy reveals underlying assumptions (14). Using the association of commitment with monogamy and "fear of commitment" with non-monogamy, he argues that these concepts overlap rather than being entirely separate since they "are equally available to individuals living both types of lifestyle," which "suggests that this logic only *seems* central" (16; emphasis in the original). This recognition provides a broader perspective to better understand the limitations of compulsory monogamy and binary views of sexuality.

Within this context, we can incorporate the perspective offered by the above conceptualization of non-monogamy into the tools that *lo cuir* provides for dismantling normative frameworks, specifically those that regulate intimacy and desire through binary oppositions such as monogamy versus non-monogamy. In doing so, *lo cuir* becomes a lens through which we can critique not only heteronormativity but also the norms that structure affective and sexual arrangements. This aligns with what Berlant and Warner describe as "queer world-making," a process involving the creation of intimacies that "bear no necessary relation to domestic space, to kinship, to the couple form, to property, or to the nation" (558). In this light, Schippers introduces the term *polyqueer sexualities*, which she defines as intimate and sexual relationships that transcend dyadic configurations and, when embraced collectively, can help dismantle part of the systems of oppression inherent in compulsory monogamy (26). Nonetheless, she warns that as non-monogamy becomes more mainstream, there is a risk of missing the opportunity to develop poly sexualities that challenge, rather than reinforce, normative understandings of relationships (24). Thus, while compulsory monogamy favors dyadic configurations and stigmatizes alternatives, it is important not to idealize non-monogamies as the solution to the problems of compulsory monogamy.

Scholars note that simply challenging sexual exclusivity is not enough to subvert monogamy, as it only addresses one aspect of the issue (Vasallo 31). Rambukkana emphasizes the importance of recognizing not only the external critiques of non-monogamy but also the need for internal criticism, particularly one that does not ignore the power dynamics within non-monogamous practices (120, 124). He explains that favoring one model of intimacy over others limits our understanding, but by acknowledging how intimacies can be "privileged or oppressed in nuanced and intersecting ways, maybe we can start to formulate discursive alternatives to oppressive normativities in ways that actively seek to avoid reifying privilege" (145). Therefore, non-monogamies can help us to rethink social, sexual, and romantic relationships if we remain aware of their intersecting systems.

In the context of Mexico and Latin America, Norma Mogrovejo has been a prominent voice in the discussion of non-monogamy from a lesbian perspective.[2] She highlights the colonial implications of Western constructions of sexual exclusivity and views non-monogamy as a way for women to reject emotional and financial dependence, and to exercise freedom by abandoning exclusivity in desire, bodies, and relationships (*Contra-amor* 15). Despite her critique of compulsory monogamy, I find limitations in her work similar to those identified by Rambukkana, such as a lack of critical engagement with privilege in terms of race and class, despite her recognition of monogamy's colonial implications. As with *lo cuir*, discussions of non-monogamy are dynamic and continuously evolving, unlike the rigidity of normative relationship configurations. Their potential to highlight and contest monogamy makes them a valuable starting point for questioning systems of oppression.

"I Don't Have to Play the Part of the Liberated Woman": *Amora* (1989) by Rosamaría Roffiel

I begin my literary analysis with Rosamaría Roffiel's (b. 1945, Veracruz) *Amora,* deliberately returning to the origins of sapphic literature in Mexico.

Examining the text from a contemporary perspective allows us to appreciate its significance while acknowledging the changes that have occurred since its publication. As critics have noted, *Amora* is a novel of its time, aiming to establish a political feminist lesbian identity (Cañedo 64; Olivera Córdova, *Entre amoras* 8–9). Although the protagonist, Guadalupe, is vocal about her beliefs, César Cañedo argues that the novel ultimately portrays "the good lesbian," in contrast to the "perverse lesbians" depicted in works like Artemisa Téllez's *Crema de vainilla* (54). Despite the Manichean view of lesbian archetypes, Jorge Luis Gallegos Vargas points out that, when we consider the context of 1980s Mexico, Guadalupe is a woman who defies the constraints of patriarchal culture (80). For Téllez, Roffiel's novel serves as a validation of relationships between women—not only romantic but all kinds—and as a celebration of femininity that highlights and strengthens bonds among women ("A Chloe le gustaba Olivia" 178). While today *Amora* may be perceived as lacking in transgressive elements and too focused on normalizing lesbian characters, it is still a crucial text in the history of *cuir* representation in Mexico.

Revisiting Roffiel's novel enables us to explore sapphic literature through Ann Cvetkovich's concept of the archive of feelings, providing a perspective on the evolution of *cuir* women's writing and considering its production and reception (7). Despite its importance in LGBTQ+ Mexican literature, the novel faced severe criticism for its perceived formal shortcomings. Ignacio Trejo Fuentes dismissed it as a feminist pamphlet, criticizing Roffiel's lack of novelistic experience (Olivera Córdova, *Entre amoras* 126). Antonio Marquet deemed it "lethargically conventional" (*letargosamente convencional*) and "excessively discursive" (*excesivamente discursiva*), arguing that the story was burdened by tedious dialogues and a melodramatic tone that he felt the author should have avoided (83). Critics' focus on formal flaws illustrates a disregard for the ideological discussions embedded in the text through its characters (Olivera Córdova, *Entre Amoras* 127). This is also reflected in the difficulties Roffiel encountered after the novel's publication and the broader discomfort *Amora* elicited in both Mexican society and the literary sphere.

Released by Editorial Planeta in 1989 and followed by a second edition in 1990 (Olivera Córdova, *Entre amoras* 105), *Amora* was a commercial hit, securing its place as the third-best seller behind Gabriel García Márquez's *El general y su laberinto* and Laura Esquivel's *Como agua para chocolate* (Marquet 83). As noted in my introduction, despite its success, the novel faced censorship. Elena Poniatowska described Roffiel's struggles, complimenting her writing and noting, "You don't know how hard it has been for her to burst through that layer of ostracism, of rejection. For example, her books, one called *Amora* instead of *amor*, they took it out of bookstores, would not distribute it, would not circulate it, that was all very hard" ("No sabes lo difícil que ha sido para ella reventar toda esa capa de ostracismo, de rechazo. Por ejemplo, a sus libros, un libro que se llama Amora, en vez de amor, lo sacaban de las librerías, no lo distribuían, no lo circulaban, todo eso fue muy difícil"; 77–78). Despite distribution challenges, *Amora* was circulated through photocopies and later republished by presses like Pax and Sentido Contrario, and Horas y Horas in Spain (Olivera Córdova, *Entre amoras* 106). Deborah Shaw notes that, despite criticism, the novel's existence is significant for challenging heterosexual norms in Mexican women's literature and representing a previously marginalized minority (51). Critics' dismissal of the novel as a "pamphlet" reflects a male-centered bias in literary scholarship that remains present.

Amora follows Guadalupe, a writer who falls for Claudia, a younger woman exploring her sexuality. Living with friends Citlali and Mariana and working with a rape survivor support network, Lupe reflects on her feminist and lesbian identity and critiques patriarchal norms. Her ideals lead her to question romantic love, understood as a fundamentally—but not exclusively—heterosexual relationship model based on complementarity, along with the idealization of the couple, marriage, and fidelity (Mogrovejo, *Contra-amor* 15). Regardless of being criticized for its feminist stance, the novel portrays Lupe's struggle with non-monogamy in a context where men's infidelity is accepted but women are expected to be faithful. Although Lupe critiques romantic love, she ends up idealizing monogamy. I contend that *Amora* reflects both limited views on non-monogamy and a reimagining of kinship beyond the traditional heterosexual family.

Influenced by its setting, Roffiel's novel engages with the romanticization of love through Mexican cultural imagery. Lupe's views on heteronormative relationships are connected to what Monsiváis describes as "sentimental education" (*educación sentimental*), which uses media to shape Mexican identity and reinforce stereotypes about gender, sexuality, and race. For instance, he views music as an "accomplice" to shaping intimacy. He argues that dominant behaviors are inevitably intertwined with the rhythms, melodies, and life philosophies embedded in songs (*Aires de familia* 42). This is true for Lupe, as she suggests that for women to love differently from heteronormative standards, they must "[c]hange the *ranchera* songs and the *boleros* for our own music, invented by us and our partner. How I would like to get a spread in all the newspapers, something like an invitation to lesbians who still repeat the patterns of domination so common in heterosexual love relationships: let's love differently, without slitting our veins" ("Cambiar las canciones rancheras y los boleros por una música propia, inventada por nosotras y nuestra compañera. Cómo me gustaría sacar un desplegado en todos los periódicos, algo así como una invitación a las lesbianas que aún repiten los patrones de dominación tan comunes en las relaciones amorosas heterosexuales: amemos diferente, sin cortarnos las venas"; 33). This passage illustrates how the protagonist calls for a departure from the traditional *rancheras* and *boleros* that often equate love with suffering. Monsiváis highlights this dynamic, noting that *ranchera* music lets the macho express sorrow without losing his masculinity, as "sobs do not feminize, there are tears as virile as punches" ("los sollozos no afeminan, hay lágrimas tan viriles como puñetazos"; *Amor perdido* 91). Consequently, Lupe seeks to not only question heteronormativity and conventional views of love but to also distance herself from elements of Mexican identity that reinforce these stereotypes. Yet, as her relationship with Claudia evolves, she realizes that achieving this is more difficult than she initially expected.

From their first meeting, Lupe and Claudia form a strong connection, with the former sometimes acting as a mentor. During one of their conversations, the protagonist criticizes marriage as being deceitful, proposing that as people grow apart, they should become friends rather than suffer in romantic relationships (39). Her seemingly nonchalant demeanor contrasts with her unease when Claudia reveals that she is seeing two men simultaneously without feeling conflicted, causing her to reflect, "Each one of Claudia's sentences gives me goosebumps. What am I getting into, Saint Josefa Ortíz de Domínguez?"[3] ("Cada frase de Claudia me pone la carne de gallina. ¿En dónde me estoy metiendo, Santa Josefa Ortíz de Domínguez, en dónde?"; 40). Despite Lupe's vision of alternative approaches to romance, she finds herself resistant to non-monogamy. This struggle reveals how entrenched monogamy is, making any divergence appear anomalous or deviant (Barra Ruatta 41). Her struggle underscores the difficulty of breaking free from established societal views on relationships. In this regard, most critiques of the novel fail to recognize that Roffiel's character is not merely a 1980s feminist trope but a portrayal of the nuanced internal conflicts of human nature.

Claudia forces Guadalupe to reassess her beliefs about love. Despite being unhappy with an open relationship, she agrees to it to keep Claudia; as she explains, "Pensé que mi amor iba a cambiarlo todo" ("I thought my love was going to change everything"; 91). This acceptance reflects a move from a pragmatic perspective to an idealistic one, wishing to reshape

Claudia to meet her expectations and succumbing to the idealization of her lover. Furthermore, Lupe's friend Graciela reveals the troubling imbalance in Lupe and Claudia's relationship, where Claudia's male lovers are oblivious to Lupe, which the protagonist recognizes as unfair (91). Unlike discourses on polyamory, which stress transparency and consent among all parties (Schippers 15), Claudia's relationship with Lupe deviates from these principles because when one partner has more knowledge about the relationships than the others, it creates a power imbalance (Rambukkana 120). Claudia's relationship is unequal, as her male lovers are unaware of her relationship with Guadalupe. Thus, Lupe and her friends' critiques of non-monogamy reflect a misunderstanding of its possibilities rather than a nuanced analysis.

Even though Lupe consents to the relationship—albeit unhappily—Claudia's openness with her does not balance the power dynamic just because she is made aware of Claudia's other lovers. Rambukkana notes that while honesty is crucial in non-monogamy, it does not fully address issues with power and privilege (120). These forms of privilege are evident in Claudia's preference for men and her repeated claims to Lupe that she feels uneasy about being with a woman. She insists she is heterosexual and wants to marry a man and have children (93). Even as Claudia rejects monogamy, her bourgeois background and need to adhere to heterosexual norms lead her to favor her male lovers, despite one of them being married. This demonstrates the persistence of inequalities that ethical non-monogamy seeks to address, particularly when viewed through a *cuir* lens critical of cisgender male privilege and in the context of Mexico's acceptance of male infidelity.

The conflict with Claudia makes Guadalupe doubt her feminist principles and efforts to subvert patriarchy. She reflects, "At times, I think that I am not being coherent, that I don't have to play the part of the liberated woman. In the depths of my being there is a tiny voice that tells me that Claudia, sooner or later, will come to her senses" ("A veces pienso que no estoy siendo coherente, que no tengo por qué jugar a la mujer liberada. Lo que pasa es que en el fondo de mi ser hay una vocecita que me repite que a Claudia, tarde o temprano, le va a caer el veinte"; 118). Romantic love has been constructed through a series of myths that serve to sustain it and attempt to rationalize it (Flores Fonseca 288). Therefore, Lupe's struggle reveals that her efforts to subvert romantic love are undermined by her own acceptance of the myth of omnipotence—the belief that love can overcome any obstacle and should be placed above all else (Herrera Gómez 295), a notion she previously criticized.

In 1970s and 1980s Mexico, certain circles of feminist lesbians engaged with non-monogamy, meaning that these ideas were not new in militant groups at the time of *Amora*'s publication. Yan María Yaoyólotl Castro, cofounder of Lesbos, Mexico's pioneering lesbian feminist group, described her approach by stating, "Claiming that I am a woman and I love all women broke the mold of monogamy, the mold of the couple, of saying that she is my woman and no one can touch her, it breaks with private property . . . we question compulsory heterosexuality, monogamy, marriage and the family; that is, the four pillars of women's oppression" ("Decir soy mujer y amo a todas las mujeres, rompía el esquema de la monogamia, el esquema de la pareja, y el decir es mi mujer nadie la toca, rompe con la propiedad privada . . . nosotras cuestionamos la heterosexualidad obligatoria, la monogamia, el matrimonio y la familia; es decir, los cuatro pilares de la opresión de la mujer"; quoted in Fuentes Ponce, *Decidir sobre el propio cuerpo* 131). Lupe's feminist approach to romantic relationships, initially focused on equality and respect, contrasts with the Marxist and anti-capitalist perspectives present in other groups. These differences highlight her character development and the diversity within feminist lesbian circles at the time.

In the end, Guadalupe's embrace of suffering as part of true love reinforces the romantic standards that she originally critiqued. The novel concludes with the two women getting back together, as the protagonist explains that Claudia broke up with her male partners, "[n]ot because I asked her to, but out of her own will. She says that when she was with them she thought about me. That our love became an urgent need for her" ("No porque yo se lo pidiera sino por convicción propia. Dice que cuando estaba con ellos pensaba en mí. Que nuestro amor se le convirtió en una urgente necesidad"; 159). This sudden resolution highlights the idea that love triumphs over difficulties, even though Lupe suffered through an uncomfortable situation out of fear of losing her lover. The ending suggests that Claudia's non-monogamy was merely a phase of confusion or a lack of awareness that Lupe was her true love. Consequently, the text's approach to compulsory monogamy reveals how it does not fully grasp the potential of unconventional relationships to confront systems of oppression and myths about romantic love.

Amora and *Cuir* Kinship

Even though the representation and critique of non-monogamy in Roffiel's novel are flawed, the text challenges traditional family structures by emphasizing Guadalupe's relationship with her female friends. Through these connections, she builds community and kinship while creating supportive networks with others dedicated to feminism and whose values are exemplified through their commitment to the aid of rape survivors. The narratives of gender violence that Lupe and her friends discuss visibly affect them and reveal their frustration with the lack of justice for women in 1980s Mexico. However, contemporary readers might find these narratives uncomfortably familiar. As noted in my introduction, the organizers of the Marcha Lencha intended *lenchitudes* to serve as a means of community-building, but also of resistance against the epidemic of gender violence and feminicide. *Amora* predates the vocabulary for issues like feminicide, yet its focus on mutual support highlights the enduring relevance of feminist efforts against gender violence, tying it to the objectives of *lenchitudes*.

Latin America is facing what scholars like Rita Segato describe as a war against women. Verónica Gago explains that this concept does not refer to a conventional war but to increasing violence and systemic inequalities. She emphasizes the need to broaden our understanding of misogynist violence to include issues like wage disparity, financial exploitation, the criminalization of migrants, and the disproportionate incarceration of marginalized women, among other problems (65–66). In the case of contemporary Mexico, feminist movements have demanded justice and the right to safety for women and girls, especially as feminicide and violence have become common.

In 2019, seventeen-year-old Estefanía was raped by police in Mexico City. Fed up with the normalization of violence and the authorities' active role in attacks against women, feminist groups protested at the Procuraduría General de Justicia (roughly an equivalent to the State Attorney General's Office) by destroying its glass doors, spray-painting the building, and throwing pink glitter, a symbol that became an iconic part of feminist demonstrations. As Raquel Gutiérrez Aguilar explains, the glitter became part of a process of collective *acuerpamiento*, along with the emergence of the slogan *la policía no me cuida, me cuidan mis amigas* ("the police don't protect me, my girlfriends do"; 7). These events unfolded long after *Amora* was published, and the escalation of violence has called for more drastic forms of protest than those depicted in the novel. However, I contend that Guadalupe and her friends represent a form of kinship and companionship that remains crucial today.

To illustrate this, I turn to the term *acuerpar*, which feminists in Latin America have embraced in recent years. María José Méndez translates it as *giving one's body* and defines it as reflecting a commitment to collective care through a wide range of actions like protests, event organization, mutual support, and the creation of community (38, 46).[4] Even though this concept was not yet coined when Roffiel wrote her novel, her protagonist's bond with her friends reflects similar core feminist values. The work done by Lupe and her friends with rape survivors exposes their frustrations with authorities who show impunity, such as judges releasing rapists or blaming women for their assaults. Consequently, *la policía no me cuida, me cuidan mis amigas* proves to be relevant both in the 1980s and today.

In the case of Roffiel's protagonist, her approach to both independence and companionship through sorority is revealed when Claudia questions whether she spends most of her time alone. Lupe's reply—that she is not alone because she has herself and her girlfriends—shows her prioritization of friendships and self-connection (10). In this regard, Cañedo suggests that the novel presents various possibilities, such as Lupe sharing her living space with friends, that reflect alternative models of horizontal love and sorority among women (68). Moreover, Guadalupe's assertion that she is never truly alone echoes Cristina Rivera Garza's view that a feminist life is grounded in the knowledge of constant companionship rather than loneliness ("La primera persona" 173). Lupe's values and reliance on community are illustrated in her cohabitation with friends Citlali and Mariana, as she notes, "The three of us have formed a family and have made a temple out of our space" ("Las tres hemos formado una familia y hemos hecho de nuestro espacio un templo"; 24). By naming her relationship with Citlali and Mariana as family, Lupe echoes Kath Weston's idea that queer individuals use chosen families to "renegotiate the meaning and practice of kinship from within the very societies that had nurtured the concept" (35). The protagonist's creation of a home alongside her friends represents a rejection of traditional family structures in favor of her own *cuir* family.

Gago perceives a destabilization of the structures of obedience that are often present in the monogamous heteronormative family as a result of women's increasing autonomy and the waning image of men as sole providers and bearers of power (76). Even though Gago's insights reflect current social changes, *Amora* remains a pioneering work in challenging traditional structures, especially when considering the crucial role that the family played in the configuration of *mexicanidad*. Just as Lupe rejects *boleros* and *rancheras*, she discards elements associated with Mexican identity that conflict with her independence and values.

Despite its critique of traditional norms, Roffiel's novel remains closely tied to middle-class Mexican life, as Guadalupe often mentions food, locations, crafts, and elements of popular culture. For example, when describing her blonde hair and blue eyes, she remarks, "At least they named me Lupe and not Jacqueline or Jessica. Horror! There is no doubt that the conquest left its mark. And we feel so Mexican!" ("Siquiera me pusieron Lupe y no Jacqueline o Jessica. ¡Horror! No cabe duda que la conquista dejó sus huellas. ¡Y nosotras que nos sentimos tan mexicanas!"; 24). While Guadalupe's remarks do not offer a profound critique of race and class, her recognition of *mexicanidad* indicates its importance to her, albeit on her own terms. Roffiel's decision to name her protagonist Guadalupe is deliberate. By doing so, she engages with Catholic imagery and challenges the desexualized and maternal aspects represented by the figure of the Virgin. Hence, the author introduces us to a *cuir* Guadalupe who actively speaks about her sexuality and defies heteronormative family ideals.

The protagonist builds what Foucault refers to as a "way of life" in the context of queer friendships, which he argues can be shared by people of diverse backgrounds and ages and can produce deep connections that are unlike those found in formal institutions (*Essential Works* 137). Foucault posits that it is the concept of queer alliances characterized by affection, friendship, and companionship, rather than just sexual encounters, that most unsettles power structures. He notes that "institutional codes can't validate these relations with multiple intensities, variable colors, imperceptible movements and changing forms" (136). Though Guadalupe's friends are not all *cuir*, they are feminist women who avoid the institutional norms Foucault describes.

Lupe explains that their dynamic is "like having a family that you choose, that you love because it comes from the heart and not because you have to. Of course, sometimes problems arise, but there is always dialogue, ways to fix them. We love and accompany each other without the need to oppress one another" ("como tener una familia que tú escoges, que amas porque te nace y no porque tienes que. Claro que a veces surgen problemas, pero siempre hay diálogo, arreglos. Nos queremos y nos acompañamos sin necesidad de oprimirnos"; 50). By saying "porque te nace," Lupe ironically underscores that this love and kinship are *born* out of relationships that are freely chosen, rather than from the duty-bound nature of biological family ties.

Rivera Garza argues that feminist praxis involves existing alongside others whom we depend on, and that "no one has a room of their own if there is no house and, around and inside the house, a community that constitutes it and affects it" ("nadie tiene un cuarto propio si no existe una casa y, alrededor y dentro de la casa, una comunidad que la constituye y la afecta"; "La primera persona" 164). Despite *acuerpar* being a recent concept, the way Lupe's friends figuratively build their house shows that the need for mutual support and care has always existed, reinforcing the novel's relevance in addressing women's solidarity, especially as long as gender violence remains one of Mexico's biggest problems. As we grow increasingly distant from *Amora*'s publication date and continue to expand our understandings of the role of *lo cuir* in challenging oppression, the novel remains a crucial starting point for literary explorations of *lenchitudes* in Mexico.

"Romantic Stability":
Del destete al desempance. Cuentos lésbicos y un colado (2008)

Gilda Salinas's (b. 1949, Mexico City) *Del destete al desempance. Cuentos lésbicos y un colado* is a collection of short stories that defy conventional genre expectations by eschewing traditional plot structures (Bisbey 170). Instead, the stories often resemble *crónicas*, or journal entries (Madrigal, "Un carnaval" 95; Bisbey 170; Fuentes Ponce, "Los personajes" 62). Viewed as a whole, the texts form a continuous narrative recounted by a nameless first-person narrator who describes her experiences in bars and nightclubs as well as her relationships with women from the 1970s through the 1990s (Bisbey 170). The playfulness and humor of the book are complemented by its oral narrative style, which incorporates Mexican slang and expressions, along with terms specific to the lesbian community of the time, such as *libáis* for lesbians—referencing the popular jeans brand—or *ambientalistas* for women who are part of *el ambiente*, or queer circles (Madrigal, "Un carnaval" 98). The collection's title, *Del destete al desempance. Cuentos lésbicos y un colado*—translated by Bisbey as *From Weaning to the Digestif: Lesbian Stories and a Stowaway*—reflects its division into two parts.

In the first part, "El destete," the narrator explores the sapphic nightlife of Mexico City, immersing herself in pleasure and enjoyment with other women. The second part, "El desempance," consisting of the two final stories, employs the symbol of the digestif that concludes a satisfying meal. Here, it represents the protagonist's arrival at "romantic stability," or a monogamous relationship (Madrigal, "Un carnaval" 94). This section provides several vignettes from Salinas's work to reveal the narrator's views on monogamy. I contend that the protagonist's ultimate dismissal of her youth experiences and her reverence for monogamy as a sign of success contribute to the discourse supporting compulsory monogamy and romantic love as necessary for a fulfilling life.

A central element of *Del destete al desempance* is its portrayal of *cuir* spaces such as bars and clubs. Madrigal notes that Salinas documents a range of now-closed sites, making the protagonist a "nostalgic claimant of the spaces that served as scenarios for more than one anecdote" ("reclamante nostálgica de los espacios que sirvieron de escenarios para más de una anécdota"; "Un carnaval," 96). Therefore, Salinas's short stories create an archive of spaces significant to *cuir* women that captures the "ephemeral and unusual traces" (8) left by queer cultures, similar to Cvetkovich's archive of feelings. Set against the backdrop of late twentieth-century Mexico City, *el ambiente*, recreated by the memories of the protagonist, is defined by Anahi Russo Garrido as a queer environment "that is always lived as a collective experience. It is a circuit of sexual, symbolic, or material exchanges that meets in visible spaces associated with queer lives or in more imperceptible spontaneous places" (21). While Madrigal rightly identifies the protagonist's nostalgia for such spaces, these memories also serve to highlight the contrast with her present-day ideals of romantic stability. This portrayal renders these places significant only in the narrator's youth, suggesting they are at odds with adulthood and dismissing those who continue to find community in bars and clubs as failing to achieve a perceived standard of maturity.

Although Salinas's protagonist is enthusiastic about exploring her sexuality with multiple women, the shadow of monogamy lingers in her thoughts. This is evident in "Los años verdes," where she describes her youth as "[g]reen years, intensive sexual courses, the discovery of what it is and what it is for, in that regard, yes, very studious" ("Años verdes, cursos sexuales intensivos, el descubrimiento de qué es y para qué sirve, en eso sí muy aplicada"; 16). By calling this period of her life the "green years," she directly alludes to youth as a time when she could reject the expectations of adulthood, as she had not yet ripened or matured. This allows her to evade norms that seek to "discipline behavior and manage human development with the goal of delivering us from unruly childhoods to orderly and predictable adulthoods" (Halberstam, *Queer Art* 3). Rather than adhering to the structure of formal education, she is driven by her rebelliousness to excel in her exploration of sexuality, becoming "muy aplicada" in this area.

Meanwhile, Bisbey notes that the narrator's perspective aligns with traditional Mexican attitudes that categorize women as either chaste wives or mistresses for sexual enjoyment (174). This view illustrates the enduring Virgin/Malinche dichotomy discussed earlier, demonstrating that even texts that contribute to a *cuir* archive can perpetuate misogyny through the oversimplification of women by confining them to two possible roles. In Salinas's narrative, after experiencing a breakup with her girlfriend over her infidelities, the protagonist tries to change her ways. She explains, "I rented a tiny house in that beloved backwater town to prove the seriousness of the new me: a faithful and selfless little Mexican wife. I needed to tear off the label of 'take one free' even if the soap hurt" ("renté una mini casa en ese querido pueblo bicicletero para demostrar la seriedad de mi nueva yo: fiel y abnegada esposita mexicana. Necesitaba arrancarme la etiqueta de 'tome una gratis' aunque doliera el jabón"; 17). This attempt to radically change her behavior demonstrates that monogamy is a fundamental aspect of what is perceived as "normalcy" in relationships, with heterosexuality as its standard (Schippers 12). In the absence of a heterosexual relationship, however, the protagonist aims to replicate heteronormative patterns.

By linking monogamy with Mexican womanhood and selflessness, she envisions her transition into a traditional wife as a potentially painful cleanse, underscoring her struggle to conform to social norms. Even though a part of her is reluctant to change, she ultimately succumbs—and eventually fails to remain faithful. The character illustrates the double standard discussed at the beginning of this chapter, demonstrating how deeply ingrained the narrative associating masculinity with permissible infidelity and femininity with fidelity and selflessness is in Mexico, even within sapphic texts. By speaking in terms of *abnegación*, she suggests that women in monogamous relationships must give up their personal desires, showing a lack of nuance in her view of romance.

After her failed attempt at monogamy and selflessness, the narrator continues to see herself as playing a masculine role, reinforcing *machista* attitudes toward infidelity. This is exemplified in "Noches de vino . . . qué rico vino," where she reacts violently upon finding her girlfriend having sex with another woman. She explains her rage by saying, "No, I am not jealous, but I am also not an idiot, I said before launching myself with all the artillery on the intruder, nobody's guest, slut, treacherous and pantyless" ("No, no soy celosa, pero tampoco pendeja, dije antes de lanzarme con toda la artillería sobre la intrusa, invitada de nadie, facilota, traicionera y sin calzones"; 26). Not only does she physically attack her girlfriend's lover, but by asserting that she is not a *pendeja*, she implies a recognition of the deceit involved in infidelity—an act that she herself repeatedly engages in. Moreover, by insulting the other woman as a *facilota* and *traicionera*, she perpetuates the misogynistic discourse surrounding women's sexuality, particularly the tendency to blame the woman with whom a partner has cheated.

In addition, the protagonist's concern with her girlfriend's infidelity is tied to her own desire for sexual pleasure and control over her partner. This becomes clear when she again catches her girlfriend with another woman, but her reaction is markedly different this time, as she states that "[i]f the enemy is in your bed . . . clothes off and make room for me" ("Si el enemigo está en tu cama . . . fuera trapos y háganme hueco"; 27). Regarding this change in attitude, Fuentes Ponce suggests that it reflects a broader shift of the time, when *cuir* women sought relationships beyond monogamy. For her, the story's ending with a ménage à trois represents a move away from monogamous norms and a celebration of pleasure ("Los personajes" 60–61). While it is true that this openness within the protagonist reveals a willingness to explore her sexuality with multiple partners, her reaction to the second encounter differs because she chooses to participate in the threesome. By joining in, she asserts control, instructing the other women to make room for her rather than asking. Fuentes Ponce correctly observes that women of the time were open to experimenting with non-monogamy, as supported by Yan María Yaoyólotl. However, the portrayal of the encounter as a one-time, spontaneous event within the protagonist's youth suggests a perception of non-monogamous practices as associated with immaturity.

In "El cofre del tesoro," the protagonist engages in her most substantial reflection on relationships beyond monogamy. While at the club with a woman she's cheating on her partner with, she reflects on her desire to be with both of them: "Oh, how wonderful it would be if I could bring them together so that the three of us could be happy . . . why is it that when I am with this one, I miss the other one and when I am with the other one too. And I also said that because I was so wasted that I didn't even know which one I was with" ("Ay, qué maravilla que pudiera juntarlas para que las tres fuéramos felices . . . por qué será que cuando estoy con estra extraño a la ostra y cuando estoy con la ostra también. Y decía eso también porque la peda era tan honda que ya no sabía ni con cual estaba"; 91). This excerpt highlights two key issues. First, despite Fuentes Ponce's argument that the protagonist explores non-monogamy, she ultimately does not view it as a viable relationship option. Her desire to be with both women is framed as a fantasy that she blames on being drunk. At the same time, rather than proposing a consensual open relationship with clear boundaries, she continues to see other women behind her partner's back. Thus, any serious, transparent consideration of non-monogamy is dismissed. Second, as Bisbey contends, the last line in this quote reveals that the women are essentially interchangeable for her (174), implying that she does not regard her current relationship as serious enough to adhere to the monogamy she allegedly aspires to.

The final story, titled "El desempance," consolidates the narrator's series of vignettes, offering a reflection from a present time years after the earlier tales. The text serves as a conclusion to the protagonist's youthful escapades. Although the character is initially configured as the antithesis of the "good lesbian" seen in *Amora* due to her stories of sexual exploration, infidelity, and heavy alcohol consumption, Salinas's protagonist ultimately transitions into a character whose lifestyle is non-threatening to heteronormativity. At the same time, she distances herself from the tragic portrayals of sapphism, reflecting on how reading Radclyffe Hall's *The Well of Loneliness* (1928) made her expect a life of sadness. Nonetheless, she highlights how "[t]here was no such suffering, and if there was, I don't remember . . . solitude is a green tea after breakfast: the first cup can be kind of boring, but the fifth becomes a pleasure" ("No hubo tal sufrimiento, y si lo hubo ya no me acuerdo . . . la soledad es un té verde después del desayuno: la primera taza puede ser medio aburrida, pero la quinta se vuelve un disfrute"; 101). In this way, despite their differences, *Del destete al desempance* mirrors *Amora* in its triumphalist representation of lesbian characters who are proud of their sexual orientation, moving away from the tragic lesbian trope (Cañedo 55). Both texts similarly highlight independence and their characters' ability to find fulfillment in being alone as a symbol of self-realization.

Paradoxically, the characters in both texts achieve this state of contentment mainly through monogamy. Salinas's protagonist credits her relationship with being the source of her happiness:

Romantic stability was the key that allowed me to be born and grow in my profession, the lock that made me mature as a person and the door that taught me to share what I am and what I have, so that my partner can do the same with me; that is why now that we are about to celebrate twenty years together—with ups and downs and mild bronchitis, but on route at a steady pace—I turn my head back and I feel full.

("La estabilidad amorosa fue la llave que me permitió nacer y crecer en mi profesión, la cerradura que me hizo madurar como persona y la puerta que me enseñó a compartir lo que soy y lo que tengo, para que mi compañera pueda hacer lo mismo conmigo; por eso hoy, que estamos a punto de cumplir veinte años juntas—con altibajos y bronquitis leves, pero en la ruta a paso seguro—vuelvo la cabeza hacia atrás y me siento plena"; 104–105)

Bisbey argues that this alignment with sentiment and the idealization of monogamy signal a departure from machismo and show "the privileging of stereotypically feminine discourses (open expressions of love, tenderness, an emphasis on domestic life) over masculine ones (cynicism, braggadocio)" (179). These changes reflect the broader narrative prevalent in Mexico, where men—embodied by the masculine traits of the character in the text—view infidelity as natural. The protagonist distances herself from this perception in her shift toward characteristics associated with femininity, also leading her perspective to align with the notion that "true love" is the ultimate sign of success, a gendered ideal imposed by patriarchal capitalism to dictate women's desires (Schneebaum 112). In this way, the protagonist views romantic love as a panacea that extends to other aspects of her life, such as her career. This idealization contradicts her earlier view on solitude, which she finds appealing once she is in a stable relationship, as she knows that despite moments of enjoyable alone time, she still has a partner at the end of the day.

This is further evidenced by how the narrator attributes her transformation to her partner, whom she credits with leading her away from infidelity: "I thought I would continue like that until the end of my days because a leopard never changes its spots . . . but suddenly la Norteña appeared and began to fill all my voids and my desires to go wild were silenced all by themselves and left me with neither the taste of longing nor the itching in my grabby hands" ("Pensé que así seguiría hasta el fin de mis días porque genio y figura . . . pero de pronto apareció la Norteña y me fue llenando todos los huecos y se me fueron extinguiendo las ganas de darle vuelo a la hilacha, solitas hicieron mutis y no me dejaron ni el sabor de la añoranza ni la picazón en las manos tentonas"; 102). The protagonist's view of her partner as filling voids perpetuates the myth of the better half or soulmate, which is rooted in the belief that we become romantically involved with someone who is predestined for us—unique, and our best and only option—because they complement us (Flores Fonseca 288). In that regard, she falls into the imagined utopia of romantic love, which captivates individuals with promises of self-realization, plenitude, and perpetual happiness (Herrera Gómez 296). The abrupt shift between "El desempance" and the rest of the vignettes creates a sense that the latter belongs to a different text.

This contrast highlights the book's portrayal of sapphic life as a dichotomy between a life of excess and instability and the relief and joy of finding "the one" and settling into a monogamous relationship. "El desempance" comes across as a conclusion that reproduces the heteronormative trope of women needing to be rescued by a prince charming, though here the narrative involves two women, with one being metaphorically saved from a chaotic, selfish life. With this in mind, and especially considering her past infidelities and self-indulgence, the protagonist ultimately finds fulfillment only when she surrenders her individuality to merge with her partner, a common expectation placed on women. Although Salinas's text partly celebrates *cuir* spaces and the exploration of sexuality, its idealization of dyadic romantic relationships ultimately configures it as a celebration of homonormativity.

Queerness/*Lo cuir* and Motherhood

Family and motherhood are topics that often generate debate in discussions of queerness. While some activists and scholars see them as important for securing rights for the LGBTQ+ community, others argue that parenting departs from queerness, given its historical ties to patriarchal gender roles and capitalism. Much like my exploration of non-monogamy, rather than taking a definitive stance, in this final section I will focus on the representation of sapphic motherhood in Criseida Santos Guevara's (b. 1978, Monterrey) novel *Rhyme & Reason* (2008). Drawing from Halberstam's postulates, I argue that the text establishes a queer temporality that embraces what capitalist, heteronormative frameworks would deem as failure. Prior to my analysis, I will discuss key arguments regarding motherhood and queerness/*lo cuir*, and then place sapphic motherhood within the context of Mexico.

In her work on queer kinship, Kath Weston asserts that when we think about *the family*, we are not considering a fixed institution but rather a cultural category with the potential to embody either assimilation or subversion, depending on its context. She explains that LGBTQ+ families are "one element in a broader discourse on family whose meanings are continuously elaborated in everyday situations" (199–200). For those who see reproductive practices as capable of subverting heteronormativity, the idea of queering an institution like motherhood is viewed as a process that could "profoundly destabilize existing social relations, institutions, and discourses" (Gibson 2). Writing from the Mexican context, Sara Espinosa Islas concurs with this potential, explaining that, for her, lesbian motherhood questions the heteronormative understanding of the family structure as being inseparable from parental and blood ties (23–24). Under this perspective, sapphic motherhood would challenge the belief that a child can have only one "real" mother, a concept that Shelley M. Park refers to as *monomaternalism* (3). Furthermore, she explains that, given the historical roots of queer theory and activism during the AIDS crisis, it seems unlikely that all forms of caregiving inevitably result in homonormativity. If this is the case, Park asks, why would caring for children pose a particular threat to queerness? (19). Still, the inclusion of parenting in queerness is largely contextual, depending on whether these arrangements replicate the status quo.

The question of blood ties brings the role of assisted reproductive technologies in sapphic families to the forefront. Feminist critiques have pointed out that these advancements can introduce new forms of control and exploitation of women's bodies, particularly when intersecting with systemic racism and classism. These technologies have primarily focused on addressing infertility in heterosexual couples, with the aim of reinforcing, rather than challenging, heteronormativity (Tam 3; Vela Barba 196–97).[5] Moreover, they are typically accessible only to affluent, predominantly white populations from the Global North, perpetuating power dynamics that exclude marginalized groups and those lacking financial means. Despite these valid and crucial concerns, assisted reproductive technologies inevitably disrupt not only the methods of achieving reproduction but also our understanding of parenthood, especially in societies that view roles like *mother* and *father* as inherently tied to reproduction (Vela Barba 210, 196). While conversations about the diverse impacts, both positive and negative, of these advancements are bound to continue, they are valuable in considering how family relationships may be subverted.

Similarly to the debate over same-sex marriage, the idea of legitimacy pervades the discourse on queer motherhood and family. As LGBTQ+ families strive for validation and the expansion of the definition of kinship, they encounter the pervasive influence of heteronormative ideas about parenthood, underscoring the state's role in determining family legitimacy (Kimport 97). Scholars and activists have pointed out the risks associated with requiring state legitimation to define personhood, noting that this process often entails the exclusion of others (Butler, "Is Kinship" 17). However, others such as Nikita Dhawan have underscored the thin line between being critical of the state and falling into state-phobia, which she argues, drawing from Foucauldian thought, is conducive to neoliberal ideas that coalesce "critique of the state and critique of domination, with the state being characterized as the origin of all violence" (64). Dhawan warns that such state-phobia can unintentionally mirror neoliberal logic, which similarly rejects state intervention and authority, thereby creating an overlap between progressive critiques of state power and neoliberal critiques of regulation and redistribution. Thus, she concludes that rather than simply taking a stance for or against the state, the more complex issue is how to reshape it, considering that its institutions and policies are the outcome of various forms of governance (67). Finally, Dhawan argues that in many countries of the Global South, queer activists and scholars are fighting for the constitutional recognition of sexual rights, viewing them as essential to social justice. At the same time, she challenges the tendency of some queer theorists from the Global North to dismiss these rights as appeasement politics, which underscores a privileged perspective (61). This is a crucial point, as it draws attention to the need for acknowledging contextual differences.

On the other hand, if we consider Halberstam's notion of queer temporality, he frames the reluctance to integrate into dominant society as an act of defiance against patriarchal and capitalist powers. This becomes key when we acknowledge that reproduction is necessary for capitalism to continue, as this economic system relies on current generations to have and raise children to create the workers of tomorrow (Schneebaum 112). Thus, Halberstam explains that while not all LGBTQ+ individuals choose to live in radically different ways from heterosexuals, the appeal of queerness as a form of self-definition in recent years stems from its capacity to generate new life paths and alternative connections to time and space, especially in relation to (re)productive lifestyles (*Queer Art* 1–2). The various discussions around family and motherhood from a *cuir* perspective demonstrate the complexity of these issues—which differ depending on the context. For Weston, those who reject perceived assimilation "into a predominantly heterosexual society tend to identify 'the family' solely with procreation and heterosexuality, while those who believe that gay kinship offers an authentic alternative often accept at face value ideologies that depict chosen families as independent of all social constraint" (198). These differing views emphasize the complexities of queering kinship and the struggle to escape heteronormativity while relying on state recognition.

Sapphic Motherhood in Mexico

Lesbian activism in Mexico has intersected with movements advocating for motherhood as a right, most notably with the establishment of GRUMALE (Grupo de Madres Lesbianas) in 1995,[6] born out of the need for mutual support among lesbian mothers. While the group is no longer active, others have taken its place, with the Red de Madres Lesbianas en México being one of the most visible—and of which Santos Guevara is a member. In the case of GRUMALE, its members gathered to share their life experiences and to discuss and question heterosexual norms (Espinosa Islas 57). In legal terms, following the 2010 protections granted to same-sex couples, the Mexican Supreme Court validated the right of sapphic couples to adopt (Beltrán y Puga 59). However, similarly to the situation with same-sex marriage, the civil codes of several states have refused to amend their laws to make adoption accessible to LGBTQ+ couples.

In the specific case of lesbian couples, the non-birthing mother often must go through an adoption process to be legally recognized as a parent. In the event of divorce, judges typically favor the birth mother when awarding custody, reflecting how legal concepts of motherhood in Mexico are shaped by a patriarchal vision of the family (Beltrán y Puga 68). In a personal interview, Ana de Alejandro, also a founder of the Red de Madres Lesbianas en México, who used to be married to and had children with Santos Guevara, explained that the two had to pursue strategic litigation in 2013 to have her then-wife legally recognized as a mother to their children without undergoing the process of adoption. They were among twelve lesbian couples who went to the *registro civil* (registry office) in Mexico City to demand legal recognition of both mothers, successfully doing so with the support of lawyers and activists.

Interestingly, to avoid the adoption process for the non-birthing parent, the mothers utilized a procedure called *reconocimiento de hijos* (recognition of children). This is one of the oldest processes in the Mexican civil code, originally intended for fathers to legally recognize children they had not acknowledged at birth. By utilizing this process, the group of lesbian mothers repurposed a mechanism originally meant to "restore" the heteronormative family, turning it into a way to legitimize their families under the law (Vela Barba 203–204). However, this reveals how, despite the existence of legal devices for same-sex parenthood in Mexico, the recognition of these rights remains particularly challenging for non-heterosexual couples.

In chapters 2 and 3, I explored how the figure of the mother, particularly the *madre abnegada*, helped shape Mexican national identity by reinforcing the family institution. Despite significant changes in the composition of families at the end of the twentieth and the beginning of the twenty-first century, an "ahistoric" image of the family persists in various sectors of the population and in the collective imagination, partly due to the central role that Catholic tradition has played in Mexico (Melgar 94). Nonetheless, the battles between conservative groups and those advocating for LGBTQ+ rights reveal the tension between the influence of Catholicism and Mexico's status as a secular state. For this reason, even though many LGBTQ+ and feminist activists question marriage and parenthood as heteronormative institutions, some see legal triumphs as signs of the strengthening of the secular state established by the Constitution (Beltrán y Puga 69). Still, in the context of Mexican families, Lucía Melgar highlights that laws alone are not enough to change mindsets and behaviors deeply ingrained in cultural patterns, social customs, and norms (98). Therefore, while legal changes and access to rights are essential, the *cuir* potential of *lencha* motherhood lies in its ability to challenge rigid notions of the family as a patriarchal institution.

For Espinosa Islas, lesbian mothers in Mexico navigate two opposing paths: one dictated by traditional gender expectations and the other shaped by their lived experiences (26–27). I consider *lencha* motherhood as potentially destabilizing of the former. By consciously choosing to have and raise children without men, *lencha* mothers bring to life the patriarchal fear identified by Rich: that of men being marginalized and losing access to women. At the same time, they disrupt the concept of male lineage, which is intrinsically tied to reproduction and its connection to heterosexual marriage (Vasallo 34). In this sense, *cuir* motherhood/parenting challenges the patriarchal family structure, which is characterized by gender inequality and subordination to the father and traditionally viewed as beginning with marriage (Melgar 100). While these circumstances and the debates they spark evolve alongside Mexican society, examining their *cuir* potential in cultural production demands an analysis that sheds light on the tension between *lo cuir* and heteronormativity as a site of possibilities.

"This Idea of Yours of Having Children": *Rhyme & Reason* (2008) by Criseida Santos Guevara

Rhyme & Reason is set against the backdrop of these very questions regarding sapphic motherhood. The novel tells the story of Claudia de Samos, a young woman who, after studying Hispanic literature the United States, returns to her hometown of Monterrey, Nuevo León, with her girlfriend, Felicia, who is pregnant with twins they plan to co-parent. Cristina Mondragón notes that although *Rhyme & Reason* can be classified as a "lesbian novel" due to its themes, it goes beyond issues of gender and sexuality, addressing broader conflicts such as existential anguish (232). This angst in the novel is closely tied to the inner turmoil that the possibility of motherhood provokes in the protagonist.

Santos Guevara develops a character who is in a continuous struggle against societal expectations and her own wishes. According to Mondragón, in *Rhyme & Reason*, sapphic motherhood does not constitute a problem for the characters, as it is represented without any mention of the conflicts it might cause in the extratextual reality (231). While this interpretation is accurate in noting the omission of the social repercussions of *cuir* motherhood in the novel, she overlooks the internal conflict that parenting poses for the protagonist. From the outset, Claudia reveals to the reader that her decision to become a mother is not her own, but is driven by her fear of being alone if she does not agree to her partner's wishes: "And I meditated on it for a few months, I thought about it carefully and came to the same conclusion: lonely with her, but lonelier without her, and I accepted, I got into this business of having children, of growing up because a shitting burden needs an adult and not a human being nearing thirty, still feeling like a teenager" ("Y lo medité unos cuantos meses, lo pensé bien y llegué a la misma conclusión: sola con ella, pero más sola sin ella, y acepté, me metí en esto de tener hijos, de crecer porque un bulto cagón necesita un adulto y no un ser humano rayando los treinta, todavía con ínfulas de puberta"; 61). This fear of solitude, as Herrera Gómez argues, is one of the most significant characteristics in the idealization and perpetuation of romantic love (383). Simultaneously, it highlights the pervasiveness of compulsory monogamy, which plays a crucial role in the marginalization of those who are not part of a couple (Schippers 14). The protagonist is surrounded by an aura of alienation that, unlike the tragic lesbian trope, stems not from societal rejection, but from her own refusal to meet social norms. In this sense, Claudia represents the antithesis of individuals who seek institutional recognition.

Moreover, her reference to motherhood as the reason for her transition from adolescence to adulthood is significant. As Halberstam posits, the concept of a prolonged adolescence challenges the conventional binary formulation that clearly separates childhood from adulthood; hence, this narrative emphasizes a distinct transition marked by the adult responsibilities associated with reproduction (*In a Queer Time and Place* 153). Likewise, the character's view of the child as a "bulto cagón" illustrates how she subverts the characteristics typically attributed to women, such as the myth of the maternal instinct and virtues such as patience, tolerance, and self-sacrifice (Palomar Verea 16). In this way, the protagonist is configured in opposition to the mythical constructions of motherhood.

Although Claudia initially agrees to co-parent, as her relationship with Felicia becomes strained, she begins to have second thoughts, fearing the loss of her freedom (90). She thus associates parenting with a lack of independence. Fuentes Ponce examines how social views on motherhood have changed, arguing that what was once seen as an aspiration has now become an action controlled and decided by women—I would add that this access to choice varies widely depending on specific circumstances like access to reproductive healthcare. Fuentes Ponce concludes that the possibility of non-biological motherhood becomes a voluntary act that fosters affective relationships and obligations, thus potentially functioning as an act of empowerment (*Decidir sobre el propio cuerpo* 399). However, in the context of the novel, the fact that the protagonist agrees to motherhood not out of her own volition but to please her partner creates a parallel between her relationship and society's expectations of women, momentarily compelling her to follow "straight temporality"—one that follows capitalist reproductive norms.

Nonetheless, as her doubts grow, the protagonist begins to accept her lack of desire to be a mother or to stay in the relationship. This is evident after the birth of the twins: "When I saw Felicia's joy, when I saw her lying on the bed, eager to meet her offspring, I almost let out tears, and it wasn't some corny shock, it wasn't happiness, it was a vague and annoying feeling, a thick fog, a foolish desire to hide under the bed and never come out again" ("Cuando vi la alegría de Felicia, cuando la vi postrada en la cama ansiosa por conocer a sus vástagos, las lágrimas casi se me escaparon, y no era una conmoción cursi, no era felicidad, era un sentimiento vago y molesto, una bruma espesa, un deseo tonto de esconderme debajo de la cama y no volver a salir nunca más"; 157). The difference in the women's reactions is clear, and the birth of the babies only strengthens Claudia's resolve to escape the situation. Once again, she defies the norms that dictate that women must take on the role of mothers. As Marta Lamas explains, viewing motherhood as a "natural" role for women leads to the perception that those who do not wish to be mothers are engaging in an "unnatural" act. A societal need, such as reproduction, is imposed on individuals, and women who resist the notion that gender dictates their fate are labeled perverse, selfish, and sometimes even criminal (112). This can be tied to the construction of the *madre abnegada*, which Claudia refuses to embody, choosing to prioritize her desires over motherhood.

In her influential text *Contra los hijos* (2014), Lina Meruane analyzes how society's persistent questions of when a woman will have children, along with the naturalized assumption that every woman eventually will, instills in women the fear that, without children, they will always be perceived as incomplete. However, she argues that there is a thought even more unsettling to society: "that that woman has considered a convincing why-not-to-have children or that she is responding to her lack of desire to have them. That she is satisfied and even celebrates the idea that not every woman should be a mother, and that she declares herself a permanent member of that club" ("que esa mujer haya meditado un convincente por-qué-no-tener-hijos o que esté respondiendo a su nulo deseo de tenerlos. Que esté conforme e incluso celebre la idea de que no toda mujer debe ser madre y que ella se declare socia permanente de ese club"; 19). This fear, then, arises from the possibility that women could *choose* not to have children and, rather than feeling incomplete, might embrace childlessness as a lifestyle, positioning themselves as individuals who consciously opt to live outside of the frames of reproduction. By doing so, women challenge the constant societal messages that they must follow certain behaviors for self-fulfillment, showing an agency that disrupts the power structures intent on maintaining gender hegemony.

The novel concludes with Claudia abandoning her partner and children, refusing to conform to reproductive time. While this represents a rejection of normative expectations for women, it is important to recognize that leaving Felicia with newborn twins also reinforces narratives that permit non-birthing parents—typically men—to evade responsibility. Claudia's choice to leave after the children have been born places a significant burden on her partner. At the same time, it is important to recognize that social expectations are deeply tied to gender. While absent fathers have been socially tolerated in Mexico, women face far greater scrutiny and are quickly deemed "bad mothers" (Palomar Verea 19). Nonetheless, Claudia's lack of commitment and her inability to make timely decisions contribute to her characterization as someone living in a state of prolonged adolescence.

Santos Guevara offers her readers an open ending, where the protagonist chooses to live her life free of attachments. Claudia reflects on her future, stating, "Claudia de Samos, gentlemen, rules, wherever she walks, on her knees through la Villa or on the Cerro de la Silla. Yes, yes, they will say mass, 'I saw her at the Plaza La Silla, walking in Valle Oriente, betting at El Caliente drinking a hot Pacífico with her loser friends in one of those snotty cantinas where you leave ten as a tip" ("Claudia de Samos, señores, rifa, por donde camina, de rodillas por la Villa o en el Cerro de la Silla. Sí, sí, dirán misa, 'la vi en Plaza La Silla, paseando en Valle Oriente, apostando en El Caliente' tomando una Pacífico caliente con sus amigos fracasados en una pinche cantina de esas fresas donde dejas diez de propina"; 162). This excerpt highlights how she embraces failure after deciding to leave her family. She sees herself as aimlessly wandering and gathering with friends she also considers losers. Halberstam contends that heteronormative common sense equates success with the accumulation of capital, family, ethical behavior, and hope, while other, queer or counterhegemonic perspectives associate failure with nonconformity, anticapitalist practices, non-reproductive lifestyles, and negativity (*Queer Art* 89). This refusal to conform is embodied by the protagonist through her choice to pursue an uncertain path, where she avoids settling in one place, gambles, and embraces a life of perceived instability.

Moreover, Claudia's rejection of motherhood and disavowal of children are evocative of Lee Edelman's critique of the Child as a metaphor that "marks the fetishistic fixation of heteronormativity: an erotically charged investment in the rigid sameness that is central to the compulsory narrative of reproductive futurism" (21). Accordingly, the protagonist turns away from procreation, refusing to engage in the system of reproduction that upholds family relations as intrinsic to personhood and fulfillment. In doing so, she embraces the pessimism that frames *cuir* subjects as non-reproductive and therefore outside the status quo. For Edelman, this gives way to queer negativity, which resists justification, as any attempt to justify it would reinforce the supposedly positive social values it seeks to challenge. He contends that the value of queer negativity lies in its very disruption of society's definitions of value—such as reproduction, capitalism, and normative relationships—thereby making this negativity radical (6). With this in mind, *Rhyme & Reason* sets itself apart from the works of Salinas and Roffiel through its subversive approach to relationships and its rejection of idealized configurations that uphold normativity.

As I have shown, while the literary works I examine differ in their portrayals of monogamy and kinship, it is through these varied perspectives that they offer insight into how cultural production is shaped by these nuanced structures within the context of sapphic relationships. Some of these texts resist normative expectations, while others depict characters who engage in practices that normalize *cuir* representation. These approaches demonstrate a range of perspectives, and the significance assigned to them within these works underscores how *lenchitudes*, conceived as a spectrum of experiences and sites of enunciation, are influenced and transformed by both interpersonal relationships and their positioning relative to state institutionalization and social perceptions. Deconstructing issues of kinship and monogamy allows us to better understand how sapphic narratives contribute to our comprehension of *lo cuir* in the context of Mexico.

Conclusion

Lenchitudes Ahead

This study focuses on literary representations, yet there are other significant forms of cultural production that also shed light on the evolving portrayal of sapphic individuals and communities. In an era increasingly defined by social media, *cuir* people leverage these platforms to challenge the gender binary and heteronormativity. TikTok, in particular—despite its problematic aspects—has become a space where younger users interrogate and reshape identity politics. An increasing number of content creators in Mexico, including Marcha Lencha organizer Sofía J. Poiré, are advancing the concept of *lenchitudes* or popularizing terms like *sapphic* to reframe how we think about women loving women, offering a break from more traditional identity labels.

Similarly, as the film and television industries expand to try to reach and represent more diverse audiences, films such as Ángeles Cruz's *Nudo mixteco* (2021) and Astrid Rondero's *Los días más oscuros de nosotras* (2017), and the adaptation of Guillermo Osorno's 2014 book into a streaming series, *Tengo que morir todas las noches* (2023), provide critical material for studying the development of sapphic characters in media. Equally important, though often overlooked by scholars, is Mexico's comedy scene, which has given visibility to *cuir* women such as La Kikis, Ana Julia Yeyé, Adriana Chavez, and Alejandra Ley. The cultural shifts reflected in Mexican cultural production, alongside the growing representation of sapphic and *cuir* individuals, open up a significant avenue for future scholarly investigation and engagement.

By centering literature, this project addresses the pressing need to foreground women's writing in a literary landscape still dominated by an *editopatriarcado.* As I have noted, authors like Artemisa Téllez, Rosamaría Roffiel, and others writing about sapphic experiences often encounter challenges and prejudice, even from within the LGBTQ+ community. In contrast, writers like Cristina Rivera Garza and Valeria Luiselli have gained visibility, offering insight into the complexity of contemporary Mexican literature written by women and its circulation. This project brings these diverse authors into conversation, despite differences in their visibility, styles, and narrative foci, to examine how sapphic representation and *cuir* potential intersect with contemporary women's writing. Furthermore, *Lenchitudes* interrogates what these representations teach us about normative structures, including the gender binary, women's sexuality, and power dynamics.

My goal is to situate this book within the ever-changing LGBTQ+ community in Mexico. It is important to recognize and celebrate the activism and contributions of sapphic and *cuir* individuals, whose roles in history have often been erased by patriarchal and heteronormative perspectives. However, precisely because of the diversity within these stories, I seek to examine how subjects and social movements engage with and address these differences. As Mexico continues to be shaped by broader narratives of neoliberal consumerism, and as many are excluded from the capitalist appropriation of LGBTQ+ culture, I am reminded of the need to think beyond singular categories. These circumstances often lead me back to the *crónicas* of Chilean writer and performance artist Pedro Lemebel, where he describes feeling like *the other* in New York City's gay scene and sees *gay* as synonymous with *white.* Lemebel highlights that those in the Global South must find their own ways of naming and understanding themselves. In this spirit, I hope *Lenchitudes* not only links activism and literary studies but also contributes to the evolving body of *cuir* knowledge emerging from Latin America and its diaspora.

Notes

Introduction

1. I consider LesVoz important due to its contributions to lesbian culture in Mexico. Founded in 1994 as a lesbian feminist press and magazine, it has supported the distribution of texts such as Rosamaría Roffiel's *Amora* (1989) and reported on issues that have affected lesbian and bisexual women. Nonetheless, their social media posts reflect an active investment in violent transphobic discourses.

2. Although I am specifically discussing marches here, lesbian and feminist organizations such as Lesbos and OIKABETH have been working toward visibility since the 1970s. For more on the development of these organizations and the many others involved in political demands for lesbians in Mexico, see Adriana Fuentes Ponce's *Decidir sobre el propio cuerpo. Una historia reciente del movimiento lésbico en México* (2015).

3. In a conversation with Poiré, she recounted that the Marcha Lencha began to take shape after she expressed her frustrations on Twitter, prompting singer-songwriter Renee Goust to propose a Mexico City Dyke March. She also explained that Goust fostered collaboration with the New York City Dyke March organizers, who provided valuable planning resources to the Marcha Lencha team.

4. During my research for this book, I was able to interview three of the Marcha Lencha organizers: Poiré, Medina, and de Alejandro. Sofía J. Poiré is a Mexican activist who works on socio-environmental justice projects, while having mostly focused her activism on gender and sexual diversity. Ana de Alejandro is a social justice advocate and founder of the Red de Madres Lesbianas en México. Raquel Medina works as a graphic designer.

5. Throughout this book, I use the term *cuir* to situate my analysis within the Latin American context, while also engaging with scholarly work at the intersection of Latin America and queer studies. However, when citing or discussing scholars who do not write from this position, I use the term *queer*. For more on the debate surrounding *lo cuir* in Latin America and its possibilities as a theoretical framework, see Alejandra Márquez, "Cuir-ing Queer: Speculations on Latin American Notions of Queerness" in the *Routledge Handbook of Queer Rhetoric*.

6. Both *tortillera* and *tamalera* are slang terms for *lesbian* in Mexico. According to Zatarain Olivas and Nuñez Noriega, these terms stem from a perception of these jobs as placing women in the traditional male role of provider and associate them with lower socioeconomic status. They note the regional use of the word *tamal* (and its superlative *tamalón*) to refer to vulvas. Furthermore, they point out that the act of making *tortillas* and *tamales*, where the clash of hands against the *masa* creates a sound similar to applause, is linked to the sound allegedly produced when two women rub their genitals together (35–36).

7. In 2010, Berkins and fellow activists like Diana Sacayán fought for a national law in Argentina that would ensure personal documents reflected individuals' self-recognized gender identity, resulting in its approval in 2012. Their efforts were further realized—albeit posthumously—with the 2021 passing of the *Ley de Acceso al Empleo Formal para personas Travestis, Transexuales y Transgénero*, or *Ley Diana Sacayán-Lohana Berkins*, which mandates that at least 1 percent of the state's full-time employees be *travesti*, transsexual, or transgender.

8. All Spanish-to-English translations in this book are my own unless otherwise specified.

9. *Machorra* is a term historically used as an insult toward masculine-presenting women in Mexico, but it has since been reclaimed as a form of self-identification.

10. I use the term *feminicide* instead of *femicide*—coined by Diana Russell to describe the murder of women and girls due to their gender—to align with Rosa-Linda Fregoso and Cynthia Bejarano's work. These scholars seek to illustrate the shift in meanings that takes place when the term is transferred from its English-language use to a Spanish-speaking context, while also approaching violence beyond notions that equate gender and biological sex (3–4). They expand Russell's definition by arguing that *feminicide* refers specifically to the murder of women and girls as a consequence of gendered structures of power (5). In addition, *feminicide* better reflects the term *feminicidio*, widely used in Mexico. My choice to use this term is both a political and a theoretical decision, as it highlights the importance of knowledge produced in the Global South (4). Finally, Fregoso and Bejarano's use of *feminicide* draws attention to the particular realities of Latin America, where state complicity in gender violence is exacerbated by "the intersection of gender dynamics with the cruelties of racism and economic injustices in local as well as global contexts" (5).

11. In my conversation with Poiré, she explained that her vision of *lenchitudes* encompasses those impacted by the social stigma associated with being seen as a *lencha*. She noted, however, that the term's definition is not fixed. The Marcha Lencha organizing committee reflects this multiplicity, with Poiré emphasizing shared oppression as a way to focus on lived experience, while others frame *lenchitudes* around self-identification. Consequently, trans men may, if they choose, see

themselves represented under the umbrella of *lenchitudes*, a perspective embraced across these varied viewpoints.

12. I consider the publications and debates emerging from the Cuir Américas Working Group to be especially productive. This group, composed of scholars and activists, engages in ongoing conversation about knowledge production from Latin America and its diasporas regarding *lo cuir*. For more on this group, see María Amelia Viteri's "*Intensiones:* Tensions in Queer Agency and Activism in Latino América."

13. Because *Lesbian Death* is written from a US perspective, Sullivan critiques what they perceive as the failures of second-wave feminism in this specific context, particularly gender essentialism and whiteness. They draw attention to Finn Enke's argument that "in less than one generation, the 'second wave' became aka 'white feminism' and 'trans-exclusionary feminism,' and now, *1970s feminists* is often used as a shorthand genealogy of today's racist and trans-exclusionary feminists" (10). However, both Sullivan and Enke are careful to note that this immediate association risks overlooking the contributions of feminist, lesbian, queer, trans, and queer of color activists during that period (Enke 11; Sullivan 15).

14. *Sapphic* has been circulating in Mexican academia as an alternative to *lesbian*. My first encounter with this term in the Mexican context occurred in 2017, during the Tercer Coloquio Internacional de Escrituras Sáficas, held at the Colegio de México, in which I participated. However, the first colloquium was organized in 2010.

15. Although Sappho has often been embraced as a lesbian icon, her sexuality has been questioned, as it is presumed that she died by suicide after being abandoned by her male lover, Phaon. This narrative has led to her being embraced by women who do not identify as lesbians (Andreadis 17, 29). Therefore, the figure of Sappho provides a wider understanding of female sexuality.

16. Lesbian characters had appeared in Mexican film decades before the changes of the 1990s. In the 1970s, Mexican cinema was widely regarded as having reached a low point, with films relying heavily on nudity and sexual content to attract audiences. As a result, sapphic characters were often portrayed as inherently sexual in these cinematic productions. Such is the case of *Las reglas del juego* (1970, dir. Mauricio Wallerstein), or *El festín de la loba* (1972, dir. Francisco del Villar), starring actress Isela Vega, or Abel Salazar's *Tres mujeres en la hoguera* (1979). The hypersexualization of lesbian characters was also exploited by horror films, which frequently depicted them as satanic agents of evil, as seen in cult classics like *Satánico Pandemonium/La sexorcista* (1973, dir. Gilberto Martínez Solares) and *Alucarda, la hija de las tinieblas* (1975, dir. Juan López Moctezuma) (Mercader 9–10). These examples demonstrate that, although sapphic characters were present, these films were created by men and framed through the male gaze, bearing no resemblance to how *cuir* women perceived themselves.

17. Argos, owned by Epigmenio Ibarra, the producer of *Las Aparicio*, is well known for creating *telenovelas* and other media with a strong political and social focus. Argos began as a production unit for TV Azteca and contributed to the network's early success with productions like *Nada personal* (1996), the first *telenovela* to openly address politics and corruption in Mexico, and *Mirada de mujer* (1997–1998), which highlighted the injustices faced by women in a patriarchal Mexican society.

18. Roffiel has expressed an affinity for writers in the US, particularly black and Chicana lesbians ("Entrevista con Rosamaría Roffiel" 105), which is notable considering that "Chicana/o literature is [indeed] barely known/read" in Mexico (Joysmith 147).

19. Chicanas have been actively exploring lesbian cultural production and theorizing the intersection of sexuality and identity since the 1980s. For further insight into these contributions, see works such as Carla Trujillo's *Chicana Lesbians: The Girls Our Mothers Warned Us About* (1991), Catrióna Rueda Esquibel's *With Her Machete in Her Hand: Reading Chicana Lesbians* (2006), and Marivel T. Danielson's *Homecoming Queers: Desire and Difference in Chicana/Latina Cultural Production* (2009), in addition to the foundational works of Anzaldúa and Moraga.

20. See Elena Madrigal's "Ficcionalización de la experiencia lésbica en tres cuentos de autoras mexicanas."

21. Although Elena M. Martínez published *Lesbian Voices from Latin America* in 1996, it addresses authors from multiple Latin American countries and is not exclusively dedicated to Mexican writers.

22. For a more comprehensive list of Mexican literary representation of lesbian characters, see Ernesto Reséndiz Oikión's essay "Las lesbianas en treinta y cuatro obras de autores mexicanos." This piece is part of *Un juego que cabe entre nosotras* (2014), a collection on Latin American sapphic literature edited by Elena Madrigal and Leticia Romero. Although the project received support from the LGBTQ+ bookstore Somos Voces (formerly known as Voces en Tinta), the book was never printed and was instead distributed as a PDF file on a CD-ROM.

23. This concept is exemplified by Gabriela Damián Miravete in a piece for *Gatopardo*. In it, she recounts the 2021 ceremony where Cristina Rivera Garza was awarded the Premio Xavier Villaurrutia for her book *El invencible verano de Liliana*, which tells the story of her sister, a victim of feminicide in 1990 at the hands of her ex-boyfriend. During the event, writer and editor Felipe Garrido expressed disappointment that Rivera Garza did not explore the mind of her sister's murderer, which he claimed readers would have found fascinating. He then proceeded to list three works—all written by men—that he considered notable for their depictions of men who murder women: Ernesto Sábato's *El túnel* (1948), Jorge Luis Borges's "La intrusa" (1966) and Edmundo Valadés's "El compa" (1967). Garrido remarked that "the reading of these works will contrast, illuminate, and make more profound that of *El invencible verano de Liliana*" ("la lectura de estos

tres textos contrastará, iluminará, hará más profunda la de *El invencible verano de Liliana*"; quoted in Damián Miravete).

24. While I discuss *machismo*, particularly in relation to *lencha* masculinities, it is important to acknowledge that the term has often been used—especially in the US—to marginalize certain forms of masculinity. As Benjamin Cowan explains, whereas figures like Samuel Ramos and Octavio Paz considered the relationship between masculinity, inferiority, and national identity, US scholars sought to formalize the link using modern social science techniques. Relying on the supposed superiority of their empirical methods, they adopted the concept of *machismo*, giving it scientific legitimacy, which in turn pathologized Latin American gender and sexual cultures (609). In my analysis, however, I draw on critics like Matthew C. Gutmann and Carlos Monsiváis to contextualize *machismo* and its role in shaping Mexican national identity.

Chapter 1

1. While I use the term *sapphic desire* throughout this book to challenge the concept of *lesbian* as a fixed identity, I employ *lesbian* when engaging with Ahmed's arguments and the work of other critics who use this word.

2. For more on Dávila's influence on writers like Rivera Garza, Cecilia Eudave, and Guadalupe Nettel, refer to Carmen Alemany's "El legado de Amparo Dávila en narradoras mexicanas actuales" (2021).

3. Rivera Garza later expanded this writing practice into the concept of *desapropiación* (disappropriation), challenging traditional views of originality by integrating the work of others into her own as a form of dialogue. This approach views writing as a communal act and questions the idea of single authorship (Rivera Garza, *Los muertos indóciles* 91, 267).

4. This section references Sarah Booker's translation of *La cresta de Ilión*. Page numbers are listed in the same order as the quotations, with those corresponding to the English text followed by those from the original Spanish version, for the reader's reference.

5. Rivera Garza named these characters after Dávila's short story "Moisés y Gaspar," from *Tiempo destrozado* (1959).

6. Despite his boredom, the doctor does experience pleasure when one of the women anally penetrates him during their encounter. According to Lila McDowell Carlsen, this moment enacts both female and male sexual roles, which "corresponds with a shedding of phallogocentric constraints of being either purely female/woman or male/man" (234).

7. This uneasiness in the home due to an unexpected guest is reminiscent of Amparo Dávila's most well-known short story, "El huésped," from *Tiempo destrozado*.

8. Even though the novel is not explicitly set in Mexico but rather between the fictional Ciudad del Norte and Ciudad del Sur, some critics have suggested that the northern city may metaphorically symbolize the United States, while the southern city represents Mexico (Cruz Jiménez 76). Nonetheless, Rivera Garza incorporates cultural and historical references to Mexico, such as the inclusion of Dávila and the choice to name a patient who dies by suicide by jumping out of a window Juan Escutia. This is significant because Juan Escutia was one of the six Niños Héroes (Boy Heroes) who died during the US invasion that led to the Battle of Chapultepec in 1847. He is famously said to have wrapped himself in the Mexican flag and jumped from the top of the Chapultepec Castle to protect it from enemy forces. Therefore, while the text transcends issues of national identity, I find the use of the Virgin and Malinche archetypes useful when analyzing gender and sexual transgressions.

9. Although Antonia takes on a new name, Antón, throughout the text the narrator refers to her using both masculine and feminine pronouns and adjectives. In my analysis, I refer to the character as a woman to better highlight her reflections on gender and sapphic desire.

10. The issues of race and class are not deeply explored in this text and, as I have explained, lie beyond the scope of this book. However, it is worth noting that Antonia's fascination with urinals suggests a somewhat naïve position of privilege, given that many working-class women are often the ones tasked with cleaning them.

11. As with *La cresta de Ilión*, translated by Sarah Booker, all English quotes from *Los ingrávidos* come from its translation by Christina MacSweeney, and page numbers correspond to the English and Spanish versions.

Chapter 2

1. As mentioned in my acknowledgments, an early version of my analysis of Madrigal's short story was published in *Clepsydra*. I wish to note that, in that article, I mistakenly listed the title of the story as "¡Pantera, Pantera!"

2. The contributions of Chicana writers are essential in reclaiming Malinche "as a vital, resonant site through which to respond to androcentric ethnonationalism and to claim a gendered oppositional identity and history" (Pratt, "Yo soy la Malinche" 861). Gloria Anzaldúa, for her part, criticizes the association between Malinche and *la chingada* in relation to the space occupied by Chicanas. Contrary to Paz, she examines the racial dimension of turning Malinche into a figure of betrayal: "[t]he worst kind of betrayal lies in making us believe that the Indian woman in us is the betrayer. We, *indias y mestizas*, police the Indian in us, brutalize and condemn her. Male culture has done a good job on us" (22).

3. The Ball of the 41, or *Baile de los 41*, refers to the police raid that took place in 1901 and that Carlos Monsiváis called the birth of homosexuality in

Mexico ("Los iguales, los semejantes" 89). In it, authorities detained men during a party, with many of them dressed in stereotypically feminine garments such as dresses. For more on the event and its repercussions in Mexican society, see Irwin, McCaughan, and Nasser's *The Famous 41: Sexuality and Social Control in Mexico, 1901* (2003).

4. This will be illustrated in contrast with the characters exhibiting masculine traits throughout this chapter. However, a notable example is Sara Levi-Calderón's *Dos mujeres*, where the protagonists, Valeria and Genovesa, "are youthful in appearance, slim, extremely attractive; they delight in feminine rituals such as bubble baths, shopping, and lunching with the girls" (Duncan 75). Cynthia Duncan argues that *Dos mujeres* configures its characters as "lesbian chic," which she defines as the use of women to bolster male fantasies about lesbianism, resulting in their appropriation by men to fulfill their sexual fantasies (75).

5. The concept of the macho and machismo is a complex one, as masculinities in Mexico are constantly changing and are dependent on aspects related to geography, class, ethnicity, and generational differences, among others (Gutmann, "Los hombres cambiantes" 726). Nonetheless, Monsiváis explains how, although the image of the macho was key in establishing a national identity, especially during the Golden Age of Mexican Cinema, it became outdated and rejected by the middle and upper classes (*Escenas* 103–108). Despite the growing rejection of machismo, Gutmann explains that "whereas the beliefs and practices of many ordinary men do not accord nearly with this monochromatic image, ordinary men and women are themselves often acutely aware of and influenced in one way or another by the dominant, often 'traditional' stereotypes about men" (*The Meanings of Macho* 14).

6. The alleged inclusion of domestic employees as part of the family is deeply problematic and reflects the complex issues of race, class, ethnicity, and gender present in these dynamics. Regarding these close affective ties, Elizabeth Osborne and Sofía Ruiz-Alfaro explain that they "blur the limits of the labor relationship/contract," adding that this ambiguity can become "a threat to the employer's power, which they attempt to eradicate through separations between them and the workers" (7).

7. While many women in the United States proudly proclaim having once been tomboys, I have yet to encounter a woman in Mexico who would gladly admit to having been a *marimacha* in the same way.

8. By referring to *el club de Tobi*, the novel references the comic strip and later animated series *Little Lulu*, and, more specifically, the character Tubby (translated into Latin American Spanish as Toby Tapia), who was known for being a leader of the boys' club "The Fellers" (*el Club de Toby* in Latin America).

9. This same year, *lucha libre* as a whole was banned from being shown on television, a prohibition that continued until 1991 (Van Bavel 21).

10. *Albur* is the name given to the Mexican tradition of oral battles that, relying on double entendres and sexual innuendos, pit two people against each other to see who can outwit whom. While it was typically reserved for men, its

popularity eventually saw the incursion of women, with the late Lourdez Ruiz, *la reina del albur*, becoming its most notable figure.

11. *Luchadores* are also typically divided into *máscaras* (masks) and *cabelleras* (hair). If a masked fighter is defeated in a match, they lose their mask and their faces are seen publicly, which serves as an act of domination that strips them of their hero persona. In the case of *cabelleras*, the loser's hair is usually cut off in a similar ritual. However, in the case of Pantera, it is worth noting that she does not wear a mask, therefore showing that she is not hiding behind a masculine character but that her masculinity is visible both in and out of the ring.

12. Although "De un pestañazo" is loosely based on Amelio Robles, it does not aim to represent the historical figure. Therefore, the story uses both masculine and feminine pronouns and adjectives for the protagonist. To avoid arbitrary distinctions, I have opted to use the singular *they* when referring to Enríquez's character in my analysis while retaining the original gender in Spanish quotations.

13. Unlike Enríquez's character, who disregards government recognition, Cano explains that Amelio Robles earned the respect and friendship of influential government officials through his skills on the battlefield. This network was crucial for his recognition by state and federal institutions ("Gender and Transgender" 183). She also notes the existence of a birth certificate for Robles from the Civil Registry Office of Zumpango del Río that lists him as Amelio Malaquías Robles Ávila. Though this document is apocryphal and elusive, it demonstrates Robles's respected status among the powerful (188).

14. Another similarity between Ansiedad and Robles is their peaceful life after leaving the armed forces. Robles lived to the age of ninety-four and became a respected elder in his hometown of Xochipala, Guerrero, where the local school was named after him (Cano, "Gender and Transgender" 179).

Chapter 3

1. In the case of the *vagina dentata*, Raitt explains that she must be "neutralized by 'pulling the teeth' from her vagina or by killing her first and then remaking her as a nonthreatening, procreative partner" (418).

2. Pratt traces these *ensayos de género* back to the nineteenth century. Some of the examples that she uses are Gertrudis Gómez de Avellaneda's "La mujer" (1860), Clorinda Matto de Turner's "Las obreras del pensamiento en América Latina" (1895), *La mujer y su expresión* (1936) by Victoria Ocampo, and Castellanos's *Sobre cultura femenina* (1950) and *Mujer que sabe latín* (1973) (76).

3. In *Rosario Castellanos, intelectual mexicana* (2019), Claudia Maribel Domínguez Miranda explains that Castellanos was not part of the intellectual elite that Paz belonged to, although she was well regarded in the public sphere (77). For Domínguez Miranda, Paz's attitude toward women intellectuals of his

time was dismissive, as he rarely commented on works written by women (with some exceptions, like Sor Juana Inés de la Cruz and Josefina Vicens). She notes how in *Generaciones y semblanzas* (2006), a compilation of his body of work, he mentions only his wife, Elena Garro, and Castellanos when it would have been a grave mistake to omit their work. Following Castellanos's death in 1974, Paz wrote about the qualities he admired in her, none of which had to do with her intellectual contributions, but rather with her value as an honest and just woman (75–76).

4. It is worth noting that by the time Paz published *El laberinto de la soledad*, he was already an established intellectual, while Castellanos was a much younger student completing her master's degree. Therefore, *Sobre cultura femenina* was more of a point of departure and "clearly an academic exercise that worked through traditional male authorities, whom she soon outgrew" (Ahern 40). Nonetheless, I consider it important to highlight that women were indeed writing about their experiences in Mexico at the time. Despite the thesis's limitations as a first major work, Castellanos's defense of it was said to abandon all solemnity, causing her professors—Eusebio Castro, Paula Gómez Alonso, Eduardo Nicol, Leopoldo Zea, and Bernabé Navarro—and audience members to laugh uncontrollably at her intelligent use of humor (Cano, *Sobre cultura femenina* 32), showcasing the wit that would become a hallmark of her later works—a quality rarely seen in her contemporaries.

5. Although it is beyond the scope of this study, I would be remiss not to mention that some of the narrative works I examine tend toward an idealization of whiteness. While in this chapter, and specifically in the work of Téllez, whiteness can be associated with how authors configure characters as akin to the femme fatale, a study focusing on race in *cuir* women's literature is necessary and would contribute to the ongoing conversation regarding its role in perpetuating or undermining power structures in the context of Mexico.

6. For an in-depth analysis on the relationship between BDSM and *lo cuir* in contemporary Mexican literature, see Francesca Dennstedt's book, *Cuir Dissidence: Tracing Restorative Criticism and Breaking Bonds with the Mexican Canon*, Nashville: Vanderbilt University Press, 2025.

7. Although homophobia in postrevolutionary Cuba is a complex and often divisive subject that falls outside of the scope of my study, Alonso's short story reveals some of the fears and anxieties surrounding the association of communist circles with homophobia following state campaigns to disenfranchise homosexuals (Guerra 269) and the control that the government has had on *cuir* Cubans (White 3). In an interview with Jorge Cabezas Miranda, Alonso highlights her experiences in Cuba during the *Proceso de rectificación de errores y tendencias negativas* (Process for Rectifying Errors and Negative Trends) of the 1980s, which the author notes produced a sense of freedom of expression. This, she explains, came to an end after the 1988 beating and imprisonment of a group of dissident poets and the subsequent harassment of artists at the hands of the police, leading

to the massive exile of Cubans in the 1990s (160–61). For more on this subject, see Hamilton (*Sexual Revolutions in Cuba: Passion, Politics, and Memory*, 2012), Ocasio ("Gays and the Cuban Revolution: The Case of Reinaldo Arenas," 2002), Stout (*After Love: Queer Intimacy and Erotic Economies in Post-Soviet Cuba*, 2014), Lumsden (*Machos, Maricones, and Gays: Cuba and Homosexuality*, 1996), and Bejel (*Gay Cuban Nation*, 2001).

8. *Lolita* is still a controversial text, as some feminist critics see a lack of condemnation of Humbert's sexual violence and pedophilia (Patnoe 83). On the other hand, critics such as Eric Goldman consider that the novel "reveals the damage that a misogynist myth can inflict on a young woman" (102). I find it important to note these different readings of Nabokov's novel, which show the text's complexity, a characteristic that I find absent in both of the texts I analyze.

9. Information regarding this award, which now seems defunct, is scarce. Some websites report that it is sponsored by Novelistik, whose website has been deactivated. Their X account defines it as a community of readers, editors, and writers, but there is no other information that would indicate it is still active. An entry in the Enciclopedia de la Literatura Mexicana claims that the award was organized by Novelistik, Ediciones Quimera, Librerías Gandhi, and web news portal *Animal politico*, and lists 2015 as the only year when it was granted, although Pérez de la Torre's novel was published in 2016.

Chapter 4

1. For more on these ongoing changes, see Natalia Tenorio Tovar, "Repensando el amor y la sexualidad: una mirada desde la segunda modernidad" (2012).

2. Although I value Mogrovejo's contributions to the discussion on non-monogamy among lesbians in Latin America, I do not condone her trans-exclusionary stance, which she has expressed openly. For example, in an interview with Martha Canseco after the release of an updated edition of her book *Un amor que se atrevió a decir su nombre* (2000), she claimed that the feminist movement's support for trans inclusion has led to the erasure of the lesbian perspective. She added that "this queer tendency has also contributed to the disappearance of the lesbian perspective, and it turns out that the lesbian perspective is absolutely radical and questions a heteronormative political regime that is the one on which state institutions are based and this is why it is uncomfortable, very uncomfortable" ("toda esa tendencia queer también ha aportado a la desaparición de la perspectiva lésbica y resulta que la perspectiva lésbica absolutamente radical y cuestionadora de un régimen politico heteronormative que es en el que se basan las instituciones del estado y por eso resulta incómodo, muy incómodo"; "Un amor"). Thus, while I include her views on non-monogamy in this chapter, as noted in my introduction, this project stands against the exclusion of trans women and non-binary people.

3. Roffiel humorously queers Catholic saints by replacing them with notable women throughout the novel. According to Aralia López González, Lupe turns to a "profane pantheon" of figures such as Saint Flora Tristán and Saint Josefa Ortiz de Domínguez, along with playful invocations like the Virgin of the Perpetual Orgasm (304).

4. Méndez explains that although "[i]ndigenous feminists in Central America deploy the term *acuerpar* in ways that overlap with some of its uses in Latin America—particularly their emphasis on the *cuerpo* (body) that roots *acuerpar* etymologically—they orient the concept of *acuerpar* around decolonizing practices," especially in relation to land (46).

5. According to GIRE (Grupo de Información de Reproducción Elegida), an NGO advocating for reproductive rights in Mexico, many administrative entities that regulate access to IVF restrict its availability to married heterosexual couples experiencing fertility issues (Vela Barba 203).

6. The chapter of GRUMALE founded in 1995 had a predecessor with the same name, established in 1986 and cofounded by writer Nancy Cárdenas. However, the group eventually dispersed. GRUMALE (1995) kept the same name in order to establish continuity with the first group's work (Espinosa Islas 58; Mogrovejo, *Un amor* 205).

Bibliography

Ahern, Maureen. *A Rosario Castellanos Reader.* U of Texas P, 1988.

Ahmed, Sara. *Queer Phenomenology: Orientations, Objects, Others.* Duke UP, 2006.

Ahmed, Sara. *The Cultural Politics of Emotion.* 2004. Edinburgh UP, 2014.

Alonso, Odette. "Odette Alonso y Carlos Alberto Aguilera: Dos voces 'antagónicas' de la última poesía cubana." Interview by Jorge Cabezas Miranda. *Confluencia*, vol. 27, no. 1, 2011, pp. 157–70.

Alonso, Odette. "Un puñado de cenizas." *Con la boca abierta y otros cuentos.* Voces en Tinta, 2017, pp. 29–53.

Andreadis, Harriette. "The Sappho Tradition." *The Cambridge History of Gay and Lesbian Literature*, edited by E.L. McCallum and Mikko Tuhkanen. Cambridge UP, 2014, pp. 15–33.

Anzaldúa, Gloria. *Borderlands/La Frontera: The New Mestiza.* Aunt Lute Books, 1987.

Arredondo, Gabriela F., Aída Hurtado, Norma Klahn, Olga Nájera-Ramírez, and Patricia Zavella, editors. *Chicana Feminisms: A Critical Reader.* Duke UP, 2003.

Ballester Pardo, Ignacio. "Un acercamiento a la poesía homoerótica en México a través de Odette Alonso y César Cañedo." *Amoxcalli, revista de teoría y crítica de la literatura hispanoamericana*, vol. 4, no. 8, 2021, pp. 57–81.

Barra Ruatta, Abelardo. *Amores bárbaros: El poliamor y el asedio a la monogamia patriarcal.* Prometeo Libros, 2021.

Barrera, Reyna. *Sandra, secreto amor.* Plaza y Valdés, 2001.

Bartra, Roger. *La jaula de la melancolía.* 1986. Random House, 2007.

Beltrán y Puga, Ana. "El laberinto del amor: el matrimonio entre personas del mismo sexo y la movilización LGBTI en México." *Acción colectiva e incidencia LGBT en México*, edited by Carlos Arturo Martínez Carmona and Alejandro Natal Martínez. El Colegio Mexiquense, 2021, pp. 53–77.

Benjamin, Jessica. "Master and Slave: The Fantasy of Erotic Domination." *Powers of Desire*, edited by Ann Snitow, Christine Stansell, and Sharon Thompson. Monthly Review Press, 1983, pp. 280–99.

Berkins, Lohana. "Travestis. Una identidad política." *Hemispheric Institute*, hemisphericinstitute.org/es/emisferica-42/4-2-review-essays/lohana-berkins.html#_edn1. Accessed 3 May 2023.

Berlant, Lauren. *Desire/Love*. Punctum Books, 2012.

Berlant, Lauren. "Intimacy: A Special Issue." *Critical Inquiry*, vol. 24, no. 2, 1998, pp. 281–88.

Berlant, Lauren, and Michael Warner. "Sex in Public." *Critical Inquiry*, vol. 24, no. 2, 1998, pp. 547–66.

Bing, Jane M., and Victoria L. Bergvall. "The Question of Questions: Beyond Binary Thinking." *Rethinking Language and Gender Research: Theory and Practice*, edited by Jane M. Bing and Victoria L. Bergvall. Routledge, 1996, pp. 1–30.

Bisbey, Brandon P. *Between Camp and Cursi: Humor and Homosexuality in Contemporary Mexican Narrative*. State U of New York P, 2022.

Blanco-Cano, Rosana. "Intimacy, Lesbian Desire, and Representation in Contemporary Mexican Film: *Así del precipicio*." *Intimacies and Cultural Change: Perspectives on Contemporary Mexico*, edited by Daniel Nehring, Rosario Esteinou, and Emmanuel Alvarado. Ashgate Publishing Limited, 2014, pp. 57–76.

Bond Stockton, Kathryn. *The Queer Child: On Growing Sideways in the Twentieth Century*. Duke UP, 2009.

Booker, Sarah. "On Meditation and Fragmentation: The Translator in Valeria Luiselli's *Los ingrávidos*." *Revista Canadiense de Estudios Hispánicos*, vol. 41, no. 2, 2017, pp. 273–95.

Bornay, Erika. *Las hijas de Lilith*. Ediciones Cátedra, 1995.

Bourdieu, Pierre. *La dominación masculina*. 1998. Translated by Joaquín Jordá. Anagrama, 2000.

Breckenridge, Janis. "Plotting Lesbian Desire: Self-Conscious Storytelling and Female Homoeroticism." *Letras Femeninas*, vol. 36, no. 1, 2010, pp. 141–59.

Burgueño Duarte, Luz Berthila, and Laura Sánchez González. "Feminicidios de mujeres trans en México." *Intersticios Sociales*, no. 25, 2023, pp. 115–45.

Butler, Judith. *Gender Trouble: Feminism and the Subversion of Identity*. Routledge, 1990.

Butler, Judith. "Is Kinship Always Already Heterosexual?" *Differences: A Journal of Feminist Cultural Studies*, vol. 12, no. 1, 2002, pp. 14–44.

Calasso, Roberto. *La locura que viene de las ninfas*. Translated by Teresa Ramírez Vadillo and Valerio Negri Previo. Sexto Piso, 2008.

Cano, Gabriela. "Gender and Transgender in the Mexican Revolution: The Shifting Memory of Amelio Robles." *Women Warriors and National Heroes: Global Histories*, edited by Joan Judge, Adrian Shubert, and Boyd Cothran. Bloomsbury, 2020, pp. 179–96.

Cano, Gabriela. "*Sobre cultura femenina* de Rosario Castellanos." Fondo de Cultura Económica, 2005, pp. 9–34.

Cano, Gabriela. "¿Qué hay detrás de las siglas LGBTTTIQ?" *Revista de la Universidad de México*, no. 846, 2019, pp. 6–10.

Cano, Gabriela. "Unconcealable Realities of Desire: Amelio Robles's (Transgender) Masculinity in the Mexican Revolution." Olcott, Vaughan, and Cano, pp. 35–56.

Cañedo, César. "*Amora* y *Crema de vainilla*, momentos clave de la novela lésbica mexicana en 25 años." *Interdisciplina*, vol. 10, no. 27, 2022, 53–78.

Cárdenas Pérez, Ricardo. *Género, poder y lucha libre femenil en el México contemporáneo*. Universidad de la Ciénega del Estado de Michoacán de Ocampo, 2020.

Cárdenas Pérez, Ricardo. "Representaciones y roles femeninos en el cine mexicano de luchadoras." *Balajú, revista de cultura y comunicación*, no. 7, vol. 4, 2017, pp. 37–59.

Carrillo, Héctor. *Pathways of Desire: The Sexual Migration of Mexican Gay Men*. U of Chicago P, 2017.

Carrillo Juárez, Carmen Dolores. *Amparo Dávila en su proceso de recepción*. Ediciones Eón, 2023.

Castañeda, Marina. *La experiencia homosexual*. Paidós, 1999.

Castellanos, Rosario. *Mujer que sabe latín . . .* 1973. Fondo de Cultura Económica, 1984.

Castellanos, Rosario. *Sobre cultura femenina*. 1950. Fondo de Cultura Económica, 2005.

Castillo, Debra A. *Easy Women: Sex and Gender in Modern Mexican Fiction*. U of Minnesota P, 1998.

Cázares, Nancy. "Feminismo Transexcluyente. Crece descontento ante realización de foro transodiante en la UNAM." *La Izquierda Diario*, 25 March 2022, laizquierdadiario.mx/Crece-descontento-ante-realizacion-de-foro-transodiante-en-la-UNAM. Accessed 23 July 2023.

Ciasullo, Ann M. "Making Her (In)Visible: Cultural Representations of Lesbianism and the Lesbian Body in the 1990s." *Feminist Studies*, no. 27, vol. 3, 2001, pp. 577–608.

Clavel, Ana. *A la sombra de los deseos en flor: ensayos sobre la fuerza metafórica del deseo*. Universidad Autónoma de la Ciudad de México, 2008.

Clavel, Ana. *Cuerpo náufrago*. Alfaguara, 2005.

"Comunicado Conjunto 102/2022." Secretaría del Trabajo y Previsión Social, 11 December 2022, gob.mx/stps/prensa/en-2023-mexico-superara-el-promedio-de-los-salarios-minimos-en-america-latina. Accessed 22 January 2023.

Connell, R.W. *Gender and Power: Society, the Person, and Sexual Politics*. Stanford UP, 1987.

Connell, R.W. *Masculinities*. U of California P, 1995.

Cowan, Benjamin Arthur. "How Machismo Got Its Spurs—in English." *Latin American Research Review*, vol. 52, no. 4, 2017, pp. 606–22.

Craig, Traci, and Jessica LaCroix. "Tomboy as Protective Identity." *Journal of Lesbian Studies* no. 15, vol. 4, 2011, pp. 450–65.

Cruz Jiménez, María Encarnación. "Transgresiones de tiempo y espacio en *La cresta de Ilión* de Cristina Rivera Garza." *Explicación de Textos Literarios*, vol. 36, no. 1–2, 2007, pp. 65–77.

Cvetkovich, Ann. *An Archive of Feelings: Trauma, Sexuality, and Lesbian Public Cultures*. Duke UP, 2003.

Damián Miravete, Gabriela. "Contra el patriarcado editorial: otras formas de escribir y leer." *Gatopardo*, 8 August 2022, gatopardo.com/arte-y-cultura/libros/cristina-rivera-garza/. Accessed 7 June 2023.

De Alejandro, Ana. Interview. Conducted by author. 9 August 2023.

De la Mora, Sergio. "Fascinating Machismo: Toward an Unmasking of Heterosexual Masculinity in Arturo Ripstein's *El lugar sin límites*." *Journal of Film and Video*, no. 44, vol. 3, 1992, pp. 83–104.

De la Mora, Sergio. "Response to Chapter Five: The Lessons of Chicana Lesbian Fictions and Theories." Arredondo et al., pp. 178–83.

De la Mora, Sergio. "*Roma*: Reparation Versus Exploitation." *Film Quarterly*, vol. 72, no. 4, 2019, pp. 46–53.

Dennstedt, Francesca. "'Between Utopian Longings and Everyday Failures': Imagining a Latin American Cuir Future." *Arizona Journal of Hispanic Cultural Studies*, vol. 22, 2018, pp. 29–47.

Dhawan, Nikita. "Homonationalism and State-Phobia: The Postcolonial Predicament of Queering Modernities." Viteri and Lavinas Picq, pp. 51–68.

Díez, Jordi. *The Politics of Gay Marriage in Latin America: Argentina, Chile, and Mexico*. Cambridge UP, 2015.

Doane, Mary Ann. *Femmes Fatales: Feminism, Film Theory, Psychoanalysis*. Routledge, 1991.

Domínguez Miranda, Claudia Maribel. *Rosario Castellanos, intelectual mexicana*. Universidad Autónoma Metropolitana, 2019.

Domínguez Ruvalcaba, Héctor. *Latinoamérica Queer*. Translated by Sonia Verjovsky Paul. Editorial Ariel, 2019.

Domínguez Ruvalcaba, Héctor. *Modernity and the Nation in Mexican Representations of Masculinity: From Sensuality to Bloodshed*. Palgrave Macmillan, 2007.

Doucet, Pauline. "*Cuerpo náufrago* de Ana Clavel: Iniciación a la virilidad, entre reproducción y deconstrucción de las nociones de género." *Revell*, vol. 3, no. 20, 2018, pp. 52–77.

Driscoll Lynch, Joan. "Incest Discourse and Cinematic Representation." *Journal of Film and Video*, vol. 54, no. 2/3, 2002, pp. 43–55.

Duggan, Lisa. "The New Homonormativity: The Sexual Politics of Neoliberalism." *Materializing Democracy: Toward a Revitalized Cultural Politics*, edited by Russ Castronovo and Dana D. Nelson. Duke UP, 2002, pp. 175–94.

Duncan, Cynthia. "Eroticism and Sexual Transgression in '*Dos mujeres* and *Amora*': Shaping the Voice of Lesbian Fiction in Mexico." *Confluencia*, vol. 26, no. 2, 2011, pp. 72–84.

Echenberg, Margo. "Rosario Castellanos Pushes the Boundaries in *Sobre cultura femenina*." *Hispanófila*, vol. 190, 2020, pp. 3–19.

Edelman, Lee. *No Future: Queer Theory and the Death Drive*. Duke UP, 2004.

"El INBAL rendirá homenaje a la escritora Iliana Godoy." Secretaría de Cultura de México, 19 Feb. 2020. Press release. Accessed 10 May 2024.

"Ella Mexico 2021 Program." *Ella Mexico Lesbian Festival*, ellafestivalmexico.com/program. Accessed 2 January 2022.

"Ella Festival Partners." *Ella International Lesbian Festival*, ellafestival.com/partners/. Accessed 2 January 2022.

Enke, Finn. "Collective Memory and the Transfeminist 1970s." *Transgender Studies Quarterly*, vol. 5, no. 1, 2018, pp. 9–29.

Enríquez, Victoria. "De un pestañazo." *Con fugitivo paso*. Candy Ediciones, 1997, pp. 69–81.

Epps, Brad. "Retos, riesgos, pautas y promesas de la teoría queer." *Revista Iberoamericana*, vol. 74, no. 225, 2008, pp. 897–920.

Erazo, Adrienne. "Blurring Borders: Construction of Narrative and Gender in Ana Clavel's *Cuerpo náufrago*." *Chasqui*, vol. 46, no. 2, 2017, pp. 227–40.

Espinosa Islas, Sara. *Madres lesbianas. Una mirada a las maternidades y familias lésbicas en México*. Egales, 2007.

Espinoza Romo, Alejandra Viridiana, Fredi Everardo Correa Romero, and Luis Felipe García y Barragán. "Percepción social de la infidelidad y estilos de amor en la pareja." *Enseñanza e Investigación en Psicología*, vol. 19, no. 1, 2014, pp. 135–47.

Esquibel Rueda, Catrióna. *With Her Machete in Her Hand: Reading Chicana Lesbians*. U of Texas P, 2006.

Estrada, Oswaldo. "Against Representation: Women's Writing in Contemporary Mexico." *Hispanófila*, no. 157, 2009, pp. 63–78.

Estrada, Oswaldo. "Asignaciones de género y tareas de identidad en la narrativa de Cristina Rivera Garza." *Cristina Rivera Garza. Ningún crítico cuenta esto . . .*, edited by Oswaldo Estrada. Ediciones Eón, 2010, pp. 179–201.

Estrada, Oswaldo. *Ser mujer y estar presente*. Universidad Nacional Autónoma de México, 2014.

Faderman, Lillian. "The Return of Butch and Femme: A Phenomenon in Lesbian Sexuality of the 1980s and 1990s." *Journal of History of Sexuality*, no. 2, vol. 4, 1992, pp. 578–96.

Falconí Trávez, Diego. "Maricas y mariquismos. Aprendizajes y un esbozo." *Revista de la Universidad de México*, no. 846, 2019, pp. 22–27.

Farrimond, Katherine. " 'Stay Still So We Can See Who You Are': Anxiety and Bisexual Activity in the Contemporary Femme Fatale Film." *Journal of Bisexuality*, vol. 12, no. 1, 2012, pp. 138–54.

Finnegan, Nuala, and Jane E. Lavery. *The Boom Femenino in Mexico: Reading Contemporary Women's Writing*. Cambridge Scholars Publishing, 2010.

Flores, Valeria. *Notas Lesbianas. Reflexiones desde la disidencia sexual.* Hipólita Ediciones, 2005.

Flores Fonseca, Verceli Melina. "Mecanismos en la construcción del amor romántico." *La ventana,* no. 50, 2019, pp. 282–305.

Foucault, Michel, and Paul Rabinow. *The Essential Works of Michel Foucault, 1954–1987.* The New Press, 1997.

Fraile Gómez, Diego. "Homoerotismo." *Barbarismos* queer *y otras esdrújulas,* edited by R. Lucas Platero, María Rosón, and Esther Ortega. Edicions Bellaterra, 2017, pp. 239–246.

Fraser, Nancy. "Rethinking the Public Sphere: A Contribution to the Critique of Actually Existing Democracy." *Habermas and the Public Sphere,* edited by Craig Calhoun. MIT Press, 1992, pp. 109–42.

Fregoso, Rosa-Linda, and Cynthia Bejarano. *Terrorizing Women: Feminicide in the Americas.* Duke UP, 2010.

Fuentes Ponce, Adriana. *Decidir sobre el propio cuerpo. Una historia reciente del movimiento lésbico en México.* La Cifra Editorial y Universidad Autónoma Metropolitana, 2015.

Fuentes Ponce, Adriana. "Los personajes lésbicos en cuentos de autoras mexicanas contemporáneas." *Graffylia,* no. 25, 2017, pp. 56–66.

Gago, Verónica. *La potencia feminista o el deseo de cambiarlo todo.* Bajo Tierra Ediciones, 2020.

Gallegos Vargas, Jorge Luis. "*Amora:* El inicio de la literatura sáfica en México." *Dossiers Feministes,* no. 21, 2017, pp. 75–88.

Garber, Marjorie. *Vice Versa: Bisexuality and the Eroticism of Everyday Life.* Simon & Schuster, 1995.

Garonzik, Rebecca. "Queering Feminism: Cristina Rivera Garza's *La cresta de Ilión* and the Feminine Sublime." *Cuaderno Internacional de Estudios Humanísticos y Literatura,* no. 14, 2010, pp. 45–56.

Gay, Roxane. "Ugly Beautiful." *Lolita in the Afterlife: On Beauty, Risk, and Reckoning with the Most Indelible and Shocking Novel of the Twentieth Century,* edited by Jenny Minton Quigley. Vintage Books, 2021, pp. 49–58.

Gaytán, Marie Sarita. "The Rise of the *Madre Abnegada* (Selfless Mother). Sara García and the National Maternal." *Meridians,* no. 18, vol. 1, 2019, pp. 17–40.

Gibson, Margaret. "Introduction: Queering Motherhood in Narrative, Theory, and the Everyday." *Queering Motherhood: Narrative and Theoretical Perspectives,* edited by Margaret Gibson. Demeter Press, 2014, pp. 1–23.

Gil, Eve. "Arsénico y caramelos." *La dulce hiel de la seducción,* compiled by Ana Clavel. Cal y Arena, 2007, pp. 69–89.

Giroux, Henry A. "Nymphet Fantasies: Child Beauty Pageants and the Politics of Innocence." *Social Text,* vol. 16, no. 4, 1998, pp. 31–53.

Godoy, Iliana. "Baños de pureza." *Ritual de excesos.* Editorial Fontamara, 2005, pp. 43–56.

Goldman, Eric. "'Knowing' Lolita: Sexual Deviance and Normality in Nabokov's *Lolita*." *Nabokov Studies*, vol. 8, 2004, pp. 87–104.

Guerra, Lilian. "Gender Policing, Homosexuality and the New Patriarchy of the Cuban Revolution, 1965–70." *Social History*, vol. 35, no. 3, 2010, pp. 268–89.

Gutiérrez Aguilar, Raquel. "Prólogo a la edición mexicana." *La potencia feminista o el deseo de cambiarlo todo*, by Verónica Gago, Bajo Tierra Ediciones, 2020, pp. 7–10.

Gutmann, Matthew C., editor. *Changing Men and Masculinities in Latin America*. Duke UP, 2003.

Gutmann, Matthew C. "Los hombres cambiantes, los machos impenitentes y las relaciones de género en México en los noventa." *Estudios sociológicos*, vol. 11, no. 33, 1993, pp. 725–40.

Gutmann, Matthew C. *The Meanings of Macho: Being a Man in Mexico City*. U of California Press, 1996.

Halberstam, J. *Female Masculinity*. Duke UP, 1998.

Halberstam, J. *In a Queer Time and Place*. New York: New York U P, 2005. Print.

Halberstam, J. *Masculinidad femenina*. Translated by Javier Sáez. Egales, 2008.

Halberstam, J. *The Queer Art of Failure*. Duke U P, 2011.

Hall, Stuart. *Representation: Cultural Representations and Signifying Practices*. Sage Publications, 1997.

Hanisch, Hugo E. "El patrimonio en derecho romano." *Revista Chilena de Derecho*, vol. 6, no. 1/6, 1977, pp. 11–92.

Hanson, Helen, and Catherine O'Rawe. *The Femme Fatale: Images, Histories, Contexts*. Palgrave Macmillan, 2010.

Harris, Laura, and Liz Crocker. *Femme Feminists, Lesbians and Bad Girls*. Routledge, 1997.

Hart, Lynda. *Fatal Women: Lesbian Sexuality and the Mark of Aggression*. Princeton UP, 1994.

Herrera Gómez, Coral. *La construcción sociocultural del amor romántico*. Editorial Fundamentos, 2010.

Hershfield, Joanne. *Mexican Cinema/Mexican Woman, 1940–1950*. U of Arizona P, 1996.

Hemmings, Clare. "Waiting for No Man: Bisexual Femme Subjectivity and Cultural Repudiation." Munt, pp. 90–100.

Hind, Emily. *Dude Lit: Mexican Men Writing and Performing Competence, 1955–2012*. U of Arizona P, 2019.

Hind, Emily. "El consumo textual y *La cresta de Ilión* de Cristina Rivera Garza." *Filología y lingüística*, vol. 31, no. 1, 2005, pp. 35–50.

Hoechtl, Nina. "If Only for the Length of a Lucha: Queer/ing, Mask/ing, Gender/ing and Gesture in Lucha Libre." October 2012, Goldsmith's University of London, PhD dissertation, core.ac.uk/reader/17308260. Accessed 12 June 2024.

Illouz, Eva. *El consumo de la utopía romántica. El amor y las contradicciones culturales del capitalismo*. Translated by María Victoria Rodil. Katz, 2010.

Irwin, Robert McKee. "'Las inseparables' and Other Early Traces of Modern Mexican Lesbianism." *Confluencia*, vol. 20, no. 2, 2005, pp. 98–111.

Irwin, Robert McKee. *Mexican Masculinities*. U of Minnesota P, 2003.

Irwin, Robert McKee, Edward J. McCaughan, and Michelle Rocío Nasser, editors. *The Famous 41: Sexuality and Social Control in Mexico, 1901*. Palgrave Macmillan, 2003.

Joysmith, Claire. "Response to Chapter Four: (Re)Mapping *mexicanidades*: (Re)locating Chicana Writings and Translation Politics." Arredondo et al., pp. 146–54.

Kaminsky, Amy. "Hacia un verbo *queer*." *Revista Iberoamericana*, vol. 74, no. 225, 2008, pp. 879–95.

Kimmel, Michael S. "Masculinity as Homophobia: Fear, Shame, and Silence in the Construction of Gender Identity." *Theorizing Masculinities*, edited by Harry Brod and Michael Kaufman. Sage, 1994, pp. 119–41.

Kimport, Katrina. *Queering Marriage: Challenging Family Formation in the United States*. Rutgers UP, 2013.

Klein, Ana. *No hay princesa sin dragón*. Hoja Casa Editorial, 2004.

Lagarde y de los Ríos, Marcela. *Los cautiverios de las mujeres. Madresposas, monjas, putas, presas y locas*. Siglo Veintiuno Editores, 2005.

Lagarde y de los Ríos, Marcela. Interview by Nuria Coronado Sopeña. "Marcela Lagarde: 'Tenemos que decir no al borrado de mujeres diciendo sí a su existencia legal y protegida.' *Público*, 21 July 2020, publico.es/sociedad/entrevista-macela-lagarde-lagarde-decir-no-borrado-mujeres-diciendo-existencia-legal-protegida.html. Accessed 2 July 2024.

Lamas, Marta. "Maternidad voluntaria y aborto." *GénEros. Revista de investigación y divulgación sobre los estudios de género*, no. 6, vol. 2, 2009, pp. 109–22.

Lavín, Mónica. "Ladies Bar." *Manual para enamorarse*. Grijalbo, 2012, pp. 76–81.

Lavery, Jane E. *The Art of Ana Clavel. Ghosts, Urinals, Dolls, Shadows and Outlaw Desires*. Legenda, 2015.

Lavinas Picq, Manuela, and María Amelia Viteri. "Introducciones: Trastocar Narratives of Modernity." *Queering Paradigms V: Queering Narratives of Modernity*, edited by María Amelia Viteri and Manuela Lavinas Picq. Peter Lang, 2016, pp. 1–18.

Lemebel, Pedro. *Loco afán: crónicas de sidario*. Anagrama, 1996.

Levi, Heather. "Lean Mean Fighting Queens: Drag in the World of Mexican Professional Wrestling." *Sexualities*, vol. 1, no. 3, 1998, pp. 275–85.

Levi, Heather. *The World of Lucha Libre: Secrets, Revelations and Mexican National Identity*. Duke UP, 2008.

Ling, Liu. "Tragedy of Nymphic Desire in *Lolita*." *Frontiers in Art Research*, vol. 4, no. 14, 2022, pp. 67–72.

López González, Aralia. "Una profesión de fe: el amor. Recuperación de la escuela sáfica y otros alientos." *Debate Feminista*, vol. 22, 2000, pp. 300–305.

Lozano Armendares, Teresa. *No codiciarás la mujer ajena. El adulterio en las comunidades domésticas novohispanas. Ciudad de México, siglo XVIII*. Universidad Nacional Autónoma de México, Instituto de Investigaciones Históricas, 2005.

Luibhéid, Eithne. Introduction. *Queer Migrations: Sexuality, U.S. Citizenship, and Border Crossings*, edited by Eithne Luibhéid and Lionel Cantú Jr. U of Minnesota P, 2005, pp. ix–xlvi.

Luiselli, Valeria. *Faces in the Crowd*. Translated by Christina MacSweeney. Coffee House Press, 2014.

Luiselli, Valeria. *Los ingrávidos*. Sexto Piso, 2011.

Macías, Anna. *Against All Odds: The Feminist Movement in Mexico to 1940*. Greenwood Press, 1982.

Macías-González, Víctor M., and Anne Rubenstein. *Masculinity and Sexuality in Modern Mexico*. U of New Mexico P, 2012.

Macfarlane, A.J. "Love and Capitalism." *The Cambridge Journal of Anthropology*, vol. 11, no. 2, 1986, pp. 22–39.

MacLachlan, Bonnie. Introduction. *Virginity Revisited: Configurations of the Unpossessed Body*, edited by Judith Fletcher and Bonnie MacLachlan. University of Toronto Press, 2007, pp. 3–12.

Madrigal, Elena. "A dos, de tres caídas." *Contarte en lésbico*. Éditions Alondras, 2010, pp. 109–14.

Madrigal, Elena. "Un carnaval para el yo lésbico: Los cuentos de Gilda Salinas." *Lectora*, no. 17, 2011, pp. 93–103.

Madrigal, Elena, and Leticia Romero. *Un juego que cabe entre nosotras. Acercamientos a la crítica y a la creación de la literatura sáfica*. Voces en Tinta, 2014.

Marambio, John, and Marcie Rinka. "A Myth Is Born: The Femme Fatale in the Golden Age of Mexican Cinema." Hanson and O'Rawe, pp. 170–83.

Marcha Lencha. "El comité organizador de la Marcha Lencha da a conocer nuestro pronunciamiento sobre la primera marcha lencha . . ." *Instagram*, 18 June 2021, instagram.com/p/CQSSEv5DeHF/?igshid=MzRlODBiNWFlZA==.

Marcha Lencha. "Hace un año realizamos nuestra marcha lencha virtual . . ." *Instagram*, 26 June 2021, instagram.com/p/CQltxqEDbMu/?img_index=1.

Maristany, José. "¿Una teoría queer latinoamericana? Postestructuralismo y políticas de la identidad en Lemebel." *Lectures du genre*, no. 4, 2008, pp. 17–25.

Marquet, Antonio. "La pasión según Roffiel." *Revista de la Universidad de México*, no. 469–70, 1990, p. 83.

McDowell Carlsen, Lila. " 'Te conozco de cuando eras árbol': Gender, Utopianism, and the Border in Cristina Rivera Garza's *La cresta de Ilión*." *Symposium*, vol. 64, no. 2, 2010, pp. 229–42.

Medina, Raquel. Interview. Conducted by author. 8 August 2023.

Melgar, Lucía. "Familia: en resignificación continua." *Conceptos clave en los estudios de género. Volumen 1*, coordinated by Hortensia Moreno and Eva Alcántara. Universidad Nacional Autónoma de México, 2019, pp. 91–103.

Méndez, María José. "*Acuerpar*: The Decolonial Feminist Call for Embodied Solidarity." *Signs: Journal of Women in Culture and Society*, vol. 49, no. 1, 2023, pp. 37–61.

Mercader, Yolanda. "La diversidad sexual en el cine mexicano." *V Jornadas de Sociología de la UNLP*. Universidad Nacional de la Plata, 2008, aacademica. org/000-096/155.pdf.

Meruane, Lina. *Contra los hijos*. Tumbona Ediciones, 2014.

Miranda, Láurel. "Transphobic Discourse Is the Real 'Trojan Horse' of Mexican Feminism." *GlobalVoices*, 5 March 2021, https://globalvoices.org/2021/03/05/transphobic-discourse-is-the-real-trojan-horse-of-mexican-feminism/. Accessed 4 June 2023.

Möbius, Janina. "De La Malinche a Miss Janeth—de La Guadalupe a Lady Apache: Imágenes de mujeres dentro y fuera del ring de Lucha Libre." *El otro héroe. Estudios sobre la producción social de memoria al margen del discurso oficial en América Latina*, edited by Antje Gunsenheimer, Enrique N. Cruz, and Carlos Pallán Gayol. Bonn UP, 2020, pp. 162–78.

Mogrovejo, Norma, editor. *Contra-amor, poliamor, relaciones abiertas y sexo casual: Reflexiones lesbianas del Abya Yala*. Ediciones Desde Abajo, 2016.

Mogrovejo, Norma. "Lo queer en América Latina: ¿lucha identitaria, post-identitaria, asimilacionista o neocolonial?" *Cartografías queer: sexualidades y activismo LGBT en América Latina*, edited by Daniel Balderston and Arturo Matute Castro. U of Pittsburgh, 2011.

Mogrovejo, Norma. *Un amor que se atrevió a decir su nombre. La lucha de las lesbianas y su relación con los movimientos homosexual y feminista en América Latina*. Plaza y Valdés, 2000.

Mogrovejo, Norma. "'Un amor que se atrevió a decir su nombre,' libro académico sobre el movimiento lésbico." Interviewed by Martha Canseco. *AmecoPress*, 7 October 2021, vocesfeministas.mx/un-amor-que-se-atrevio-a-decir-su-nombre-libro-academico-sobre-el-movimiento-lesbico/.

Mondragón, Cristina. "El viaje a la animalidad: *Rhyme & Reason* de Criseida Santos Guevara." *Nuevas narrativas mexicanas 2: desde la diversidad*, edited by Marco Kunz and Cristina Mondragón. Linkgua Digital Ediciones, 2014, pp. 225–39.

Moi, Toril. *What Is a Woman? And Other Essays*. Oxford U P, 1999.

Monsiváis, Carlos. *Aires de familia*. Anagrama, 2000.

Monsiváis, Carlos. *Amor perdido*. Ediciones Era, 1977.

Monsiváis, Carlos. "Crónica de aspectos, aspersiones, cambios, arquetipos y estereotipos de la masculinidad." *Desacatos*, no. 15–16, 2004, pp. 90–108.

Monsiváis, Carlos. "La mujer en la cultura mexicana." *Mujer y sociedad en América Latina*, edited by Lucía Guerra-Cunningham. Editorial del Pacífico, 1980, pp. 101–17.

Monsiváis, Carlos. "Los iguales, los semejantes, los (hasta hace un minuto) perfectos desconocidos (A cien años de la redada de los 41)." *Que se abra esa puerta: Crónicas y ensayos sobre la diversidad sexual*. Paidós, 2010, pp. 77–107.

Monsiváis, Carlos. "Mexican Cinema: Of Myths and Demystifications." *Mediating Two Worlds*, edited by John King, Ana M. López, and Manuel Alvadaro. British Film Institute, 1993, pp. 139–46.

Monsiváis, Carlos, and Marta Lamas. *Misógino feminista*. Debate Feminista, 2013.

Moraga, Cherríe L. *Loving in the War Years. Lo que nunca pasó por sus labios*. 1983. Cambridge: South End Press, 2000.

Morgan, Tracy. "Butch-Femme and the Politics of Identity." *Sisters, Sexperts, Queers: Beyond the Lesbian Nation*, edited by Arlene Stein. Plume, 1993, pp. 36–46.

Mulvey, Laura. *Visual and Other Pleasures*. 1989. Palgrave Macmillan, 2009.

Munt, Sally, editor. *Butch/Femme. Inside Lesbian Gender*. Cassell, 1998.

Munt, Sally. Introduction. Munt, pp. 1–11.

Muñoz, José Esteban. *Cruising Utopia: The Then and There of Queer Futurity*. New York UP, 2009.

Navarrete, Federico. *México racista. Una denuncia*. Penguin Random House, 2016.

Nuñez Noriega, Guillermo. *Just Between Us: An Ethnography of Male Identity and Intimacy in Rural Communities of Northern Mexico*. U of Arizona P, 2014.

Olcott, Jocelyn, Mary Kay Vaughan, and Gabriela Cano, editors. *Sex in Revolution: Gender, Politics, and Power in Modern Mexico*. Duke UP, 2006.

Olivera Córdova, María Elena. "*Amora:* literatura de compromiso sociosexual." Madrigal and Romero, pp. 131–38.

Olivera Córdova, María Elena. *Entre amoras. Lesbianismo en la narrativa mexicana*. CEIICH-UNAM, 2009.

Olivera Córdova, María Elena. "Masculinidades en mujeres en la literatura latinoamericana." *Interdisciplina*, vol. 5, no. 11, 2017, pp. 127–44.

Olivera Córdova, María Elena. "Narrativa lésbica mexicana." *Connotas. Revista de crítica y teoría literarias*, no. 4–5, 2005, pp. 133–43.

Olivera Córdova, María Elena. *Narrativa sáfica latinoamericana: una lectura tortillera*. 2014. Universidad Autónoma Metropolitana Unidad Iztapalapa, master's thesis.

Olivera Córdova, María Elena. "Ni ángeles ni demonios." *Jornadas Anuales de Investigación 2009*. CEIICH-UNAM, 2010, pp. 271–77.

Ortiz, Roberto. "Recuerda, Notes on Alfonso Cuarón's *Roma*." *Mediático*, special dossier on *Roma*, 24 December 2018, reframe.sussex.ac.uk/mediatico/2018/12/24/special-dossier-on-roma-recuerda-notes-on-alfonso-cuarons-roma/.

Osborne, Elizabeth, and Sofía Ruiz-Alfaro. Introduction. *Domestic Labor in Twenty-First Century Latin American Cinema*, edited by Elizabeth Osborne and Sofía Ruiz-Alfaro. Palgrave Macmillan, 2020, pp. 1–21.

Palomar Verea, Cristina. "'Malas madres': la construcción social de la maternidad." *Debate feminista*, vol. 30, 2004, pp. 12–34.

Palou, Pedro Ángel. *El fracaso del mestizo*. Paidós, 2014.

Pâquet, Lili. "The Corporeal Female Body in Literary Rape-Revenge: Shame, Violence, and Scriptotherapy." *Australian Feminist Studies*, vol. 33, no. 97, 2018, pp. 384–99.

Park, Shelley M. *Mothering Queerly, Queering Motherhood*. State U of New York P, 2013.

Patnoe, Elizabeth. "Lolita Misrepresented, Lolita Reclaimed: Disclosing the Doubles." *College Literature*, vol. 22, no. 2, 1995, pp. 81–104.

Paz, Octavio. *El laberinto de la soledad*. 1950. Penguin Books, 1997.

Pereda, Javier, and Patricia Murrieta-Flores. "The Role of Lucha Libre in the Construction of Mexican Male Identity." *Networking Knowledge: Journal of MeCCSA Postgraduate Network*, no. 4, vol. 1, 2011, pp. 1–19.

Pérez de la Torre, Mildred. *Lo hice por amor*. Quimera, 2016.

Perlongher, Néstor. *Plebeian Prose*. Translated by Frances Riddle. Polity Press, 2019.

Phelan, Shane. "Public Discourse and the Closeting of Butch Lesbians." Munt, pp. 191–99.

Pierce, Joseph. "I Monster: Embodying Trans and Travesti Resistance in Latin America." *Latin American Research Review*, vol. 55, no. 2, 2020, pp. 305–21.

Pierce, Joseph, María Amelia Viteri, Diego Falconí Trávez, Salvador Vidal-Ortíz, and Lourdes Martínez-Echazábal. "*Queer*/Cuir de las Américas: Traducción, decolonialidad y lo inconmesurable." *El lugar sin límites*, no. 5, 2021, pp. 1–20.

Pietrak, Mariola. "El mingitauro: La identidad de género y su representación en *Cuerpo náufrago* (2005), de Ana Clavel." *Brumal, revista de investigación sobre lo fantástico*, vol. 8, no. 1, 2020, pp. 35–48.

Pisano, Margarita. *El triunfo de la masculinidad*. Ediciones Pirata, 2000.

Platero, Lucas. "La masculinidad de las biomujeres: marimachos, chicazos, camioneras y otras disidentes." *Jornadas Estatales Feministas de Granada. Mesa Redonda: Cuerpos, sexualidades y políticas feministas*, 2009.

Plaza-Morales, Natalia. "Exploración y lectura de la figura mítica de la ninfa en la literatura: *Las ninfas a veces sonríen* de Ana Clavel." *Revista de literatura hispanoamericana*, no. 75, 2017, pp. 56–70.

Poiré, Sofía J. "Día de la visibilidad lésbica: ¡Amor de lenchas y sáficas!" *Malvestida*, 26 April, 2023 https://malvestida.com/2023/04/amor-de-lenchas-y-saficas/?amp=1. Accessed 3 June 2023.

Poiré, Sofía J. Interview. Conducted by author. 4 August 2023.

Poniatowska, Elena. "Una charla con Elena Poniatowska." Interviewed by Iliana Alcántar, Marisol Castillo, Marisol Pérez, and Melissa Strong Carrillo. *Mester*, vol. 32, 2003, pp. 72–84.

Pratt, Mary Louise. "'No me interrumpas': Las mujeres en el ensayo latinoamericano." *Debate feminista*, no. 21, 2000, pp. 70–88.

Pratt, Mary Louise. "'Yo soy la Malinche': Chicana Writers and the Poetics of Ethnonationalism." *Callaloo*, vol. 16, no. 4, 1993, pp. 859–73.

Price-Glynn, Kim. *Strip Club: Gender, Power, and Sex Work*. New York UP, 2010.

Quevedo y Zubieta, Salvador. *México Marimacho: Novela Histórica Revolucionaria*. Ediciones Botas, 1933.

"¿Quiénes son las lenchitudes? Marcha Lencha te lo explica." *Homosensual*, 20 April 2023, homosensual.com/lgbt/lesbianas/que-son-las-lenchitudes-marcha-lencha-te-lo-explica/. Accessed 3 May 2023.

Quinn, Patrick J. *Patriarchy in Eclipse: The Femme Fatale and the New Woman in American Literature and Culture, 1870–1920*. Cambridge, 2015.

Raitt, Jill. "The *Vagina Dentata* and the *Immaculatus Uterus Divini Fonti*." *The Journal of the American Academy of Religion*, vol. 48, no. 2, 1980, pp. 415–31.

Rambukkana, Nathan. *Fraught Intimacies: Non/Monogamy in the Public Sphere*. U of British Columbia P, 2015.

Ranea Triviño, Beatriz. *Desarmar la masculinidad: los hombres ante la era del feminismo*. Catarata, 2021.

Raynor, Cecily. *Latin American Literature at the Millennium: Local Lives, Global Spaces*. Bucknell UP, 2021.

Reséndez Fuentes, Andrés. "Battleground Women: *Soldaderas* and Female Soldiers in the Mexican Revolution." *The Americas*, vol. 51, no. 4, 1995, pp. 525–53.

Reséndiz Oikión, Ernesto. "Las lesbianas en treinta y cuatro obras de autores mexicanos." Madrigal and Romero, pp. 140–72.

Rich, Adrienne. *Compulsory Heterosexuality and Lesbian Existence*. 1980. Only Women Press Ltd., 1981.

Ríos, Sofía. "Representation and Disjunction: Made-up Maids in Mexican *Telenovelas*." *Journal of Iberian and Latin American Research*, no. 21, vol. 2, 2015, pp. 223–33.

Rivera Garza, Cristina. *The Iliac Crest*. Translated by Sarah Booker. Feminist Press, 2017.

Rivera Garza, Cristina. *La cresta de Ilión*. Tusquets, 2001.

Rivera Garza, Cristina. "La primera persona del plural." *Tsunami I*, edited by Gabriela Jáuregui. Sexto Piso, 2019, pp. 159–73.

Rivera Garza, Cristina. *Los muertos indóciles. Necroescrituras y desapropiación*. Tusquets, 2013.

Rizki, Cole. "Latin/x American Trans Studies Toward a Travesti-Trans Analytic." *TSQ: Transgender Studies Quarterly*, vol. 6, no. 2, 2019, pp. 145–55.

Rodríguez Dorantes, Cecilia. "Entre el mito y la experiencia vivida: las jefas de familia." *Familias y mujeres en México: del modelo a la diversidad*, edited by Soledad González Montes and Julia Tuñon. El Colegio de México, 1997, pp. 195–238.

Roffiel, Rosamaría. *Amora*. Editorial Planeta, 1989.

Roffiel, Rosamaría. "Entrevista con Rosamaría Roffiel." Interviewed by Clary Loisel. *Revista de literatura mexicana contemporánea*, vol. 8, no. 16, 2002, pp. 101–107.

Rojas, Olga, Diana Córdoba, and Daniel Nehring. "Gentlemen Have No Memory: Some Considerations about Male Infidelity in Mexico." *Sociology in a Changing World: Challenges and Perspectives*, edited by Gregory Katsas. Athens Institute for Education and Research, 2009, pp. 349–62.

Rojas Martínez, Olga Lorena. "Masculinidad y vida conyugal en México. Cambios y persistencias." *Géneros: Revista de investigación y divulgación sobre los estudios de género*, no. 10, 2011–2012, pp. 79–104.

Roof, Judith. *A Lure of Knowledge: Lesbian Sexuality and Theory*. Columbia UP, 1991.

Rubenstein, Anne. "The War on 'Las Pelonas': Modern Women and Their Enemies, Mexico City, 1924." Olcott, Vaughan, and Cano, pp. 57–80.

Rubin, Gayle. "Of Catamites and Kings: Reflections on Butch, Gender, and Boundaries." *Persistent Desire: A Femme-Butch Reader*, edited by Joan Nestle. Alyson Publications, 1992, pp. 466–82.

Rueda Esquibel, Catrióna. *With Her Machete in Her Hand: Reading Chicana Lesbians*. U of Texas P, 2006.

Ruiz-Alfaro, Sofía. "A Threat to the Nation: México Marimacho and Female Masculinities in Postrevolutionary Mexico." *Hispanic Review*, no. 81, vol. 1, 2013, pp. 41–62.

Rupp, Leila J. *Sapphistries: A Global History of Love Between Women*. New York UP, 2009.

Russo Garrido, Anahi. *Tortilleras Negotiating Intimacy: Love, Friendship, and Sex in Queer Mexico City*. Rutgers UP, 2020.

Salazar, Estefani. "PRIDE 2021: Marcha Lencha en la CDMX reúne a cientos de mujeres." *La Razón*, 28 June 2021, razon.com.mx/ciudad/pride-2021-marcha-lencha-cdmx-reune-cientos-mujeres-fotos-439586. Accessed 12 May 2022.

Saldaña Tejeda, Abril. "Racismo, proximidad y mestizaje: el caso de las mujeres en el servicio doméstico en México." *Trayectorias*, vol. 15, no. 37, 2013, pp. 73–89.

Salinas, Gilda. *Del destete al desempance. Cuentos lésbicos y un colado*. Trópico de Escorpio, 2008.

Samuelson, Cheyla Rose. "Towards a Transnational Criticism: Bridging the Mexico-US Divide on Valeria Luiselli." *Chasqui*, vol. 49, no. 2, 2020, pp. 176–94.

Sánchez Bringas, Ángeles, Sara Espinosa, Claudia Ezcurdia, and Edna Torres. "Nuevas maternidades o la deconstrucción de la maternidad en México." *Debate Feminista*, vol. 30, 2004, pp. 55–86.

Sánchez Prado, Ignacio. *Screening Neoliberalism: Mexican Cinema 1988–2012*. Vanderbilt UP, 2014.

Sánchez Prado, Ignacio, Anna M. Nogar, and José Ramón Ruisánchez Serra, editors. *A History of Mexican Literature*. Cambridge UP, 2016.

Santillán Ramírez, Iris Rocío. "El feminicidio en México. El mal que nos aqueja." *Alegatos*, no. 113, 2023, pp. 7–34.

Santos Guevara, Criseida. *Rhyme & Reason*. Tierra Adentro, 2008.

Savage, Shari L. "Lolita: Genealogy of a Cover Girl." *Studies in Art Education*, vol. 56, no. 2, 2015, pp. 156–67.

Schippers, Mimi. *Beyond Monogamy: Polyamory and the Future of Polyqueer Sexualities*. New York UP, 2016.

Schneebaum, Alyssa. "All in the Family: Capitalism, Patriarchy and Love." *GEXcel Work in Progress Report 8*, edited by Sofia Strid and Anna G. Jónasdóttir. Centre of Gender Excellence, 2010, pp. 109–16.

Segato, Rita. *La escritura en el cuerpo de las mujeres asesinadas en Ciudad Juárez. Territorio, soberanía y crímenes de segundo estado*. Universidad del Claustro de Sor Juana, 2006.

Shaw, Deborah. "Erotic or Political: Literary Representations of Mexican Lesbians." *Journal of Latin American Cultural Studies*, vol. 5, no. 1, 1996, pp. 51–63.

Sinclair, Marianne. *Hollywood Lolitas: The Nymphet Syndrome in the Movies*. Henry Holt and Company, 1988.

Smith, Paul Julian. *Mexican Screen Fiction*. Polity Press, 2014.

Smyth, Cherry. "How Do We Look? Imagining Butch/Femme." Munt, pp. 82–89.

Straayer, Chris. "Femme Fatale of Lesbian Femme: Bound in Sexual *Différance*." *Women in Film Noir*, edited by E. Ann Kaplan. British Film Institute, 1998, pp. 151–63.

Sullivan, Mairead. *Lesbian Death: Desire and Danger Between Feminist and Queer*. U of Minnesota P, 2022.

Tam, Michelle W. "Queering Reproductive Access: Reproductive Justice in Assisted Reproductive Technologies." *Reproductive Health*, vol. 18, no. 164, 2021, pp. 1–6.

Téllez, Artemisa. " 'A Chloe le gustaba Olivia' Implicaciones de una literatura que quisiera llamarse lésbica." *Homofobia: Laberinto de la ignorancia*, coordinated by Julio Muñoz Rubio. UNAM-CEIICH, 2010, pp. 174–84.

Téllez, Artemisa. "An Interview with Artemisa Téllez." Interview by Julia Constantino. *Wasafiri*, no. 34, vol. 2, 2019, pp. 14–18.

Téllez, Artemisa. *Crema de vainilla*. Editorial Voces en Tinta, 2014.

Téllez, Artemisa. Facebook message to author. 20 December 2021.

Téllez, Artemisa, editor. *Hasta que comienza a brillar: Antología de cuento lésbico mexicano*. Penguin Random House, 2024.

Tenorio Tovar, Natalia. "Repensando el amor y la sexualidad: una mirada desde la segunda modernidad." *Sociológica*, no. 76, 2012, pp. 7–52.

Thomson, Marilyn. "Workers Not Maids—Organising Household Workers in Mexico." *Gender and Development*, vol. 17, no. 2, 2009, pp. 281–93.

Torrent Lozano, Meritxell. "De Lolitas y otros males." *Lectora*, no. 3, 1997, pp. 117–24.

"Trace, N (1)." *Merriam-Webster*, 2023, https://www.merriam-webster.com/dictionary/trace.

Tuñón, Julia, Ed. *Enjaular los cuerpos: normativas decimonónicas y feminidad en México*. Colegio de México, 2008.

Valencia Triana, Sayak. "Del *queer* al cuir: *Ostranénie* geopolítica y epistémica desde el sur glocal." *Queer y Cuir. Políticas de lo irreal*, compiled by Fernando R. Lanuza and Raúl M. Carrasco. Editorial Fontamara, 2015, pp. 19–37.

Valencia Triana, Sayak. "Teoría transfeminista para el análisis de la violencia machista y la reconstrucción no-violenta del tejido social en el México contemporáneo." *Universitas Humanística*, no. 78, 2014, pp. 65–88.

Van Bavel, Marjolein. "Morbo, lucha libre, and Television: The Ban of Women Wrestlers from Mexico City in the 1950s." *Mexican Studies/Estudios Mexicanos*, vol. 37, no. 1, 2021, pp. 9–34.

Vasallo, Brigitte. *Pensamiento monógamo. Terror poliamoroso*. La Oveja Roja, 2018.

Vela Barba, Estefanía. "Nuevas tecnologías reproductivas." *Conceptos clave en los estudios de género. Volumen 2*, coordinated by Hortensia Moreno and Eva Alcántara. Universidad Nacional Autónoma de México, 2019, pp. 195–214.

Visser, Sandra. *Romantic Children, Brazen Girls? An Exploration of the Girl-child's Representation in and around Nabokov's Lolita and Three Derivative Novels*. 2010. University of Stellenbosch, master's thesis.

Warner, Michael. *Publics and Counterpublics*. Zone Books, 2002.

Warner, Michael. *The Trouble with Normal*. The Free Press, 1999.

Wayar, Marlene. *Travesti: Una teoría lo suficientemente buena*. Muchas Nueces, 2019.

Weston, Kath. *Families We Choose: Lesbians, Gays, and Kinship*. 1991. Columbia UP, 1997.

White, Bretton. *Staging Discomfort: Performance and Queerness in Contemporary Cuba*. U of Florida P, 2020.

Zatarain Olivas, Andrea, and Guillermo Núñez Noriega. "Tortilleras, tamaleras, chanclas y lenchas: representaciones dominantes de las relaciones erótico-afectivas entre mujeres en el norte de México." *Revista de Estudios de Antropología Sexual*, vol. 1, no. 9, 2019, pp. 27–45.

Index